Cataloging the Web

Metadata, AACR, and MARC 21

Edited by
Wayne Jones, Judith R. Ahronheim,
and Josephine Crawford

Series editor
Brad Eden

ALCTS Papers on Library Technical Services
and Collections, No. 10

The Scarecrow Press, Inc.
Lanham, Maryland, and London
Published in Cooperation with the Association
for Library Collections & Technical Services,
a Division of the American Library Association
2002

SCARECROW PRESS, INC.

Published in the United States of America
by Scarecrow Press, Inc.
4720 Boston Way, Lanham, Maryland 20706
www.scarecrowpress.com

4 Pleydell Gardens, Folkestone
Kent CT20 2DN, England

British Library Cataloguing-in-Publication Information Available

Library of Congress Cataloging-in-Publication Data

Cataloging the Web : metadata, AACR, and MARC21 / edited by Wayne Jones, Judith R. Ahronheim, and
Josephine Crawford.
    p. cm. — (ALCTS papers on library technical services and collections ; no. 10)
  Includes bibliographical references and index.
  ISBN 0-8108-4143-6 (alk. paper) ✓
  1. Cataloging of computer network information. 2. Metadata. 3. Digital libraries. I. Jones, Wayne, 1959–
II. Ahronheim, Judith R. III. Crawford, Josephine. IV. Series.
Z695.24 .C38 2002
025.3'44—dc21
                                                       2001049383

Contents

Preface: Meting Out Data

Wayne Jones

My apartment is small, minimally furnished, and well organized. I have pretty much everything I want domestically within its walls. When there is something I need—the flashlight, batteries for my tape recorder, that fake check for 58 billion dollars (Canadian) from my friend Oscar—I know exactly where to go to retrieve it. There is none of that clichéd and inefficient pawing through drawers and closets, tossing clothing into a pile in the middle of the bedroom in a vain effort to find what I'm looking for.

The Web is huge, furnished with a wealth of information and services and entertainment—let's call it all "data"—and generally very badly organized. Some corners are neat and tidy and nicely arranged, and there is clean-up work in progress on a couple of rooms, but overall the place is a mess. Perhaps you have had the same experience searching the Web as I have. If I need to find a specific tidbit of information, I sigh at the daunting prospect of being able to locate it efficiently.

There are four main methods of getting the data. The first one is the hallowed and dreaded keyword search, sometimes extremely effective in getting searchers immediately to what they are looking for, but more often burdening them with an overabundance of results containing words that are not the concept they are looking for, though the spelling happens to be the same. The second method is searching through a subject hierarchy, of which many are set up and maintained by the larger search-engine and Web-portal concerns. It can be a painful, time-consuming, and frustrating exercise to drill further and further down through a massive taxonomy of data, seeing several links that look like the logical next click but never quite knowing which one will lead to what you want and which one will be a dead end from which you will have to spend even more time retreating. It's like consulting the Dewey or Library of Congress classification schemes every time you want the answer to a simple question about cars. The third method is a variation of keyword searching that can have very effective results in certain situations: phrase searching. It's useful for when you are absolutely certain of an exact phrase from the resource you are searching for, such as a line from a Lyle Lovett song or from *Hamlet*. The fourth method is not so much a method as it is an expediency: beloved bookmarks. People rely on them religiously because they often represent hours of tedious searching that nobody wants to recreate. A chill goes down your spine when you click a bookmark and discover it is dead or has moved without leaving a forwarding URL.

The chapters in this book represent substantial hope that all is not lost for meting data out of an ever-burgeoning Web. New international standards have been and are being developed so that the Web can be cataloged to some extent, so that users can get access to its content in ways that are currently not universally available. Clifford A. Lynch notes in his article that search engines can't distinguish in their results between resources *about* a person and resources *by* the person. I do a search on "Clifford A. Lynch" on Google, for example, and I retrieve 2,270 hits (on September 7, 2000), and, yes, some of them are for things by him and some are for things about him. Furthermore, some are for things by or about some *other* Clifford A. Lynch, and—even though I use phrase searching—some are for a Clifford J. Lynch, and still more are for pages that simply contain both words, "Clifford" and "Lynch." These messy results point up one of the other fundamental problems with name searching on the Web: generally speaking, there is no way to search a name as a structured heading in its authoritative form, the way I can search "Lynch, Clifford" in WorldCat and be assured that it is giving me the right results. In fact, there's generally no way to search for any kind of heading—not just names but also subjects and uniform titles—in its structured, authoritative form.

However, some of the standards-development work that is underway (if not already pretty fully developed) may eventually help alleviate this situation. Metadata schemes or element sets are out there that are being used by various communities on various parts of the Web in order to bring some order to information chaos: the Dublin Core, the Encoded Archival Description, and the Text Encoding Initiative are just three among many. The challenge for the future will be to propagate their use across a much broader portion of the Web. Not to catalog everything, of course—as Michael Gorman points out, that is neither possible nor necessary—but to provide a standard for bibliographic access not only to the corners but also to the broad surfaces of the Web. Eric Miller and Diane Hillmann describe how developments such as the Resource Description Framework and the Extensible Markup Language have the potential to be the "meta-standards" that can draw everything together. All metadata creators need not adopt the same tools or the same methods. They can continue to use the element sets that serve them and their users best, and RDF and XML have the built-in flexibility to accommodate all comers.

Older standards also have a significant role in this effort. AACR and MARC, two stalwarts that have proven their value and flexibility over the course of several decades of cataloging, are not mere useless curiosities now. Brian Schottlaender describes how AACR is being adapted for the new world of e-resources. Two of the main efforts entail incorporating seriality in a more thorough and systematic manner and harmonizing AACR with other international descriptive standards such as the International Standard Bibliographic Description and ISSN policies. Rebecca Guenther describes how the American and Canadian MARC standards, now combined and aptly redubbed "MARC 21" for the twenty-first century, are also adapting to a new world of coexistence with relative newcomers such as the Dublin Core. Crosswalks or mappings have been developed so that both the old and the new may interoperate: a bibliographic description in one format may be easily translated into the other so that both creators and users have maximum flexibility in how the data is stored and viewed.

Some of those well-arranged corners of the Web that I've mentioned are described in detail in this collection. They are practical applications of both the old and the newer standards, mini-digital libraries that exploit the latest techniques in order to provide a defined community of users with some of the best examples of bibliographic access on the Web. There are general applications for large and broad subject collections such as the National Library of Medicine or the Colorado Digitization Project, and there are specific applications, as well—sort of like digital special libraries—in which the access is provided for a focused set of e-resources: art objects, cartographic materials, music, social science data, videos. Think of them as case studies—analyses of specific populations that have lessons for the broader world.

And that is one of the main goals of this collection of papers: to give an overview of not only what is currently afoot on the Web but also what is possible. The standards are ready, or they are being developed or adapted, and now it's up to librarians and library managers and all manner of people who are interested in how information is organized on the Web to go forth and multiply. The tools and the need are there, and now is the time to clean the place up.

Acknowledgments

The chapters in *Cataloging the Web* are based on papers presented at the Preconference on Metadata for Web Resources, which was held July 6–7, 2000, at the American Library Association Annual Conference in Chicago. The preconference was jointly sponsored by the Association for Library Collections and Technical Services (ALCTS) Committee on Cataloging: Description and Access (CC:DA), the Committee to Study Serials Cataloging (CSSC), the Networked Resources and Metadata Committee (NRMC), and MARBI (the Machine-Readable Bibliographic Information Committee).

The preconference planning task force was cochaired by Mary Larsgaard and Sally C. Tseng and was further composed of Judith R. Ahronheim, Matthew Beacom, Josephine Crawford, Ellen Crosby, Brad Eden, Mary Grenci, Wayne Jones, Erik Jul, Susan Moore, Jina Choi Wakimoto, and Mary S. Woodley.

Some of the papers were transcribed from the contributors' presentations by Everett Allgood, Mary Larsgaard, John Radencich, Sally C. Tseng, Manuel Urrizola, Jina Choi Wakimoto, and Mary S. Woodley.

I

INTRODUCTION

1

Metadata and Libraries: What's It All About?

Jennifer A. Younger, transcribed by Mary Larsgaard

Metadata is a topic of intense interest among librarians, information scientists, computer scientists, and knowledge managers. Within bibliographical, archival, and other scholarly communities concerned with describing and organizing information resources, metadata enjoys a distinguished history as well as an exciting future. Metadata makes it possible for users to discover, access, and use information. Success in finding and using information is a significant factor in creating the high quality of life we seek.

In this paper, I contrast a snapshot of metadata as seen in the published journal literature and in the freely available Web-accessible literature. On the basis of major characteristics of today's world, I explore where we might be going with metadata and cataloging in the library.

A BRIEF GLIMPSE OF THE PAST

Philosophers are fond of telling us that those who ignore the past are doomed to repeat its mistakes.[1] To avoid the mistakes, whatever they are, however, is only one reason for reviewing the past. My purpose in this paper is to remind us—ever so briefly—that cataloging has a long history distinguished by the passion of its creators.

A recent article brings to our attention the rebirth of the Alexandrian Library and describes the efforts that will take place to ensure the library is fully a part of the cyber age.[2] Ptolemy, the first monarch of Egypt, aspired to collect at Alexandria "the books of all the peoples of the world."[3] Toward that end, Ptolemy wrote to kings and governors, asking them to send all works to him. When the ships arrived in port, he confiscated the manuscripts, returning only copies to the ships' captains. While this practice is not deserving of emulation, the great catalog recording Ptolemy's acquisitions serves as inspiration for all of us. By about 240 B.C. Callimachus of Cyrene had cataloged more than 500,000 scrolls.[4] No doubt, he wasn't burdened with the range of fields included in a modern bibliographic record, but still, his feat was extraordinary.

This great catalog, entitled (translated into English) *Catalogues of the Authors Eminent in Various Disciplines,*[5] bore little resemblance to modern-day catalogs. Callimachus had produced a classification but one that contained only broad categories mirroring the various sections of the library. He included only eminent Greek authors from the works on the shelves, and although his selection was extensive, requiring close to 120 scrolls, it was not a comprehensive guide to the collection. Use may not have been its most important purpose, for it could be used only by those already familiar with the library arrangement.

By the Middle Ages, the libraries of antiquity had disappeared. Of the holdings of the great Alexandrian Library, although shrouded a bit in mystery, it appears that only the books of Aristotle might have survived the final destruction ordered by the Caliph of Constantinople.[6] A picture of medieval libraries was painted in a widely read novel by Umberto Eco,[7] a renowned medievalist and historical scholar. Eco's description of medieval monastic libraries is shown, however, to be wholly in conflict with what scholars know about medieval libraries from historical sources, despite the rigorous conformity in Eco's novel to the social, mental, and religious aspects of medieval times.[8] Early monastic libraries were indeed dusty and archaic but owned ten to twenty manuscripts at most, not the 85,000 we were to assume were housed in Eco's *Aedificio,* and these were most likely stored in a book cupboard. By 1300 A.D., the largest and most up-to-date university libraries had collections of only 1,000 volumes. The librarian was almost always the person also in charge of music, and the monks and scholarly sources do not mention any duties associated with the care of or access to collections. In the end, Eco's library is seen as a metaphor for the world, and a sinister meaning emerges:

> It is a symbol of man's wrongful endeavor to control and understand what he cannot control or understand. By establishing a constructed, artificial and ultimately erroneous notion of truth, and vainly surrounding it with a myriad of treatises carefully guarded from profane use, the library and the librarians are contradicting the nature of things.[9]

Through the years, however, libraries gained—or regained—great stature for keeping knowledge safe, and librarians are seen to resemble the helpful monastic librarians whose portrait was so vividly drawn by Eco. And since medieval times, we have significantly enhanced the functionality of the library catalog. Proposing access points far beyond a single author, modern leaders have shown themselves to be as visionary as were their predecessors in developing the catalog. Sir Anthony Panizzi, Charles Jewett, Charles Ammi Cutter, Melvil Dewey, Seymour Lubetsky, David Judson Haykin, Henriette Avram, and Michael Gorman—to name only a few of the best-known experts—all contributed to the development of cataloging and catalogs.[10] The Margaret Mann Citation awarded annually by the American Library Association (ALA) Association for Library Collections and Technical Services (ALCTS) Cataloging and Classification Section recognizes the role and influence of teachers in ensuring that traditions and bibliographic principles are not lost to the library community.

These highlights come only from the Anglo-American library community. Rich, established traditions also exist in archival, museum, geographical, medical, scientific, and computing communities, all of which are making significant contributions in the metadata arena. The recognition of metadata in the plural broadens and transforms our thinking about library-developed metadata schemes, such as Anglo-American Cataloguing Rules (AACR), Library of Congress Classification (LCC), and Dewey Decimal Classification (DCC), and will propel library cataloging into the exciting world of "meta access."

METADATA IN THE JOURNAL LITERATURE

I conducted two separate keyword searches using *metadata* and *cataloging* for the purpose of comparing the body of retrieved literature on three dimensions. These are: (1) number of published and indexed articles; (2) range of dates; and (3) focus of article topics.

The search parameters for both searches were set to include all document types, all languages, and all three of the indexes in the online version of the *Web of Science*. The search covered only the most recent twenty-five years, from 1975 to 2000, because those were the only files readily available in my library. Two hundred sixty-nine documents from a database of slightly over 22,600,000 matched on the term *metadata*. The search on *cataloging* resulted in 1,351 documents.

On the first dimension, almost five times as many indexed articles turned up for *cataloging* as for *metadata*. Second, the range of dates for documents retrieved under the term *metadata* ranged from 1982 to 2000, while under the term *cataloging*, the range of dates began in 1975, seven years earlier. I did not record the author or title of first citation under *cataloging*, but it is interesting to note that, at least in this search, the first article indexed under metadata was published in *Drexel Library Quarterly*.[11]

As expected, the focus of the articles retrieved under these terms respectively reflects work emanating from different bibliographic and indexing communities. Articles retrieved by *metadata* are typified by Liston's paper in 1982 titled "Metadata Systems for Integrated Access to Numeric Data Files." Many succeeding articles were on the use of specific schemes or sets of metadata in domains defined by subject or document type, for example, the EarthKAM project, astrophysics and space sciences, museums, clinical information, and geospatial objects. There appeared to be fewer articles on general principles or topics such as the role of a digital librarian in the management of digital information systems. The papers were often published in journals specific to a field such as computing, physics, or geosciences, which addressed control of literature and objects in those fields, although several papers were from the *Journal of the American Society for Information Science* and from digital library publications.

Under *cataloging*, the articles were on the principles, rules, and use of the primary library cataloging schemes: AACR, LCC, DDC, MARC. Articles on cataloging in subject domains occurred most notably in music, art, cartography, and law, where long traditions exist of meeting specific access requirements. Many articles were on the management of cataloging and catalogs, catalog design, the role of catalogers, and trends in cataloging.

The previous categorization, however, is anecdotal, not systematic in nature. A systematic review may find greater differences or similarities than suggested here.

METADATA IN THE REAL WORLD

Using the same parameters of all document types, all languages, all sources, and all years available to me, I repeated the search under the term *metadata* on the Web, using the Google search engine. The results came to an astronomical number—172,000 hits in four-tenths of a second. The Web obviously offers access to a very large set of resources.

More important, though, it offers access to a different set of information resources than the information indexed in *Web of Science.* Google was searching freely available, Web-accessible literature located on Web sites of individuals and organizations. This information comes from a wide variety of organizations, including the W3C Consortium (World Wide Web Consortium), the Coalition for Networked Information (CNI), and the Digital Library Federation (DLF). National libraries and bibliographic agencies, such as the Library of Congress, the National Library of Australia, and the United Kingdom Office for Library and Information Networking, as well as some commercial operations, including the Association of American Publishers, all maintain Web sites. The list grows with the addition of research centers and digital library projects, for example, the Distributed Systems Technology Center (DSTC) and the Alexandria Digital Library. Professional and standards organizations such as ALCTS and the International Federation of Library Associations and Institutions (IFLA) add to the vast array of documents that we know as gray literature.

Between these two searches—one in a citation database available only by subscription and one on the Web without that requirement—a slight overlap occurred in information resources retrieved. Gray literature is defined as literature not controlled by commercial publishers[12] and often not included in commercially published citation databases. The overlap came primarily from online journals that were indexed both as published journals in *Web of Science,* for example, Milstead and Feldman's article in ONLINE[13] and articles from *D-Lib Magazine,* but also indexed on the Web because those journals were in part or in full made freely available on the Web by the publishing organization.

In this search for information on metadata, I did not search a library catalog. I expected to find most of the information on metadata in journal articles or on organizational Web sites. Although the library catalog is often a gateway to the full text of journals, the catalog does not index journal articles. Second, in cases where the library has acquired and cataloged the gray literature, those publications are then directly accessible via the catalog. By searching on the Web, though, I was not dependent on library holdings in the library catalog or on access through a library gateway to Web sites. Citation databases and search engines did the searching of individual journals and sites for me.

TODAY'S WORLD

Search engines are only one of the aspects that make the world surrounding library cataloging and catalogs very different from the one many of us encountered as new librarians. Four characteristics stand out, not because they are great revelations to us, but because they have changed the landscape so significantly. These four characteristics are the proliferation of metadata schemes; search engines; a wired, networked information environment; and library catalogs that link to full text.

At the start of the Cultural Revolution in China, Mao Tse-tung decreed: "Bai-hua-qi-fang, bai-jia-zheng-ming."[14] Translated, this is the well-known phrase "Let a hundred flowers bloom; let a hundred schools of thought contend." Although subsequent events did not always fulfill the promise of his words, Mao believed these strategies would best promote the advancement and progress in the development of arts and sciences. The recent proliferation of metadata schemes makes it seem as if someone has said, "Let a hundred metadata schemes bloom." Acronyms abound: GILS (Government Information Locator Service), CDWA (Categories for the Description of Works of Art), CDF (Channel Distribution Format), EAD (Encoded Archival Description), TEI (Text Encoding Initiative), AACR (Anglo-American Cataloguing Rules), FGDC (Federal Guidelines for Digital Content) Standard, and finally, one in words—Dublin Core. Clusters of indexers, catalogers, and computing experts weave their way through this jumbled set of characters, interpreting them for their specific needs while crosswalks equate data across schemes.[15] Without a doubt, the number of readers is increasing as the metadata literature grows larger and the metadata community more connected than it has been in the past.

Search engines are new entries in the world of metadata and much less structured than other schemes, so much so that some may not have thought of search engines as metadata schemes. Often identifying only keywords to be tagged, guides explain meta tagging and search engine processing of data in the META tag[16] to an audience of Web site creators. As with other metadata schemes, there are hundreds of search engines, some designated as meta-search engines. Search engines search vast quantities of unstructured text and return in just seconds documents with terms matching a search query.

The networked environment brings catalogs, indexes, full-text databases, and data files within easy reach. We can search multiple sources from our desktop computers, sequentially or simultaneously, choosing from a rapidly growing number of online libraries, archives, and Web sites. Some are as large as the Library of Congress; others reflect the work of a single individual and are quite small. Despite this ease of access, the characteristics of key features of the networked information environment are still being defined. Such features include: large-scale, rapid growth; the heterogeneous nature of resources; varying granularity and quality of content in resources; and multiple generations of information resources and supporting access systems. Collectively, these features create challenges for resource discovery and retrieval.[17]

Library catalog search engines don't search the Web as other search engines do, but catalog records containing hot links (URLs in MARC 856 fields) to full-text, Web-based information sources and Web sites are the norm in most library catalogs. In providing direct access to electronic resources and holdings, library catalogs now provide greater functionality than did the first and second generations of online catalogs.

WHERE ARE WE GOING WITH METADATA AND CATALOGING?

These environmental characteristics naturally will shape our thoughts about library cataloging and catalogs. We now have the opportunity to consider what roles library cataloging and catalogs can or should take in the future. In looking toward the future, I consider five topics. These are: resource discovery, access, and context; catalogs and gateways; metadata librarians; the concept of a scholars' portal; and partnerships.

Resource Discovery, Access, and Context

In regard to resource discovery, access, and context, Milstead and Feldman predict a likely mode of development for metadata, although in a future that has so many players with so many different agendas that they are hesitant in doing so.[18] In their predictions, more and more communities and subcommunities will want to be sure their resources are covered by metadata schemes. This will increase the number of metadata schemes and thus the number of registries of schemes. From this will emerge a smaller number of "standards" used by major groups, complete with guidelines for how to interpret these standards and, ultimately, the development of cross-language metadata standards. National borders will become even less relevant than they are today.

Their view points to the emergence of order from what seems at times a chaotic scene. At the University of California, Los Angeles, Ercegovac describes the Internet arena and evolving metadata traditions, identifying three patterns that have evolved since the mid-1990s.[19] These patterns give additional shape to the future predicted by Milstead and Feldman. The first is that among national metadata standards that evolved earlier in different professional traditions— for example, MARC, FGDC (geographic), TEI—there are some overlapping attributes. Ercegovac believes that constructive cooperation now exists between metadata standards developers on common attributes. Developers of crosswalks such as those between Dublin Core and MARC, or between Categories for the Description of Works of Art and eight other metadata systems,[20] know firsthand of both overlapping and unique attributes.

A second pattern is seen in the flexibility and scalability of some new metadata structures. While retaining structure, a scheme such as the Dublin Core is less structured and more flexible than the highly structured MARC, capturing the ease of application that comes with less structure but also the ability to provide more control with optional expansions—for example, into controlled subject terms. Internet search engines provide flexibility in a very limited structure, often with only two metadata elements: keywords and description (AltaVista), or where there is additional structure, it is in the form of broad subject directories only (Yahoo!).

These schemes will coexist with metadata schemes, in which a high degree of structure is needed to identify attributes unique to document types or subject domains. Such structures also provide for context-providing attributes, bibliographic collocation, listing all works of an author together, and classification—all objectives of the library catalog, which are not considered necessary or necessary to the same degree in all metadata standards.

Finally, Ercegovac points to the adoption of common formal languages—for example, SGML (Standard Generalized Markup Language) and XML (Extensible Markup Language)—to support different metadata applications such as Encoded Archival Description (EAD) and the Text Encoding Initiative (TEI). The MARC format has long been the communication structure for library-generated metadata and with the substantive investment in cooperative cataloging, MARC remains an important structure. Several years ago, Edward Gaynor wrote about the possibility of a library catalog hospitable to MARC and SGML, but this capability has not yet been developed for library catalogs.[21] A common language is important for supporting access to multiple metadata databases. It is needed, for example, in digital library support for collection registration, network discovery, user documentation, and collection management for the georeferenced collections in the Alexandria Digital Library.[22]

The growth of more metadata schemes (some of which will be less structured), registries, and common languages for support will have an effect on library metadata schemes and MARC support language. In the view of some, the Dublin Core will be important "as an engineering tool for federating library and non-library databases . . . as a lower-cost alternative for describing materials."[23] The Colorado Digitization Project has chosen Dublin Core to record core descriptive information because it is usable across the Internet and because additional elements can be added that make sense within a discipline.[24] The project participants are libraries, museums, and archives using differing metadata standards for visual resources, archival materials, and books. Beyond Dublin Core, if we are to involve ourselves successfully in the building of digital library services, we will need to track work on the Warwick Framework and the definition of additional metadata sets within that framework in order to address issues such as provenance, integrity, and management of digital content.[25]

Catalogs and Gateways

The newest versions of library catalogs provide links to online text and resources. Library gateways take this one step further by establishing an integrated path to Web-based information resources, including the library catalog and library reference services. Gateways provide options for searching and browsing networked resources, enable remote access to licensed databases by authorized users, and point to library Web sites for subject-specific information. Though some librarians have wanted to route library users to the Web via the library catalog, library users have driven the development of gateways as the front end, with their preferences for going right to the Web.[26]

Gateways also emanate from organizations other than libraries. One example is seen in the project underway to "develop an operational framework to provide the nation's teachers with 'one-stop/any-stop' access" to lesson plans, teacher guides, and other educational materials available on various federal, state, university, nonprofit, and commercial Internet sites.[27] Although some of the resources may be already available via library gateways, this gateway is being developed for a specific clientele—teachers—and with a focus on a specific set of resources.

Gateways do not make library catalogs obsolete, although I confess to listening intently in another forum to the ideas from Los Angeles on moving into the future with a national union catalog.[28] The services, however, provided by gateways may spur the development of catalogs into the management of services beyond resource discovery. Library catalogs can be searched remotely, and with appropriate governance they can support direct borrowing by regional or other consortially defined groups of users, as is done in OhioLINK. Collectively, we own 44 million items, and making those more directly obtainable is a great service to library users.[29] Catalogs offer searching capabilities beyond the browsing that can be done of lists of electronic journals, texts, and databases on library Web sites. In addition, new software tools can extend a search done in a library catalog to another database, thus increasing the value of searching done in a catalog.

A Scholars' Portal

Portals are customized gateways that anticipate the needs of a particular user group and offer directions to what this user group wants. Every group is getting one: alumni, sports fans, business college faculty and students, the general body of students, and, as recently proposed, scholars. In a paper prepared for the Association of Research Libraries, Campbell suggests several reasons why a scholars' portal is needed. He points to the undependable nature of the results of information.com services: that they do not go to the depths ordinarily reached by researchers in subject disciplines and that they are focused on broad customer bases, not the particular needs of scholars. He defines a goal as providing "highly focused search engines adapted to the technical languages of the various academic specialties."[30] In my search earlier, Google made accessible gray literature that would not necessarily have been acquired or cataloged by every library. Some help in sorting through 170,000 hits would have been greatly appreciated.

A library gateway is the beginning of the portal concept, with its focus on scholarly resources available to the local scholarly community. Gateways provide access to high-quality content and library services such as interlibrary loan and reference. A scholars' portal would take this one step further by including reference assistance in directing scholars to the most appropriate scholarly resources, developing search strategies, and evaluating the results. If done cooperatively by libraries, we would leverage our resources as we have done in sharing bibliographic records.

While reading *Time Digital,* a supplement to *Time* magazine, I was surprised to read about the value of reference librarians. The ideas being offered on searching the Web recognized that the search engines do return "weird, unexpected and seemingly endless results" for what seems a straightforward query.[31] Lake makes two suggestions: pick the right site and know how to search. He follows that with: "If you're nostalgic for the days when you could ask a reference librarian to look up a book for you, human-assisted search sites are a good starting point."[32] He has hit the nail on the head. A scholars' portal could be an online reference room, a place or tool that scholars can choose over Google or Yahoo! to explore scholarly resources, to get help and directions. Reference librarians have always directed users to indexes and other tools and educated them in how to use these tools, when to use them, and how the various tools related to each other. We have the opportunity now to extend this into the virtual environment.

Lake knows that knowledge of underlying structure and vocabulary is important in deciding how to search. He offers tips on choosing words, combining words, and looking for related pages, all quite appropriate, in that search engines and sites may not have much structure beyond keywords or weighting of keywords. Here again, as shown in the Gateway project at Cornell University, the knowledge of those in technical services needs to be brought together with that of others from public services, collection development, and information technology to produce the most effective gateway.[33]

The development of scholars' portals will bring in metadata librarians, too. Cortez identifies several research studies on information retrieval supporting his proposition that "the process of retrieval involves defining (establishing the boundary of) a subset of documents from a collection of documents, which itself has a defined boundary."[34] The project underway proposes to create a unified information access system called REEIS (Research, Economics, and Education Information System) to thirty-nine separate databases of programs, projects, and research that focus on food, agriculture, natural resources, and rural development. Accomplishing the development of this custom portal will require the development of a metadata vocabulary for indexing the databases in the catalog. The idea is that "this same metadata vocabulary will provide the means for users to construct effective and efficient search strategies to facilitate querying the individual records contained in REEIS."[35]

The lack of structured browsing and controlled vocabulary support, typically provided in library-developed catalogs and databases but lacking in Web search engines, is partially offset by the comprehensiveness, currency, and power of Web searching.[36] Hence its popularity and success. Vizine-Goetz goes on, however, to note that the developers of richly structured databases such as library catalogs and the developers of Web search engines are recognizing the benefits of their counterparts and are increasingly adopting each other's features.[37] We can expect that scholarly gateway, database, and portal projects will draw on the expertise of metadata librarians, as well as that of computing experts in designing tools for effective retrieval and access.

Metadata Librarians

Looking at the problem statements and recommended actions of the Association for Library Collections and Technical Services (ALCTS) Task Force on Meta Access,[38] we can clearly see a role for librarians. The task force report identified necessary actions in seven areas: naming; resource description and metadata; syntax and formatting; record management; education; outreach; and environmental scanning. It asked that librarians, libraries, and library organizations engage in a variety of activities for the purpose of contributing to the "big picture" of providing access to digital resources. Specifically, that we "adopt transportable, persistent locator information," "promote a coherent view of metadata from a library perspective," continue the "ongoing development of MARC/SGML mapping," and "define appropriate objectives and elements of a national bibliographic control system for the future."[39] Where appropriate forums do not exist, we should seize the opportunity to bring together a wide range of interested appropriate parties from within and outside of the library community. Within the library community there is a great history of successful collaboration on cataloging rules and bibliographic record communication, suggesting a certain ease with the idea of extending our efforts into broader access communities.

Some opportunities are already in place, requiring only that librarians and professional association committees broaden their contextual scope beyond a focus on the development of library-generated metadata schemes and systems. Librarians can participate in metadata workshops originating external to the library community, such as the 1997 workshop on metadata registries in Berkeley. Librarians can engage in the development of a simple resource description record for Internet resources, such as the international Dublin Core workshops. From the OCLC Online Computer Library Center, Stu Weibel, a proactive developer in new arenas, has encouraged librarians to bring their knowledge to the development of other metadata schemes taking place in forums beyond libraries.

Librarians knowledgeable about metadata can also promote the use of metadata standards by libraries, universities, government bodies, and other information producers in their production of digital documents. In 1998, the University of Arizona Library defined responsibilities for a metadata librarian. The position "establishes relationships with potential campus partners, takes a leadership role on campus related to academic metadata, is integral to the implementation of the Library's OCLC SiteSearch system and contributes to fulfilling the Library's obligations to strategic projects such as the Southwest Project and DAPS."[40] At the University of Michigan, the metadata specialist coordinates the development of schemas for descriptive metadata and metadata production processes for collaborative projects taking place outside of, or in conjunction with, the library.[41] This is familiar territory to those cataloging librarians active in national and international efforts to enhance descriptive and subject cataloging schemes, as well as to those instructing campus subject specialists not in libraries in the use of library schemes.

The newness of the metadata specialist concept comes from involvement with a broader definition of metadata and range of schemas and its close working relationship with other partners in the development of digital information infrastructures inclusive of multiple content formats and metadata schemas. On the international and national scenes, numerous initiatives are underway to create necessary support mechanisms. The developers of crosswalks between metadata schemes may not yet be considered "metadata specialists," but crosswalks are an excellent example of what librarians do as metadata librarians. In the near future, local systems will manage data records from many sources in a variety of formats and syntaxes, and successful system managers will add expertise in metadata into their knowledge bases.

The transformation of cataloging librarians into metadata librarians is exciting, necessary, and in process. In addition to the initiatives mentioned earlier, catalogers are recording descriptions in the Dublin Core metadata format of Web-based resources and entering them into a national database, CORC, the Cooperative Online Research Catalog.[42] With the practice database having yielded in July 2000 to a production model, the number of 145 participating libraries is likely to increase, thus expanding the ranks of "metadata catalogers." In reality, cataloging librarians have always been metadata librarians. As specialists in the development and use of schemes originating in the library community, we were called cataloging librarians, much as metadata specialists in the world of indexing were called indexers. Changing terminology from *cataloging librarian* to *metadata librarian* emphasizes the effect of the digital, networked environment and multiple metadata schemes on library catalogs and cataloging and positions cataloging librarians to work effectively in directing the functioning of library catalogs and cataloging in this environment. Not every cataloger will necessarily be directly conversant with multiple metadata schemas, but every cataloger will be working in the multiple-schema framework.

Partnerships

In today's world, teams and partnerships are standard operating practices. This collaborative mode is transforming business, and the *Wall Street Journal* day after day writes about mergers, acquisitions, and other partnerships formed for creating stronger, more able entities. In April 2000, the Advisory Council, whose members are successful executives primarily from the corporate environment, imparted the same wisdom to the University of Notre Dame University Libraries. The development of metadata schemes and digital libraries is a clear demonstration of the success of this approach.

The goal of the Alexandria Digital Library Project is straightforward: "to build a distributed digital library (DL) for geographically-referenced materials."[43] In describing the work being done, Smith lists the many partners involved in developing the catalog and metadata component of the Alexandria Digital Library. The University of California, Santa Barbara, is leading a consortium of universities, government institutions, and private corporations that involves over thirty researchers, representing a broad range of disciplines and expertise. In addition, he points out that this project is working closely with other digital library projects in developing interoperable libraries. At the University of Michigan Digital Library Project, there are likewise numerous partners and research teams involving librarians and other disciplinary experts on teams for advanced user interfaces development, collection search and retrieval, ontology definition, and user interface design and evaluation.[44]

While the large operations and funding requirements of these projects make partnerships an obvious arrangement, successful but smaller library gateway teams are also comprised of individuals with expertise in a range of functions, including cataloging, reference, and information technology experts. This is not surprising because it has long been recognized that in the implementation of library online systems, the integration of functions into an online system must be mirrored in the functional expertise of the implementation team. Metadata librarians are actively involved with other experts in developing metadata schemes and organizational gateways, such as the Gateway to Educational Materials (GEM).[45]

Where Goes Library Cataloging?

Negroponte wrote his seminal work[46] five years ago, almost a generation in the digital age. He was exploring the possibilities that "being digital" would bring for broadcast TV and newspapers, two of the most popular media delivering news and entertainment. Although each medium has its own sensory appeal, they are similar in that the underlying intelligence originates at the point of transmission, when the material is sent out to audiences. Producers and editors select the material. The audience receives it. But, he asks, what if we had "computers that read newspapers and look at television for us, and act as editors when we ask them to do so?"[47] Producers and editors would continue to produce news shows and newspapers and send them out via the usual distribution channels. But, in addition, a "point of intelligence," says Negroponte, could live in a new home appliance that would then pull from this transmission a specific selection of items—only the items of interest—to the family living there. He concludes that the future will not be one or the other of these choices but both.[48]

Likewise, we will see that our future in libraries will include both cataloging and the creation of catalogs using library-developed schemes, as well as the interaction of cataloging and catalogs with other metadata schemes and databases. While library cataloging and catalogs have always been only one tool in the vast array of indexes and databases, the networked environment and the drive toward creating digital library services bring a new emphasis to the need to connect library catalogs with other metadata repositories.

Recently, Cline described the Harvard Library Digital Initiative. It is not a separate digital library, as Harvard has chosen "to integrate digital resources as one more evolutionary stage in its libraries."[49] The Digital Initiative "intends to develop the university's capacity to manage digital information by creating the technical infrastructure to acquire, organize, deliver and archive digital library materials."[50] One important piece of the infrastructure has been the creation of Web-based union catalogs for visual information, for finding aids for access to archival collections, and for geospatial data. Collections are in libraries, museums, and archives on campus. Although not described, there are undoubtedly a variety of metadata schemes involved and metadata librarians working with archivists, visual resource experts, and computer experts, to create the digital library. Cataloging librarians will apply their knowledge of the principles of describing and organizing information resources to new situations. They will articulate how the goals of the library catalog differ from those of other databases and will establish a framework that allows a user to retrieve information successfully from multiple databases.

Library cataloging and catalogs will likely continue as discrete activities and entities but not in the same manner. They may evolve to incorporate other schema[51] or be different simply because they are Web-accessible and can be used in conjunction with other databases. With knowledge of how library-developed schemes fit into the big picture of resource discovery, access, and use, metadata librarians will develop successful interaction with other metadata schemas and indexes and, as Negroponte suggests, create a future of library and other metadata schemes.

NOTES

1. George Santayana, *The Life of Reason, or the Phases of Human Progress,* 2nd ed. (New York: Charles Scribner's Sons, 1922), 284.

2. Ron Chepesiuk, "Dream in the Desert: Alexandria's Library Rises Again," *American Libraries* 31, no. 4 (April 2000): 70–73.

3. Luciana Canfora, *The Vanished Library* (Berkeley: University of California Press, 1987), 20.

4. Peter Brush, "The Alexandrian Library as It Once Was," *American Libraries* 31, no. 4 (April 2000): 74.

5. Canfora, *The Vanished Library,* 39.

6. Ibid., 99.

7. Umberto Eco, *The Name of the Rose* (San Diego: Harcourt Brace Jovanovich, 1983).

8. J. O. Ward, "Alexandria and Its Medieval Legacy," in *The Library of Alexandria,* ed. Roy MacLeod (London: Tauris, 2000), 163–179.

9. Ibid., 172.

10. See: Maurice J. Freedman, *The Functions of the Catalog and the Main Entry As Found in the Work of Panizzi, Jewett, Cutter and Lubetzky* (Ann Arbor, Mich.: University Microfilms International, 1983); Francis Miksa, *The Subject in the Dictionary Catalog from Cutter to the Present* (Chicago: American Library Association, 1983); Wayne Wiegand, *Irrepressible Reformer: A Biography of Melvil Dewey* (Chicago: American Library Association, 1996); John Metcalfe, *Information Retrieval: British & American, 1876–1976* (Metuchen, N.J.: Scarecrow Press, 1976).

11. D. M. Liston and J. L. Dolby, "Metadata Systems for Integrated Access to Numeric Data Files," *Drexel Library Quarterly* 18, no. 3–4 (1982): 147–160.

12. Judy Luther, "GL '99 Explores 'New Frontiers in Grey Literature,'" *Library Hi Tech News* 17, no. 5 (2000): 10–15.

13. Jessica Milstead and Susan Feldman, "Metadata: Cataloging by Any Other Name," *ONLINE* 23 (January–February 1999), http://www.onlineinc.com/onlinemag/OL1999/milstead1.html.

14. John DeFrancis, *Annotated Quotations from Chairman Mao* (New Haven, Conn.: Yale University Press, 1975), 138.

15. See: Michael Day, *Metadata: Mapping between Metadata Formats,* http://www.ukoln.ac.uk/metadata/interoperability; Rebecca Guenther, *Dublin Core/MARC/GILS Crosswalk,* http://lcweb.loc.gov/marc/dccross.html; Elizabeth Mangan, *FGDC to USMARC,* http://www.alexandria.ucsb.edu/public-documents/metadata/fgdc2marc.html; Eliot Christian, "Annex B: GILS Core Elements to USMARC," in *Application Profile for the Government Information Locator Service (GILS): Version 2,* http://www.gils.net/prof_v2.

html#annex_b; Jackie Shieh, *Description of Text Encoding Initiative (TEI) Header Elements and Corresponding USMARC Fields: Appendix to TEI/MARC Best Practices,* http://etext.virginia.edu/~ejs7y/tei-usmarc.html.

16. Allan Richmond, *Web Developer's Virtual Library: Meta Tagging for Search Engines,* http://wdvl.internet.com;Location/Meta/Tag.html.

17. Clifford Lynch, Avra Michelson, Cecilia Preston, and Craig A. Summerhill, "The Nature of the NIDR Challenge," in *CNI White Paper on Networked Information Discovery and Retrieval,* chap. 1, http://www.cni.org/projects/nidr/outline.chapt1.html.

18. Milstead and Feldman, "Metadata."

19. Zorana Ercegovac, "Introduction," *Journal of the American Society for Information Science* 50, no. 13 (1999): 1166.

20. Murtha Baca, ed., *Introduction to Metadata: Pathways to Digital Information.* (Los Angeles, Calif.: Getty Information Institute, 1998).

21. Edward Gaynor, "From MARC to Markup: SGML and Online Library Systems," *ALCTS Newsletter* 7, no. 2 (1996): A–D, http://www.lib.virginia.edu/speccol/scdc/articles/alcts_brief.html.

22. Linda L. Hill, Greg Janee, Ron Dolin, James Frew, and Mary Larsgaard, "Collection Metadata Solutions for Digital Library Applications," *Journal of the American Society for Information Science* 50, no. 13 (November 1999): 1178.

23. Clifford Lynch, "The Dublin Core Descriptive Metadata Program: Strategic Implications for Libraries and Networked Information Access," *ARL Newsletter* 196 (February 1998), http://www.arl.org/newsltr/196/dublin.html.

24. Colorado Digitization Project, Metadata Working Group, *General Guidelines for Descriptive Metadata Creation & Entry,* http://coloradodigital.coalliance.org/glines.html.

25. Lynch, "The Dublin Core Descriptive Metadata Program."

26. Karen Calhoun, Zsuzsa Koltay, and Edward Weissman, "Library Gateway. Project Design, Teams and Cycle Time," *Library Resources & Technical Services* 43, no. 2 (1999): 116.

27. Stuart A. Sutton, "Conceptual Design and Deployment of a Metadata Framework for Educational Resources on the Internet," *Journal of the American Society for Information Science* 50, no. 13 (November 1999): 1182.

28. Steve Coffman, "Building Earth's Largest Library," *Searcher* 7, no. 3 (March 1999): 34–37.

29. Marifay Makssour, "United Kingdom's Wellcome Library Adds 44 Millionth Bibliographic Record to WorldCat," *OCLC News Release,* June 28, 2000, http://www.oclc.org:80/oclc/press/20000628.htm.

30. Jerry Campbell, "The Case for Creating a Scholars' Portal to the Web: A White Paper," in *Building Scholarly Communities: Association of Research Libraries, Proceedings of the 136th Annual Meeting, April 13, 2000* (Baltimore, Md.: Association of Research Libraries, 2000), 4, http://www.arl.org/arl/proceedings/136/portal.html.

31. Matt Lake, "Searching the Web," *Time Digital,* July 2000, 74, http://www.timedigital.com.

32. Ibid., 76.

33. Calhoun, Koltay, and Weissman, "Library Gateway," 114–122.

34. Edwin M. Cortez, "Use of Metadata Vocabularies in Data Retrieval," *Journal of the American Society for Information Science* 50, no. 13 (November 1999): 1218.

35. Ibid.

36. Diane Vizine-Goetz,. "Netlab/OCLC Collaboration Seeks to Improve Web Searching," *OCLC Newsletter* (July/August 1999): 30–32.

37. Ibid., 30.

38. Association for Library Collections and Technical Services, Task Force on Meta Access, *Final Report,* April 3, 1997, http://www.ala.org/alcts/publications/meta.html.

39. Ibid.

40. University of Arizona, "Metadata Librarian Position Description," June 10, 1998, http://dizzy.library.arizona.edu/library/teams/access98/meta610.htm.

41. University of Michigan, Library. "Position Description: Metadata Specialist," August 1, 1999, http://www-personal.umich.edu/~jaheim/metadataspec.html.

42. Bill Carney, "Libraries Use CORC to Catalog Useful Sites," *OCLC Newsletter* (November/December): 12–13.

43. Terence R. Smith, "A Brief Update on the Alexandria Digital Library Project," *D-Lib Magazine,* March 1996, http://www.dlib.org/dlib/march96/briefings/smith/03smith.html.

44. University of Michigan, NSF/DARPA/NASA Sponsored Digital Library Project, "Team Partners," http://www.si.umich.edu/UMDL/partners.html.

45. Sutton, "Conceptual Design and Deployment of a Metadata Framework for Educational Resources on the Internet," 1182–1192.

46. Nicholas Negroponte, *Being Digital* (New York: Knopf, 1995).

47. Ibid., 20.

48. Ibid.

49. Nancy M. Cline, "Virtual Continuity: The Challenge for Research Libraries Today," *EDUCAUSE Review* 35, no. 3 (May/June 2000): 27.

50. Ibid., 27–28.

51. Gaynor, "From MARC to Markup."

II

CATALOGING THE WEB: AACR AND MARC 21

2

AACR2 Complexities, Necessary and Otherwise: The Delsey Report, the Cardinal Principle, and (ER) Harmonization

Brian E. C. Schottlaender, transcribed by Mary Larsgaard

To describe the Anglo-American Cataloguing Rules (AACR), and the processes for their revision, as "complex" is to risk stating the obvious. To describe them as "necessarily complex," perhaps less so. Several of the code reviews undertaken in the recent past underscore the necessary complexity of both the code and its revision. This chapter presents an overview of some of these reviews, initiated primarily as a consequence of the International Conference on the Principles and Future Development of AACR held in October 1997.

Hosted in Toronto by the Joint Steering Committee (JSC) for Revision of Anglo-American Cataloguing Rules, the invitation-only conference had as its objective to review the underlying principles of AACR, with a view to determining whether fundamental rule revision is appropriate and feasible and, if so, advising on the direction and nature of those revisions.[1] The outcomes of the conference included three that are relevant here:

- Pursue the recommendation that a data-modeling technique be used to provide a logical analysis of the principles and structures that underlie AACR
- Solicit a proposal to revise Rule 0.24 to advance the discussion on the primacy of intellectual content over physical format
- Determine if there are any existing surveys on the extent of use of AACR2 outside the Anglo-American community and, if no such survey exists, conduct such a survey

Fortunately, at least one of these tasks had already been carried out in the form of surveys on the extent of use of AACR outside the Anglo-American community, documented in a thesis by Pino Buizza and in a follow-up article by Diego Maltese. While JSC, therefore, did not need to conduct such a survey itself, the committee was sensitized to the desirability of ensuring that the Anglo-American Cataloguing Rules remained in "harmony" with other international cataloging standards.

JSC commissioned Tom Delsey (National Library of Canada) to prepare a logical analysis of AACR, which he did in 1998 and 1999—working with Beth Dulabahn, Michael Heaney, and Jean Hirons (part 1). The entire *Logical Structure of the Anglo-American Cataloguing Rules* analysis is available on the World Wide Web.[2]

The objectives of what rapidly came to be called the "Delsey Model" were to:

- Help us understand more clearly how some of the structural elements of the rules relate to the key underlying principles of the code
- Help us as we chart the future development of the code to respond to emerging issues associated with the evolution of digital technologies and a networked environment[3]

The method Delsey and his colleagues used to analyze the underlying logical structure of the code involved identifying the entities/objects at the center of that structure and articulating the rules that govern the relationships between them. The outcomes and recommendations of the model are several and substantial; the executive summary alone extends to almost one hundred pages. What follows is an overview of the major points in part 1 of the analysis.

Delsey and colleagues identified five structural issues that need addressing in part 1 of AACR2, as follows.

ISSUE 1

> The wording of rule 0.24 implies that the form of the physical carrier determines the class of material to which the item belongs. However, while the form of the physical carrier is in many cases the principal criterion . . . there are in fact other criteria at play.[4]

Delsey recommended using the model developed for his study to assess options for restructuring part 1 of the code, to facilitate the integration of rules for new forms of expression and new media. One option he identified for such a restructuring is to use the ISBD(G) areas of description as the primary organizing element for the overall structure of part 1 of AACR. JSC responded to this recommendation by commissioning Bruce Chr. Johnson (Library of Congress) to develop a prototypical ISBD(G)-based reorganization. The JSC's review of the alpha prototype confirmed that reorganizing the code by ISBD(G) area of description would be as complicated (if not more so) as anticipated and, furthermore, might well be of debatable benefit. The alpha prototype did demonstrate that there are opportunities for generalizing the code by moving provisions contained in chapters 2–12 into chapter 1. The JSC has requested permission of the publishers to make the alpha prototype available for community comment via the AACR Web site.

ISSUE 2

> The code implicitly assumes that a document . . . has a physical dimension . . . rule 0.24 dictates that the "physical form of the item in hand" is the starting point for description.[5]

Delsey recommended using the model developed for his study as the basis for examining the feasibility of modifying the internal logic of the code to accommodate documents that are defined in nonphysical terms, with appropriate consultation of experts in the area of electronic document architecture. JSC responded to this recommendation by working on a Statement of Principles (presented at the JSC meeting in September 2000 and eventually to appear in AACR2, as such a statement did in the first edition) and by requesting that CC:DA (ALA/ALCTS/CCS/Committee on Cataloging: Description and Access) develop revisions for chapter 9 (Electronic Resources) and a revision of Rule 0.24. These were completed and presented to JSC in 1999 and early 2000.[6]

ISSUE 3

> . . . distinctions made in the code between "unpublished" and "published" documents are implicitly predicated on the notion of public distribution of physical copies of a document. . . . With on-line dissemination of digital objects, those same assumptions do not necessarily hold.[7]

Delsey recommended examining the issues raised with respect to the notion of "publication" in a networked context, in consultation with experts in the area of electronic documents. This matter is currently under consideration by JSC constituent organizations, where a number of discussions as to what constitutes a "published" item are proceeding.

ISSUE 4

> . . . distinctions made in the code between monographic . . . and serial publications . . . are also predicated on conventional modes of "continuing" a publication by means of issuing successive physical parts. . . . digital technology . . . introduces other options for "continuing" publications that do not entail the issuing of successive physical parts.[8]

Delsey recommended continuing the "seriality" examination initiated during the International Conference on the Principles and Future Development of AACR, using the frame of reference set out in the model developed for his study as a tool to assist in the analysis of the issues. JSC responded to this recommendation by requesting that Jean Hirons (Library of Congress) draft chapter 12 (Serials) revisions. These revisions have been submitted to JSC and are undergoing constituent review.

ISSUE 5

> Implicit in the rules is the assumption that both the source from which the data is derived and the form in which the information is represented in that source will be the same from one copy of a document to another. . . . The introduction of digital technology has effectively undercut those a priori assumptions.[9]

The ease with which digital files can be manipulated is a double-edged sword because in that very facility is the attendant reality that there are no guarantees as to constancy of digital content. Delsey recommended reviewing the current conventions and rules for reflecting change in the attributes of described items in order to determine their applicability to changes in the attributes of digital objects and to extend them as necessary to accommodate a broader range of variables. JSC responded to this recommendation by requesting that CC:DA prepare a draft appendix to the code that differentiates between major and minor changes in bibliographic information and describes under what change circumstances a cataloger should create a new bibliographic record. The CC:DA Task Force charged with this undertaking submitted an Interim Report to JSC in August 2000. As one might expect, the chapter 12 (Serials) revisions drafted by Jean Hirons likewise include provisions for recording changes in bibliographic attributes.

It came as no surprise to JSC to discover that Rule 0.24 was at the heart of the issues identified by Delsey as needing addressing in part 1. It is, after all, "The Cardinal Principle." Moreover, Delsey's "call to action" regarding Rule 0.24 was yet another in a long line of such exhortations dating back to the earliest "multiple-version" discussions. By the end of the International Conference on the Principles and Future Development of AACR, it was clear that "The Cardinal Principle" was a basic and pressing problem and that if useful discussion was to proceed, a concrete proposal was required.

> 0.24. It is a cardinal principle of the use of part 1 that the description of a physical item should be based in the first instance on the chapter dealing with the class of materials to which that item belongs. For example, describe a printed monograph in microform as a microform (using the rules in chapter 11). There will be need in many instances to consult the chapter dealing with the original form of the item, especially when constructing notes. So, using the same example, consult the chapter dealing with printed books (chapter 2) to supplement chapter 11. In short, the starting point for description is the physical form of the item in hand, not the original or any previous form in which the work has been published.
>
> In describing serials, consult chapter 12 in conjunction with the chapter dealing with the physical form in which the serial is published. For example, in describing a serial motion picture, use both chapters 12 and 7.[10]

Rule 0.24 has several functions, most notably:

- Assisting the cataloger in describing items with multiple characteristics
- Assisting the cataloger in deciding when to create new bibliographic records for similar items

There have for some years been problems with applying this rule, including:

- It requires the cataloger to give primacy to carrier type rather than to intellectual content.
- It assumes that a particular carrier type conveys a particular content type.
- It requires that the cataloger create a new bibliographic record both for a new expression and for the same expression in a different manifestation.

The CC:DA Task Force charged with developing concrete revision proposals for Rule 0.24 made three recommendations. These and JSC's responses follow.

RECOMMENDATION 1

Take a "staged approach" to revising Rule 0.24.[11]

JSC endorsed the following revision for Rule 0.24, as a first step.

> 0.24. It is important to bring out all aspects of the item being described, including its content, its carrier, its type of publication, its bibliographic relationships, and whether it is published or unpublished. In any given area of the description, all relevant aspects

should be described. As a rule of thumb, the cataloguer should follow the more specific rules applying to the item being cata-logued, whenever they differ from the general rules.[12]

RECOMMENDATION 2

Investigate further the format-variation (multiple-version) problem in Rule 0.24, including, specifically, the possi-bility of ignoring manifestation variations in determining when to make a new record.[13]

While rejecting the specific recommendation (as written), the JSC endorsed the task force's general recommendation. JSC plans to establish an interconstituency working group to pursue the issue, with a particular view toward assessing the benefits and/or deficiencies of expression-based cataloging.[14]

RECOMMENDATION 3

Add an introductory chapter to the code that includes a statement of principles, entity definitions (work, expres-sion, etc.), a discussion of format (manifestation) variations, and other information as needed.[15]

As noted previously, JSC is already working on a statement of principles. In response to the broader recommendation, JSC has requested that LA/BL—a joint committee of the [British] Library Association and the British Library, equivalent to CC:DA—draft such an introductory chapter.[16]

Finally, there is another area of discussion regarding AACR in which digital technology is front and center: namely, that surrounding "harmonizing" AACR2 (primarily chapter 9) with the International Standard Bibliographic Description (Electronic Resources) (ISBD[ER]). This sort of "harmonization" is one of JSC's principal charges and one of its most complex, operationally and politically. Would that ISBD(ER) harmonization were as simple as replacing the term *computer file* in AACR with the term *electronic resource*! Unfortunately, while general replacement of one term with the other is appropriate, wholesale replacement is not. Each occurrence of the term had to be evaluated separately. And that's just the tip of the iceberg for this complex harmony—closer to Bach than to Gregorian chant. JSC, CC:DA, and other constituent groups have been hard at it now for the better part of eighteen months. Actions thus far include:

- Thorough revision of chapter 9
- Substantial additions and revisions to the glossary and index
- Significant revisions to chapter 1 (inevitable, given its role as the foundation upon which subsequent chapters are built)[17]

There is additional work yet to do. Still under discussion are:

- The elimination of Area 3 in chapter 9
- The extension of Area 5 in chapter 9 to remote-access resources
- Wholesale reconsideration of the general material designations (GMD), ranging from their elimination to the as-signment of multiple GMDs

Beyond that, for the future—coordination and harmonization between AACR and various metadata schema: a sub-stantial challenge, with an even more substantial payoff.

NOTES

1. "Joint Steering Committee for Revision of Anglo-American Cataloguing Rules," http://www.nlc-bnc.ca/jsc/. See also Jean Weihs, ed., *The Principles and Future of AACR: Proceedings of the International Conference on the Principles and Future Devel-opment of AACR, October 23–25, 1997, Toronto, Canada* (Ottawa: Canadian Library Association; Chicago: American Library Asso-ciation, 1998).

2. Tom Delsey et al., *The Logical Structure of the Anglo-American Cataloguing Rules: Part 1,* August 1998, http://www.nlc-bnc. ca/jsc/aacrint.pdf, and *Part 2,* January 1999, http://www.nlc-bnc.ca/jsc/aacrint2.pdf.

3. Delsey, Part 1, 1.

4. Ibid., 25.

5. Ibid., 28.

6. See: ALA/ALCTS/CCS/CC:DA Task Force on Rule 0.24, *Overview and Recommendations Concerning Revision of Rule 0.24,* August 16, 1999, http://www.ala.org/alcts/organization/ccs/ccda/tf-024h.pdf; and: ALA/ALCTS/CCS/CC:DA Task Force on the Harmonization of ISBD(ER) and AACR2, *Final Report,* September 2, 1999, http://www.ala.org/alcts/organization/ccs/ccda/tf-harm3.pdf.

7. Delsey, Part 1, 30.

8. Ibid., 33.

9. Ibid., 34.

10. *Anglo-American Cataloguing Rules,* 2nd ed., 1998 rev. (Chicago: American Library Association, 1998), 8.

11. ALA/ALCTS/CCS/CC:DA Task Force on Rule 0.24, 5.

12. Joint Steering Committee for Revision of Anglo-American Cataloguing Rules, "Outcomes of the Meeting Held in Brisbane, Australia, 18–20 October 1999," http://www.nlc-bnc.ca/jsc/brisbane.htm.

13. ALA/ALCTS/CCS/CC:DA Task Force on Rule 0.24, 5.

14. Joint Steering Committee for Revision of Anglo-American Cataloguing Rules, "Outcomes of the Meeting of the Joint Steering Committee Held in San Diego, California, USA, 22–24 March 2000," http://www.nlc-bnc.ca/jsc/0003out.html.

15. ALA/ALCTS/CCS/CC:DA Task Force on Rule 0.24, 6.

16. Joint Steering Committee for Revision of Anglo-American Cataloguing Rules, "Outcomes of the Meeting of the Joint Steering Committee Held in San Diego."

17. Ibid.

3

O, Brave Old World:
Using AACR to Catalog Web Resources[1]

Matthew Beacom

INTRODUCTION

Using AACR to catalog Web resources challenges catalogers, libraries, and our profession to successfully extend our existing tools—staff, institutions, concepts, the rules, practices, and culture—to a profoundly new situation. The long-term result may be substantial modifications, such as the seriality issues currently under discussion, or radical transformations, but the short-term result has been more modest. We are making the changes we need to get the job done, and we are doing the job.

The theme of using AACR to catalog Web resources can be discussed in many ways, but I want to focus mainly on the choices we can make and do make. To that end, this chapter is organized around a handful of questions that I think need to be answered by catalogers in order to catalog Web resources:

1. Where do I start?
2. What do I catalog?
3. What about e-aggregations?
4. Is it a reproduction, edition, or neither?
5. Serial, mono, or integrating?
6. One record or two?
7. Which GMD?
8. Where do I put the URL?
9. What about access restrictions?
10. What about maintenance?

Each of these questions presents choices to the cataloger. There could be more than ten or fewer. The ten could be some other ten questions. These are certainly ten questions that are asked again and again, and they have immediate practical consequences and grander "philosophical" implications. For each question, I'll try to say something about both aspects.

WHERE DO I START?

Of course, it is best to begin at the beginning, but sometimes it is hard to say just what is the beginning.

- AACR2r 1998 rev.
- Rule interpretations: LC, utilities, local
- Indispensable guides: *CONSER Module 31; Cataloging Internet Resources,* 2nd ed.; PCC core standards
- Work of our peers: examples in OCLC, RLIN, and OPACs
- AUTOCAT and the professional literature

This may look like a reading list, and it is that. This list summarizes what you need to know or, rather, where you need to look. But it is, more important, a sign of something else. The listed sources of information, knowledge, and perhaps even wisdom are outward signs of the professional community of which you (and the rest of us) are a part. You are not alone.

WHAT DO I CATALOG?

Here is another beginning. You can't catalog something until you have something to catalog. There are four main issues or points here:

1. Do we catalog manifestations or expressions? The current rule is to catalog the item in hand (or on screen). As you may know, *AACR2 (Anglo-American Cataloguing Rules)* rule 0.24[2] is under serious discussion now and may change. But the concept of cataloging what one has (in hand or on screen) is a profound one and this cardinal principle may endure after all.

2. Selection still matters. We don't have to catalog the entire Web but just select those Web resources that are of value to our users. Just because much has changed, and changed drastically, doesn't mean that everything has. This is one service principle that hasn't changed and I don't think it will.

3. Collections aren't a thing of the past. Selecting resources yields collections of resources. It doesn't matter that the resources are not in hand or on the shelf in your building. It matters that you have chosen them and have access to them, whether they be leased, paid for, pointed to, and so on.

4. At what level of granularity will we describe a resource: article, issue, journal, aggregation, and so on? We make very similar decisions about analog resources now. We have to make those decisions about Web resources, too.

WHAT ABOUT E-AGGREGATIONS?

E-aggregations are a special case of the issue of granularity. Resources may be offered via aggregations that lump them by topic or source or at the whim of the provider. We need options to be able to present those resources in aggregations and the aggregations themselves in ways that serve readers. This will vary from library to library. Libraries and vendors need to work together creatively and flexibly. One example of this cooperation is the Program for Cooperative Cataloging's Automation Task Group on Journals in Aggregations. Its *Final Report* recommends methods for creating analytics for journal titles, supplies suggestions for machine generation of records from other information, and reports on a prototype project with EBSCO to provide analytic records for their aggregations.[3] Jake (Jointly Administered Knowledge Environment), a resource based at Yale, offers the possibility of a union database of information for resources in aggregations held at member institutions.[4]

IS IT A REPRODUCTION, EDITION, OR NEITHER?

This is one of the most important questions to ask and answer, since many other decisions about cataloging a Web resource follow upon this one. There is no one right answer. We may, as a profession, choose one answer as the best for most of us, most of the time, and then again we may not. It has happened with reproductions before.[5] But that begs the question.

What do we think Web resources are? If the same title exists in print, is a Web version of that title a reproduction, another edition, or something else—or something to which ideas about editions and reproductions don't apply?

The draft Library of Congress (LC) rule interpretation of rule 1.11A[6] sees Web resources that have print cousins (if you will) as reproductions and suggests that we catalog them more or less along the lines that LC has established for microfilms—catalog the original and cite the reproduction. The chief weakness of the draft LCRI is its lack of a clear definition of what is and what is not a reproduction with respect to electronic resources.

Other institutions treat Web resources with print cousins as reproductions only when the Web version is an image of the print. In cases where the Web version is marked up (in SGML, XML, HTML, etc.), it is cataloged as another edition. Still others see Web resources as being inherently dynamic and protean—too changeable and too easily changed to fit well with concepts such as edition or reproduction, which we created from our experiences with media that are far more fixed or static than are Web things. I think this last view is too radical. It views the impact of the Web on cataloging, publishing, and communication too much as a break with the past. Better definitions may come as IFLA's terminology of item, manifestation, expression, and work[7] becomes part of our policy-making.

A NEW RULE OF THREE: SERIAL, MONO, AND INTEGRATING

We are on the verge of a big breakthrough. AACR most likely will change its primary dichotomy of serial/nonserial to a richer, three-part distinction of what I call mono, serial, and integrating publication modes.[8] For those of us who have had to catalog as monographs full-text databases that used to be printed serial indexes, this will be a great relief. There will be practical issues regarding how to decide if a publication is one or the other of the three types, and sometimes I'm sure it will be difficult to determine. But if it quacks like a duck. . . .

ONE RECORD OR TWO?

This question is something of a misnomer, I think. It is clearer if we think of it as using a twenty-first-century version of dashed-on entries or using separate records for print and e-versions of the same title. The dashed-on technique produces complex records in the OPAC, while the separate record technique produces complex indexes. Neither is perfect. The separate-record approach may be seen as a consequence of seeing the e-version as a new edition. The CONSER option[9] is pretty straightforward—catalog it (with a new record) or refer to it from the record for the print version and link to the resource from that record. It works, but it has drawbacks for users and librarians, since it may be difficult to distinguish which characteristics of the record apply to a given electronic version and also limits institutions' ability to share records with others. LC's delineation technique uses the same basic strategy, and it is outlined in LC's draft interim guidelines.[10] Delineation compensates for some of the drawbacks of the dashed-on approach by stipulating that information necessary to the user be added to the record in notes associated with the link to the e-version. Neither approach is a viable multiple-versions approach, though each is a step in that direction.

WHICH GENERAL MATERIAL DESIGNATION (GMD)?

For textual materials, a quick and easy answer is "follow the standard"—use [computer file].[11] But why take the quick and easy way? Sure, it is "more, cheaper, faster," but it may not be better. It may not serve your users well enough. Some are anticipating the change to [electronic resource][12] and are using it. Others are creating hybrids of special material designations and GMDs ([electronic resource (map)]) or even rolling their own ([cool Web page]). Still others are not opting to use a GMD at all.

This is an issue under consideration in many quarters. Discussions on the AUTOCAT listserv reveal it to be of interest in many libraries; the Joint Steering Committee for Revision of AACR is looking into it; and an OLAC (Online Audiovisual Catalogers) group is doing so as well.

WHERE SHOULD YOU PUT THE URL?

Where should you put the URL? It depends. URLs have no place in AACR now. But thanks to MARBI (ALA's Machine-Readable Bibliographic Information Committee), we have a place for them in our catalog records! MARC supports the URL in the 856 field and now in several other fields. A proposal to add rules regarding URLs to AACR (as part of Uniform Resource Identifiers) was discussed at the ALA Annual Conference in Chicago in July 2000.[13]

One important aspect of the debate surrounding this issue is whether URLs should be treated as local holdings information or more universally applicable information (like a standard number). URIs would probably be pretty clearly seen as similar to standard numbers. They would be unique identifying elements, but URLs are less clearly so.

Whether URLs are standard numbers or not, we could cite URLs in notes such as those for mode of access, important numbers on items, and so on. The rules don't support this now, but MARC allows it in some note fields and catalogers have been doing it anyway. One good reason, though, to refrain from using URLs outside of the 856 is to minimize duplication of the same information and to keep maintenance work on URLs to a minimum.

WHAT ABOUT ACCESS RESTRICTIONS?

On the practical level, either the resource you are cataloging is freely available or it is not. If it is not, you need to tell the user. The user also needs information on who may have access and how. The former is a universal note; the latter, a local one: in MARC, a 506 and a 590 respectively. On a more philosophical level, the movement away from access restrictions based on copyright law to restrictions based on licensing agreements is a major change for all involved—content creators, users, publishers, and librarians. It has made sharing resources and sharing metadata more complicated. We don't know now where the changes in technology or social norms will lead us—to a pay-per-view model or a Napsterish model, or something less apocalyptic or utopian. This makes it difficult to determine a long-term policy for locating access information in a record.

WHAT ABOUT MAINTENANCE?

We know things change. We know that sometimes things fall apart. Web things seem to change more and more quickly. In our daily work as Web-resource catalogers, we act as if Web resources are fixed enough for us to use AACR to catalog them. We list URLs and scope and system requirements in our records, all areas subject to change. But we have also recognized the need to anticipate change. We know we are describing something that may be inherently plastic or at least easily changed. A clear example of this is the development of the "viewed on" note. Part of the catalog record describes not the object of the record but the timing of the act of cataloging it, in order to anchor the description to a particular moment of the resource's "life."

Are Web resources by their nature as networked, digital information things, too potentially dynamic, too potentially protean for our rules, our catalogs, and our accumulated wisdom to control? Our catalogs and our rules have developed over time with resources that are highly stable and difficult to change. Printed paper is durable and fixed. As resources shift to an ephemeral and plastic medium—the Web—will radically new approaches to "bibliographic" control be required?

CONCLUSION

Library catalogs are proving to be a useful tool for managing Web resources. The activities of the Toronto conference on the future of AACR[14] give evidence of the cataloging community's willingness to change in response to e-publishing. Now, AACR, MARC, and library management systems must adapt further to a pluralistic metadata and data environment.

NOTES

1. I'd like to thank Mary Larsgaard for her suggestion for the title and theme of this paper. I appreciate both the Shakespearean allusion and the focus on actual practice.

2. "Methods of Procedure [Rule] 0.24," in *Anglo-American Cataloguing Rules,* 2nd ed., 1988 rev. (Chicago: American Library Association, 1988), 8.

3. Program for Cooperative Cataloging, Standing Committee on Automation, Task Group on Journals in Aggregator Databases, *Final Report,* January 2000, http://lcweb.loc.gov/catdir/pcc/aggfinal.html.

4. "Jointly Administered Knowledge Environment (jake)," http://jake.med.yale.edu/docs/about.html.

5. "1.11: Facsimiles, Photocopies, and Other Reproductions," in *Anglo-American Cataloguing Rules,* 58–9. Note that there is no rule 9.11.

6. Library of Congress, Cataloging Policy and Support Office, *Draft LCRI 1.11A, Non-Microfilm and Electronic Reproductions,* April 14, 2000, http://lcweb.loc.gov/catdir/cpso/1_11A_cover.html.

7. IFLA Study Group on the Functional Requirements for Bibliographic Records, *Functional Requirements for Bibliographic Records: Final Report* (Munich: K. G. Saur, 1998). Also available at http://www.ifla.org/VII/s13/frbr/frbr.htm.

8. Jean Hirons, Regina Reynolds, and Judy Kuhagen, *Revising AACR2 to Accommodate Seriality: Report to the Joint Steering Committee for Revision of AACR,* http://www.nlc-bnc.ca/jsc/ser-rep0.html.

9. "31.3.5: Guidelines for Online Versions of Serials Issued in Print, CD-ROM, etc.," in *CONSER Cataloging Manual,* module 31, part 1, http://lcweb.loc.gov/acq/conser/mod31pt1.html.

10. Library of Congress, Cataloging Policy and Support Office, *Draft Interim Guidelines for Cataloging Electronic Resources [DCM B19],* January 5, 1998, http://lcweb.loc.gov/catdir/cpso/dcmb19_4.html.

11. "1.1C: General Material Designation," in *Anglo-American Cataloguing Rules,* 20.

12. International Federation of Library Associations and Institutions, "1.2: General Material Designation," in *ISBD(ER): International Standard Bibliographic Description for Electronic Resources* (Munich: K. G. Saur, 1997), 33–35.

13. American Library Association, MARBI, *Proposal No. 2000-02: Renaming of Subfield $u to Uniform Resource Identifier (URI) in Field 856 in MARC 21 Formats,* December 3, 1999, http://lcweb.loc.gov/marc/marbi/2000/2000-02.html.

14. Joint Steering Committee for Revision of Anglo-American Cataloguing Rules, International Conference on the Principles and Future Development of AACR, http://www.nlc-bnc.ca/jsc/index.htm.

SOURCES FOR FURTHER READING

International Federation of Library Associations and Institutions. *Digital Libraries: Cataloguing and Indexing of Electronic Resources,* June 21, 1999, http://www.ifla.org/II/catalog.htm.

Journal of Internet Cataloging (Binghamton, N.Y.: Haworth Press), vol. 1, no. 1 (1997), http://www.haworthpressinc.com/jic.

4

Struggling toward Retrieval: Can Alternatives to Standard Operating Procedures Help?

Sheila S. Intner

INTRODUCTION

I have always championed standard cataloging—my cataloging textbook is titled *Standard Cataloging for School and Public Libraries;* achieving recognition of standards for nonprint cataloging guided my involvement with Association for Library Collections & Technical Services' Audiovisual Committee, which I chaired back in the 1980s when ALCTS was called RTSD (Resources & Technical Services Division)—but I also recognize the value to particular audiences of nonstandard policies and practices designed to meet their unique needs. However, I believe it is much more difficult, time-consuming, costly, and limiting to stray from standard operating practice; therefore, one must have a particularly good reason to go to the trouble of doing so and derive something of great value in exchange for the additional effort and cost. For reasons why I believe this to be true, see my chapter in Weinberg's *Cataloging Heresy,* "Rejecting Standard Cataloging Copy: Implications for the Education of Catalogers."[1]

Being a cataloging educator rather than a practicing cataloger, my adherence to standards and my trust that following them are the most effective ways to maximize output and thus provide the greatest cataloging value to the library, but this has never stopped me from playing the devil's advocate and questioning their efficacy. Knowing that I have this penchant, I will address alternatives to standard cataloging operations for Web-based serials—an issue that I believe becomes more important with each passing day, as the balance of library collections shifts toward electronic resources and away from materials in other formats. Please note that, as represented here, "metadata" is confined to Web resources only and that this article is concerned solely with serials.

Two basic assumptions underlie my arguments: (1) "the goal of libraries is to serve their patrons";[2] and (2) the principles underlying bibliographic services are embodied in Cutter's "Objects," namely, that cataloging operations should produce data that enable catalogs to identify individual items and collocate related items. Cutter thought in terms of authors, titles, and subjects as the main elements to be identified and collocated, but today we have added others, such as dates, publishers, languages, and so on, to his list of three.

Assumption 1 implies that patron needs are predictable and amenable to the application of standard methods. This may have been true in the past, when scholarship was more limited and rule-bound, but it appears to be far from the rule today. The definition of "patron," once generally thought to be a white Protestant male of Anglo-Saxon descent, today describes anyone on the planet with Internet access. Similarly, the definition of "information needs," once limited in scope, genre, and format to a relatively small number of materials covering well-defined subject areas, is today anything one can envision—from the unedited footage of events captured live to global demographics sought by multinational corporations—and the boundaries among disciplines are notoriously unclear.

Assumption 2 could be abbreviated as Find and Gather, or, in catalogers' terms, Description and Collocation. But that is no longer the whole point of catalogs. Cutter's Objects assume that someone had previously selected the materials and acquired them for the library before catalogers went to work on them. Thus, to be more accurate, we must expand Cutter's Objects to Selection and Acquisition, Description and Collocation. Furthermore, we need to consider the outcome of all this activity, for which the library catalog was the primary vehicle. This can be expressed as Second Selection and Use. The first selection traditionally assumes that a librarian-selector starts with the entire universe of knowledge and culls from it that which best meets the needs of the local library, which will subsequently be acquired for use on site. The whole operation could be expressed as:

1. First Selection
2. Acquisition
3. Description
4. Collocation
5. Second Selection
6. Use

What has changed in today's library catalogs, because they are distributed via the Internet, is that they possess a whole universe of knowledge—not everything, to be sure, but enough material to look like a good imitation of everything. This makes it possible for patrons to telescope the six-stage operation involving numerous library specialists, support staff, and themselves into one giant step they can take alone. Patrons themselves can do the initial selection from the universe of knowledge, dispense with the acquisition process, and skip the middle stage, in which highly educated catalogers provided them with bibliographic systems and the need to make a Second Selection from them (often mediated for greater effectiveness by highly educated reference librarians). Instead, patrons now can move from First Selection to Use.

OBSERVATIONS ON SERIALS CATALOGING STANDARDS

As I noted in some detail in a series of columns written for *Technicalities* and republished in the book *Interfaces: Relationships between Library Technical and Reference Services*,[3] the results of applying our traditional standard practices do not enable the library catalog to offer much information about serials. The Library of Congress, which sets the standard for quality cataloging practice, uses the simplest and least informative bibliographic model for describing serials. To be cataloged as a serial is to eliminate most of the elements both librarians and patrons use to identify, locate, and select materials for use, such as authors' and editors' names, article titles, representation of contents through indexing and classification, or even a full description of the physical material itself. All the details given in the catalog record (but not those likely to change over time, like the editor, the number of issues or volumes, titles of individual articles, page numbers, etc.) relate solely to the title's first issue or, when that is not available, the earliest issue in the library's possession. Consider how much helpful information that catalog record would contain for a scientific journal that began publishing in the nineteenth century or an e-journal that publishes three times a week or every day.

Traditional operations dictate that elements expected to change over time are eliminated from the catalog record prepared by libraries. Instead, commercial organizations are entrusted with providing access to the contents of serial titles. (I call this doing the cataloging, but not many others agree.) Patrons get a little something from the library's catalog—a pointer indicating that the library owns some part of a particular serial title, though not what it is. To find serially published materials, patrons go to a non-library-produced index to find a wanted work (an article, column, editorial, chapter, or review) and note its location in detail (volume, issue, pages); compare these data against the library's serials holdings list to see if the desired part is, indeed, part of the library's collections; and, if it is, proceed to the shelf, hoping to find the material and read it. (These hopes are occasionally dashed, but most of the time patrons do succeed.)

Fortunately, this scenario is changing, thanks to the capabilities of library computers. It is no longer difficult for holdings records to be attached to bibliographic records, enabling the catalog to show if a desired part of a serial is available. But it still seems too difficult for libraries to do more than minimal descriptions or to apply subject indexing to serial parts smaller than the entire publication—all issues and all text, past, present, and future. Following the model of the monographic book, which mandates summarizing the entire item as the chosen unit for subject indexing with a handful of descriptors, serials have fared poorly in standard cataloging operations. Instead of providing intellectual access for serials, library catalogs provide inventory control, something librarians would never tolerate as sufficient for the monographic books they buy.

WHAT SHOULD THE CATALOG DO?

Returning to our theoretical discussion of what the catalog should do, I believe the current environment—Web-based e-journals forming an overabundant supply of raw material, diverse kinds of patrons with ever-more-diverse information needs, frequent blurring of disciplinary boundaries, and search practicalities that lack either the time or the logistics for continuing to employ traditional access methods effectively—dictates a fundamental shift in our thinking about serials cataloging. We must ask how we can get the catalog to provide more useful information about the things searchers seek—which will not be an entire e-serial—and a lot more personal service via librarian interfaces with patrons *at the point of their search*—not through some standard but limited precoordinated set of options that patrons have to learn by participating in years of bibliographic instruction sessions.

Interestingly, some observers see this as a gender-related issue. An article appearing some months ago in the *New York Times* special section on e-commerce stated:

> Women are looking for different information and in different ways from the traditional male audience, forcing website designers to rethink their products. . . . Hifi.com has introduced Herhifi.com, which sells the same stereos and televisions as the original website but in a different way. Links to a plain-spoken expert are displayed prominently. And, instead of listing products in traditional categories like home theater or video, with emphasis on the gadget, Herhifi.com emphasizes context, selling products by room, like kitchen and home office. Sites that cater to women generally have more prominent search tools, links to chat rooms and forums or other places where the users can ask questions—features that female Web users in surveys say more sites should adopt. "Designers should consider moving from a broadcasting model of communication to an interactive and dynamic palette where users are collaborators. . . ."[4]

I never thought of library catalogs as having a "broadcasting model of communication," but it explains what's wrong with traditional cataloging in a Web-based world. In my opinion, accommodations to "female" search psychology on the part of several e-firms suggest ways to improve serials cataloging operations and enable the catalog to do a better job of rewarding patron search efforts. We can provide more prominent search tools, multiple approaches to the representations of both descriptive and subject content (such as Herhifi.com's listings by function as well as by location), and, most of all, we can supply a link to a plain-spoken expert to whom baffled searchers can turn for advice. In fact, I believe that every time someone initiates a catalog search session for the first time, he or she should be prompted to consult with a plain-spoken expert—namely, a librarian—just as one is prompted to buy the latest offering to America OnLine subscribers during the first log-in of the day. One can always say "no." Moreover, it should not matter if that librarian spends more of her or his workday in the library answering patrons' questions at a public desk or selecting, acquiring, and organizing the library's new materials at a backroom workstation. The librarian-adviser should be able to suggest effective search strategies and stand ready to aid the searcher in the event that expected responses fail.

These suggestions, however, go beyond mere bibliographic data to bibliographic services. At one time, the primary bibliographic service rendered by any library to its patrons was preparation of the catalog; but today, we need to think more broadly. Returning to the matter of data, I believe we must change our ideas about what constitutes a valid bibliographic unit. We need to stop cataloging complete entities and start focusing on the works that patrons seek. This is not the first time we have faced this issue. Microform sets posed a similar problem for catalogers, because one physical carrier was capable of containing numerous works. Traditional bibliographic units encompassing a whole set simply didn't furnish an appropriate level of access to the works in the set. New levels of analysis had to be considered and compromises reached. Perhaps, for Web-based resources, we might need to go deeper still, turning into a new kind of back-of-the-book indexer, parsing and representing the ideas—not the sites—on the Web.

CONCLUSIONS

Clearly, we must accept that catalog records, particularly for electronic serials, are no longer merely one of many fully mediated steps in the search process, but the one and only opportunity to point searchers in the right directions to satisfy their information needs. To do this, we have to strike new balances between uniformity and flexibility. While uniformity fosters wide interchangeability—something we have prized highly—it strictly limits individuality, something the current environment demands. What questions can we ask to decide where to set a new equilibrium?

First, how predictable and stable are our client needs? The fewer anomalies we must support—such as external campuses and distance-learning students; patrons of peer libraries, consortia, regional cooperatives, and others; and totally unaffiliated patrons from here and abroad—the more stable and predictable are the sum of patron needs, and the more we should lean toward staying with uniform standards. The more anomalous our patron populations and the more we wish to customize our services to them, the more productive a move toward flexibility becomes.

Second, how fluid is the institutional environment? Those who can support flexibility should do so, positioning themselves well for the future. Those who cannot will have to work toward such capabilities, because the future is very likely to require greater flexibility.

Third, what strengths and weaknesses do current operations exhibit? Knowing them and reviewing them with regard to the advantages and disadvantages of uniformity vs. flexibility, we can design systems that foster appropriate change.

What seems clear is that we need to expand the bibliographic options for an increasingly diverse client base, and we must do much more work for searchers than we have ever done before. What is happening to librarians is not unique. It is happening outside of libraries to every other organization involved with human beings and the Internet. We can learn from what is happening around us. We can:

- Engage patrons as individuals
- Serve them with our professional knowledge
- Use technology to expand bibliographic data and service options
- Seek to achieve deeper levels of control in order to accommodate a diversity of informational materials, information needs, and information seekers

NOTES

1. Sheila S. Intner, "Rejecting Standard Cataloging Copy: Implications for the Education of Catalogers," in *Cataloging Heresy*, ed. Bella Haas Weinberg (Medford, N.J.: Learned Information, 1992), 119–130.

2. Ibid., 119.

3. Sheila S. Intner, *Interfaces: Relationships between Library Technical and Public Services* (Englewood, Colo.: Libraries Unlimited, 1993), 7–92.

4. Steven E. Brier, "Since Women Ask for Directions, the Web Is Being Remapped," *New York Times,* March 29, 2000, special "E-Commerce" section.

ANNOTATED BIBLIOGRAPHY

Boydston, Jeanne M. K., ed. *Serials Cataloging at the Turn of the Century* (New York; London: Haworth Press), 1997. 1997 state-of-the-art review; somewhat dated, but covers all the issues still being discussed and problems still unresolved.

Burke, Mary A. *Organization of Multimedia Resources: Principles and Practice of Information Retrieval* (Aldershot, England; Brookfield, Vt.: Gower, 1999). Focuses mainly on monographic resources but provides a good basic discussion of organizational issues for electronic resources.

Hill, Janet Swan. "You May Already Know the Answer," in *Head in the Clouds, Feet on the Ground: Serials Vision and Common Sense: Proceedings of the North American Serials Interest Group, Inc. 13th Annual Conference* (New York; London: Haworth Press, 1999). Suggests existing standards can handle access to electronic serials.

Intner, Sheila S. *Interfaces: Relationships between Library Technical and Public Services* (Englewood, Colo.: Libraries Unlimited, 1993). See, especially, chapters 14, "Access to Serials," 15, "Serials Catalog Records: Image and Reality," and 16, "Modern Serials Cataloging," 77–92, in which the case is made for enhanced access to serials by treating individual volumes as monographs and indexing them more exhaustively.

———. "A New Paradigm for Access to Serials," *The Serials Librarian* 19, no. 3/4 (1991): 151–161. Continues the discussion; includes selected bibliography.

Jones, Wayne. "Gimme a C! MIT's Experience with Core Cataloging of Serials," *The Serials Librarian* 37, no. 3 (2000): 41–49. Makes a strong case for eliminating at least some of the data from standard operating practices at an institution where serials are highly valued.

Nisonger, Thomas E. *Management of Serials in Libraries* (Englewood, Colo.: Libraries Unlimited, 1998). Places a very brief review of cataloging amid all the managerial issues raised in the collection, storage, and use of serials in libraries.

Olson, Nancy B. *Cataloging of Audiovisual Materials and Other Special Materials*, 4th ed. (DeKalb, Ill.; Minnesota Scholarly Press, 1998). Probably the best textbook/manual of its kind for cataloging nonbook materials; devotes one chapter to serials.

Reynolds, Regina Romano. "Harmonizing Bibliographic Control of Serials in the Digital Age," *Cataloging & Classification Quarterly* 28, no. 1 (1999): 3–19. Analyzes the current desire to harmonize cataloging standards for serials at a time in which the shift to electronic formats is impacting serials in important ways.

5

AACR2 and Seriality

Jean Hirons, transcribed by John Radencich

This chapter on AACR2 and Seriality will explain where we are in the process of rule revision of chapter 12, the goals we started out with, and the achievements in reaching these goals. As a part of this, I will focus on how we have developed new concepts for new types of material and will explain the definitions we have developed for these new types of material. Following that, I will look very briefly at the revision of chapter 12 and the potential impact these new concepts may have on current library functions. Finally, at the end I'll review where we've come from and explain where we're headed.

In addition to the revisions from CONSER, there will also be a new introduction to part 1, which is being prepared by the British Library and the Library Association. And a task force of CC:DA has prepared a new appendix of major and minor changes that we will use to determine when we need a new record. Further work will also be needed to reconcile any differences between the revised chapters 9 (Electronic Resources) and 12 (Continuing Resources).

We identified three major goals of this whole process. These were, first, to include rules for new and existing forms of material that had not previously been covered by AACR2. This is not a new problem. Loose-leafs are an example of this type of material, and they've been around a long time but are not covered by AACR2. In addition to loose-leafs, an expanding world of updating databases and Web sites needs to be covered by cataloging rules. The second goal was to accommodate seriality throughout the code. Many of us consider AACR2 to be very monographic-centric! It's something we have complained about for years and that we finally have the opportunity to address. The third goal was to harmonize AACR with ISBD(S) and ISSN. We have a golden opportunity, because ISBD(S) and ISSN are also currently going through their own revisions.

This discussion will focus on the first goal—that of including new and existing forms of material and how the revision will impact on our current library functions. What does it mean to live in a world of continuing resources and integrating resources?

First, what have we accomplished so far? We've revised chapter 12 and changed the title to "Continuing Resources." We've expanded the chapter to cover loose-leafs and electronic resources that are continuing in nature but that are not necessarily issued in a succession of parts. The rules in chapter 12 will focus only on the seriality of these resources, while chapter 9 will be used for rules regarding their electronic nature. Also, we have added new terms and their definitions, and we've revised one of our favorite old definitions—"serial." The new terms that we've added are *bibliographic resource, continuing resource,* and *integrating resource.*

The model in figure 5.1 was prepared in 1998 and served as the initial model for the revision process. It divides bibliographic resources into two very broad categories: the finite resource and the continuing resource. Those are the definitions that relate to whether a particular work has or does not have any form of seriality. Under these two categories are the "form of issuance" or how the work is actually issued. When not complete as first issued, will further material be issued successively or as updates to be integrated into the whole? In this model we recognize that there are both finite and continuing works that integrate.

Let's take a look at the new, revised concepts. The "bibliographic resource," as defined, is "the manifestation of a work that forms the basis for bibliographic description. A bibliographic resource may be in any medium or combination of media and may be tangible or intangible." It replaces the words *item,* as used in AACR2, and *publication,* which is considered too print-based. A "bibliographic resource" is basically anything that you might catalog.

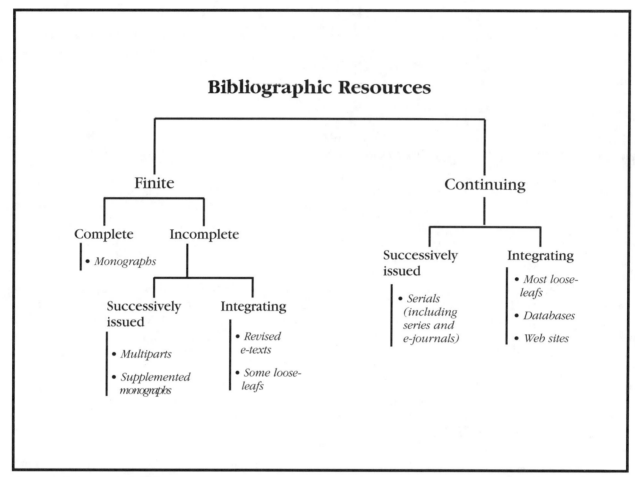

Figure 5.1   AACR type of publication model.

Within that, a "continuing resource" is "a bibliographic resource that is issued over time [usually] with no predetermined conclusion." The word *usually* is in brackets because it was not in the original proposal to the JSC but has been suggested as an addition to the definition. The concept of "continuing resources" is very broad and focuses on the seriality but not on the form of issuance. It allows for different rules for different forms of issuance and leaves a much more flexible position for handling the variety of works to be cataloged.

The definition of "serial" has undergone a "minor" rather than a "major" change! As redefined, it states: A serial is "a continuing resource in any medium issued in a succession of discrete parts, usually bearing numeric or chronological designations, that usually has no predetermined conclusion." The addition of the word *discrete* allows us to consider articles in electronic journals as parts, while saying that it "usually bears numeric or chronological designations" means we can account for unnumbered series. Finally, saying that it "usually has no predetermined conclusion" is much easier to deal with than that it "is intended to be continued indefinitely." An added advantage of this revised definition for "serial" is that it would allow newsletters of an event to be treated as serials, even though they're not going to go on forever. I want to credit the ISBD(S) working group for this addition.

What we're recognizing is that there are lots of things we want to check in and treat serially, even though they will not be issued indefinitely. We hope that this will allow a more logical and practical approach to how we catalog and treat things in our libraries. It also means that we can call an electronic journal or magazine a serial whether or not it has issues. If it calls itself that and it's got articles, let's call it a serial.

"Integrating resource" is a new category. It is defined as "a bibliographic resource that is added to or changed by means of updates that do not remain discrete and are integrated into the whole." These are neither monographic (finite) nor serial (issued in parts). Examples include items that are loose-leaf for updating and Web sites. There may also be such a thing as a cartographic integrating resource. These works require separate rules because they have only one chief source at any one time, unlike serials, which have to have a title on each issue.

We will apply a traditional latest entry convention to the cataloging of integrating resources but might term the convention *integrating entry.* I believe that the new terminology is needed to distinguish this convention from *latest entry,* which was applied to serials under earlier rules.

How has all of this been incorporated into chapter 12? We have integrated the rules for serials and integrating resources, and we have gone from the broadest sense to the most specific, by first making a rule that applies to all continuing resources, then going down to serials or integrating resources, and then finally to the more specific. Also included in the proposals to the JSC are more general rules for chapter 1.

The model in figure 5.2 shows how the rules have been integrated into the code. The big difference is that all integrating resources are described in one place, chapter 12, rather than being in both chapters 2 and 12. This is because, whether finite or continuing, integrating resources can exhibit change and the rules for how they are described would not differ according to their status of publication.

What might be the impact? The revisions extend many existing rules for serials to integrating resources. That's one result. Also loose-leafs, Web sites, and databases will no longer be thought of as monographs. We may have to continue coding them as such for some time, but we shouldn't think about them in this sense. We've got to apply a "serial mindset" to these materials.

Now for the impact these new rules will have on libraries. First, who will catalog integrating resources? No doubt, the same people who are cataloging them now, right? But who is doing it now? At a recent NASIG conference, when I asked the question, it was mainly the serial catalogers who were cataloging electronic resources. However, it is also true that at some institutions it's primarily monographic catalogers or a special group of electronic resources catalogers. Will the presence of rules for these resources in chapter 12 make any difference on who is doing the cataloging? Furthermore, will these changes have any impact on the way in which cataloging and technical services are organized in libraries? I know of one library that decided to reorganize along the lines of finite and continuing, including both acquisitions and cataloging.

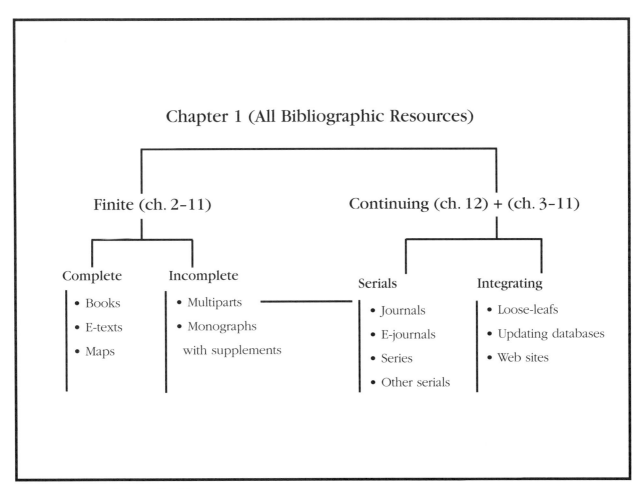

Figure 5.2   The model as realized in AACR2.

What's the impact on MARC 21? As Crystal Graham would say, "But, Jean, how are we going to code these records?" That is what it comes down to for many because the coding often determines who will and even who can catalog them. At first I really wasn't sure what the right solution to the coding was, but after the rule revisions were completed, it became clearer. The solution, as I see it, is to define a new bibliographic level code "i" that uses the serial 008, which we might rename the "seriality 008." As a result, for example, we could code a loose-leaf as still being updated or as complete; we could say when it began, when it ended; and we could code for the frequency of the updates in order to facilitate check-in. If we separately code integrating resources, they would also not be under the restrictions of serial, and particularly CONSER, records on OCLC. This solution provides a lot more flexibility.

What's the impact on cooperative cataloging? Perhaps this is the most difficult issue for me. CONSER's focus has always been on maintenance; BIBCO has not shared this focus, being a monograph program. Can BIBCO and CONSER share the work of creating and maintaining records for integrating resources? And if so, how would these records be authenticated and distributed? This is a major issue for CONSER and for the LC Cataloging Distribution Service because the CONSER database is distributed as a discrete database. Documentation is also an issue and another area in which CONSER and BIBCO might collaborate.

Finally, I'll give you a short historical review of this revision process. It was six years ago in Chicago that the AACR2000 preconference was held, so it seems fitting to review the process at this point. During that preconference, Crystal Graham gave the paper "What's Wrong with AACR2: A Serials Perspective," in which she claimed that AACR2 is inadequate for serials because it doesn't accommodate all forms of material or accommodate seriality for print or nonprint materials. In her speech she introduced us to the "bibliographic hermaphrodite," which evolved into the integrating resource.

Interestingly, the CONSER AACR Review Task Force was formed in January 1994, so this group had been around for a long time even before the preconference. Through the years it has been very instrumental in all of these revisions. This has truly been a joint effort and its work has been invaluable.

Then came the JSC conference on AACR2 in Toronto in 1997, where Crystal and I presented the paper "Issues Related to Seriality." We presented three models, each of which progressively stripped away one of the requirements for a serial. We recommended that we apply Model B (redefine serial to encompass updating publications) in an effort to move toward Model C (the "ongoing entity"). At the time we thought that Model C was too radical to propose.

Subsequently, in 1998, my colleagues and I in CONSER were charged with preparing rule revisions, but after looking at the issues, we decided to begin with a report of recommendations. Four groups were formed to discuss the redefinition of serial, description of serials, electronic serials, and title changes. We held electronic discussions with participants from all over the world: from the United States, Canada, Great Britain, Australia, and Germany. The final reports were issued in January 1999, and in May 1999 we issued the paper "Revising AACR2 to Accommodate Seriality." In this report we introduced "Modified Model C," which uses "continuing resources" as the umbrella for integrating resources and serials.

During 1998, we went through a really creative period of looking at and rejecting various concepts. We looked at the concept of "incorporating entry," which Sara Shatford Layne provided for us. The concept was a very sophisticated way of dealing with electronic journals, but we decided it was probably a little too complex for the average cataloger. Then we considered a "succession of latest entry records." Though we came up with lots of creative ideas, we always aimed for the simplest solutions. Having also started a new training program during this time, I was aware of the need for clarity and simplicity.

So what's changed along the way? We had some original concerns that don't seem quite as important now as they seemed five years ago, like keeping versions together in catalogs and having to use different rules for print and electronic versions. We've developed new concepts that have been widely reviewed and broadly accepted. I also think we have achieved a certain degree of simplicity.

So what's next? The chapter 12 revision is currently under review by JSC constituents, and there seems to be broad support for the major changes. The JSC was to meet in September 2000 in London to go over the revisions in more detail. Following that was a "meeting of experts" in November at the Library of Congress, to harmonize AACR2 with ISBD(S) and ISSN and look further at longer-term solutions. And we hope to have a revised chapter 12 in 2001.

Thanks to this revision, I believe that AACR rules are better equipped now to handle Web sites, electronic journals, databases, and printed serials. We hope that AACR will be considered an equal, if not superior, alternative to other forms of metadata. Speaking of which, to compare other metadata systems with the new AACR2, where *is* the seriality in the Dublin Core? Do other metadata standards accommodate changes over time? Do they impose the same monographic mindset on resources that are anything but static?

6

ISSN: Link and Cross-Link for Data and Metadata

Regina Reynolds, transcribed by Everett Allgood

I have been the head of the U.S. ISSN program since 1992, but I have in fact been associated with it since the mid-1970s. At that time, the ISSN was pretty tame. Identifiers were very difficult to define for people without their eyes glazing over as you tried to explain identifiers' purpose.

In recent years, because of the electronic environment with its high volume of resources and the desire for rights management, identifiers have become really hot. I can almost say that *identifier wars* are going on: ISSN, ISBN, DOI, URN, and many others. It has really become quite an exciting world, and if the ISSN did not exist, someone would have to invent it. ISSN has been in existence since the 1970s, and, coincidentally, Al Gore is not the only one reinventing himself for the twenty-first-century—so is the ISSN!

The ISSN Network has been watching the seriality discussions very closely and has become involved in the current rule-revision process, as the network is currently revising the manual of ISSN assignment rules and procedures. One of the goals of the ISSN manual's revision is to harmonize our definitions of serials and the areas we intend to cover with the ISSN, with the revised AACR2 and with the models being developed. At our directors' meetings in Paris in the fall of 1999, it was decided to enlarge the scope of what the ISSN would cover so that in the future it will include all continuing resources. For practical considerations we may have to make some exceptions, such as personal and advertising Web pages.

Certainly, the ISSN Network cannot cover continuing resources all on its own. So we will have to form partnerships, working with metadata creators and promoting the fact that we have been creating metadata for serials since 1972. The potential for partnerships is a very strong one, for surely with all of these new domains and all of these new resources we can no longer afford the handcrafted records we have all grown accustomed to.

The ISSN has also emerged as an identifier for digital manifestations. This is somewhat controversial, because the ISSN initially began as a work- or title-level identifier, but with the proliferation of manifestations the ISSN Network chose the course of assigning a separate ISSN for each manifestation. Therein lies our own very serious multiple-versions problem.

The ISSN can function as a link to both data and metadata, and this ISSN is not your father's ISSN but a new and improved version for the new century. There are several examples of the ISSN as a link to data, the ISSN transforming itself to become a URN name-space. ISSN Online has been equipped to link directly to electronic resources. The ISSN forms the basis for the title portion of the SICI code, and the ISSN's use in reference linking is a question mark.

URN

URN stands for Uniform Resource Name, and it is a standard that is being developed by the Internet Engineering Task Force. It is developing rather slowly, but those developing the URN are confident that it will have a place and that Web browsers will eventually be equipped to handle URNs. My own opinion is that instead of a clear winner in these identifier wars, we will eventually have a multiplicity of identifiers. Just as individuals have Social Security numbers and multiple telephone numbers and PINs and all the other identifying numbers linked to us within various databases, so I think there will be multiple identifiers within the electronic resources environment.

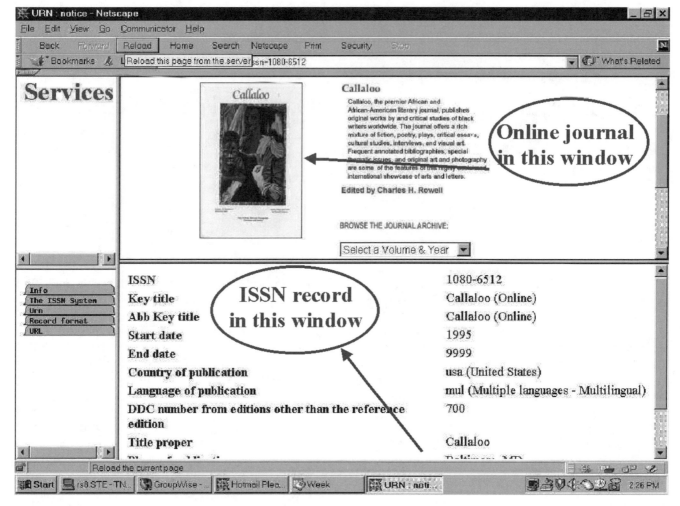

Figure 6.1   Search results using URN with ISSN.

The URN uses a resolution server to provide persistent access to a resource and/or metadata. The ISSN as a URN is currently in the development stage. The ISSN Network has developed a plug-in available for download that enables those participating in the test phase (e.g., the ISSN Centers) to type an ISSN into a browser, retrieve the corresponding record, and then link directly to that resource. The syntax will be URN:ISSN: followed by the ISSN number. The resulting split-screen (see figure 6.1) displays the online journal in the top-half of the screen, and below the metadata record, that is, the ISSN cataloging record.

Members of the ISSN Network are very excited about this project and its potential. Currently, when you type an ISSN into a browser line on the World Wide Web, you retrieve a true hodge-podge of results: anything ranging from articles citing that ISSN, to some straight uses of the ISSN, to nothing. However, by employing this URN application, an ISSN search will link directly not only to the resource itself, but also to the metadata record describing it.

ISSN Online

The URN browser remains experimental, but another currently available product is also quite exciting: ISSN Online.[1] The ISSN database is an international file with a broad chronological scope. The French in particular have been diligent in assigning ISSNs not only to current titles, but also to retrospective titles dating back to the eighteenth century. The database contains significant numbers of records from Eastern Europe and Asia and is an extremely rich source of metadata for serials from around the world. Increasingly, separate ISSNs are assigned to journals in all their various manifestations. If a print version exists, there is one ISSN. If a CD-ROM version exists, there is another ISSN. And for an online version, there is yet another ISSN.

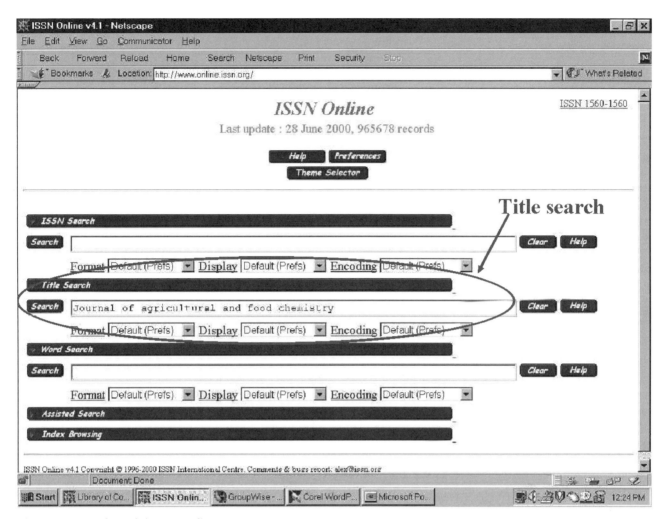

Figure 6.2   Search result in ISSN online.

As the ISSN Network embraces the concept of continuing resources, and the integrating types of resources (e.g., Web sites, databases), these records are showing up in ISSN Online, which supports a variety of search methods that can be used to search and retrieve the metadata record for serial titles. Figure 6.2 is an example of an ISSN bibliographic record.

We are hopeful that, as a result of the current harmonization efforts involving ISBD(CR)—formerly ISBD(S)—and AACR, these bibliographic records will be much more similar in the future to the catalog records we know under AACR and MARC. Even so, the fields in ISSN records are very similar to those in MARC 21 records because the ISSN Network uses a very early version of USMARC. The ISSN records for electronic resources have been equipped with MARC field 856 hotlinks to the online journals, so that clicking on the 856 (the URL) will take users directly to the resource via the ISSN.

SICI

The ISSN also forms the basis for the Serial Item and Contribution Identifier, or the SICI code. This identifier, which is a NISO standard, is capable of linking both at the issue level for checking-in and increasingly at the article level as an identifier to aid with document delivery and linking. The CARL UnCover system is using an early version of the SICI code in its document-delivery system. The California Digital Library is at least experimenting with the SICI, if not using it outright for linking. Some publishers are also printing Serials Industry Systems Advisory Committee's barcode implementation of the SICI.

Unfortunately, use of the SICI barcode is not currently widespread. It may be a bit ahead of its time, as many libraries have only recently begun taking advantage of online check-in. The Library of Congress, though, which obviously has many journals to check in, has in the past year implemented an integrated library system and would find it very helpful if serials could be checked in by simply wanding issues.

REFERENCE LINKING

The ISSN's use in reference linking is problematic at this time, but it is a very hot topic of discussion. Reference linking is the capability of linking citations in one journal article to the full text of the cited article. It is currently an intensely pursued application. Members of the publishing community are seeking ways to cooperate among themselves with regard to their rights and their relationships to make this possible. They need a link to make it possible but have not found an ideal linking mechanism to date.

The CrossRef project,[2] which is a large publisher initiative, has not found the ISSN completely successful for this purpose, partly because of the multiple-ISSN problem and partly because the ISSN is not universally available. The ISSN Network is working on solutions to both of these problems. Interestingly, at the North American Serials Interest Group annual conference in San Diego in 2000, there was a demonstration of linking under CrossRef, using the CODEN, which is another competitor in the identifier wars. The use of the CODEN avoids the multiple-versions problem that use of the ISSN presents because the CODEN still assigns only one designation per title or work. However, as most publishers are using the ISSN and not the CODEN, the developers of CrossRef had to build in a way to accommodate the ISSN. They probably accomplished this by means of an underlying table of correspondences, which lists a single CODEN and then all the ISSN for a given title, thus allowing a group of identifiers to stand for a single title. This kind of solution may be a way to alleviate the multiple-ISSN problem.

Other solutions for this problem include better utilization of the MARC field 776 (Additional Physical Form Available). This field is used to link the described title to records describing other physical forms of the title. In the ISSN database, every record for a title available in multiple formats has all of the 776 links for all the other formats. Each of these 776 field links includes its distinct ISSN within the subfield *x*. Unfortunately, many of today's OPACs fail to take advantage of the presence of these linking fields. Some do not even display 776 fields, and others do not include the ISSNs subfielded within these fields. In short, today's OPAC vendors fail to take full advantage of the linking mechanisms currently available within each ISSN record issued in multiple formats.

Another solution for the multiple-ISSN problem is to suggest that publishers print all of the ISSNs assigned to a given title on each version of each title they publish. This way, people have access to the ISSN they need and can also provide linking, cross-linking, and cross-referencing as they see fit to enable "hooks to holdings" and whatever other applications they may be using.

Another idea that has been discussed within the ISSN Network is a sample table of correspondence (mentioned previously), transparent to the users, which would underlie various applications. This table would simply contain the ISSNs of all the versions of a title, thus enabling a user who linked to any one of the versions to subsequently link to all of them.

ISSN AS A LINK TO METADATA

ISSN is also a link to metadata. As we have seen, ISSN Online represents a wealth of metadata, including an ever-growing body of metadata for online publications. The ISSN can also be used in OPAC linking and in the URN function to connect with metadata. As an OPAC link, the hook to holdings has been a very popular application of the ISSN (see figure 6.3). In this application, a link is made between a citation in an online database to the library's OPAC records—descriptive and holdings—for the serial title in the citation. I am hopeful that the current ISSN multiple-versions problem, which some libraries see as an impediment to ISSN use in hook to holdings applications, may be overcome with more constructive use of the 776 field and with correspondence tables.

Other uses of the ISSN as a link to metadata include the possibility of using the ISSN as a linking mechanism to display different physical forms and to display earlier, later, and the latest titles, such as can be seen in the ISSN Network's illustration of a family tree of serial records (see figure 6.4).

Another ISSN use as a link to metadata involves linking from a catalog record for a serial to other sources of metadata about that serial, such as Yale University's Jake (Jointly Administered Knowledge Environment).[3] This database of serial titles includes information on which services abstract or index a serial and which carry the serial in full-text. Still another example of linking to additional metadata is the potential to link to additional information about a serial as is found in serial directories such as *Ulrich's Online*. Again, the linking mechanism that can connect to the OPAC record and the additional metadata is the ISSN, which is contained in both records.

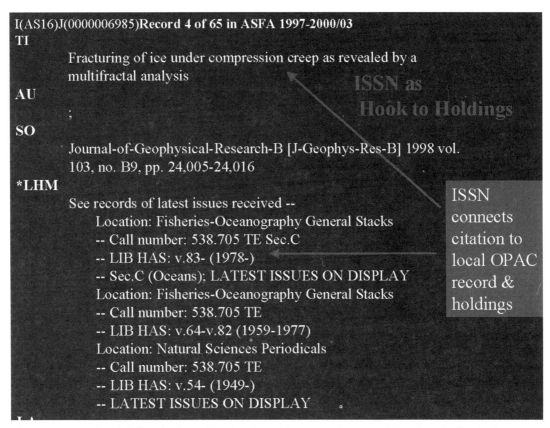

Figure 6.3 Hook to holdings in the University of Washington catalog using SilverPlatter's SilverLinker.

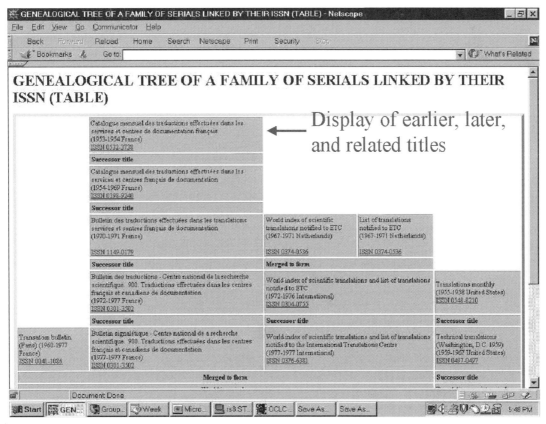

Figure 6.4 Family tree of serial records.

We can no longer afford to think of the library catalog in isolation. We must consider it a component, as referred to in the CC:DA Task Force on Metadata report,[4] that can link and connect to other sources of data and metadata. For serials, the ISSN can help in this multiple-interface environment.

The final link I want to point out is the ISSN's ability to link the publisher and the library and to help provide formatted metadata to publishers. Currently, publishers provide metadata to the National Serials Data Program (NSDP, the U.S. ISSN center) via a Web form. Catalogers at NSDP then convert this into a MARC bibliographic record in a process very similar to that used in OCLC's CORC Project. In a future potential application, we could then use CORC to format these bibliographic records into metadata the publishers would embed in their Web sites. The publishers already come to NSDP to have their ISSNs assigned. The ISSN Centers could just as easily also provide them with formatted metadata records that publishers would then embed in their Web sites, thus allowing libraries to use the headers in those resources to create OPAC records, to use CORC to obtain a better record, or to create CORC pathfinders. When the search engines can make better use of the metadata, all would benefit from better search-engine results. We could even work with a task force to provide publishers with an abridged version of the *Library of Congress Subject Headings* so that they may supply some of their own subject headings.

Far from being just a number printed on a journal issue, the ISSN is coming into its own as a linking mechanism in the online environment. Are your serial records out there unattached, unlinked, adrift in a sea of bibliographic volumes? If so, consider the ISSN as the missing link to data and metadata that can benefit you and your patrons in the electronic environment.

NOTES

1. You may visit http://www.issn.org for a free-trial of ISSN Online, which is the full online ISSN database of over 900,000 records. Subscription information is available on the Web site.
2. CrossRef, http://www.crossref.org/.
3. Jake, http://jake.med.yale.edu/.
4. American Library Association, Committee on Cataloging: Description and Access, Task Force on Metadata, *Final Report,* June 2000, http://www.libraries.psu.edu/iasweb/personal/jca/ccda/tf-meta6.html.

7

MARC 21 as a Metadata Standard: A Practical and Strategic Look at Current Practices and Future Opportunities

Rebecca Guenther, transcribed by Jina Choi Wakimoto

This chapter describes the MARC 21 format, how it has evolved to accommodate electronic resources, and how it relates to the Dublin Core Metadata Element Set. It considers metadata crosswalks and how they are used for the interoperability of different metadata schemes with different structures. The chapter suggests future opportunities for MARC standards and MARC data in the emerging environment of multiple metadata standards for different purposes.

MARC 21

MARC is probably the oldest and most widely used metadata standard. It is a data record structure that is highly standardized and widely adopted throughout the world and has been in use since 1968. As such, it follows national and international standards: Z39.2, the U.S. national standard for information interchange, and ISO 2709, the international standard for the same.

Large bibliographic systems know MARC and know what to do with it; millions of bibliographic records are using it. The content designations in MARC records are used to serve various needs of the library. MARC 21 is a format that defines an element set and defines semantics of content designators, that is, the definitions of fields, subfields, indicators, and indicator values. However, the content of the elements is defined by other standards, such as Anglo-American Cataloguing Rules, 2nd ed. (AACR2) or International Standard Bibliographic Description (ISBD). Another example is subject thesauri that are used as content standards in subject (6xx) fields. MARC 21 is a data structure that carries metadata, a set of elements, and their definition, and it allows for the information to be shared.

MARC 21 is not a new format but rather is a result of a harmonization effort between USMARC and CANMARC (formerly used in Canada), which was completed in 1997. The two formats are now jointly published under the new name, which was chosen to indicate its international scope and worldwide use and its pointing to the future, the twenty-first century.

There are many reasons for using MARC 21 to catalog Internet resources. It allows for incorporating these records into our familiar library catalogs so that they can be used along with records for other more traditional resources. MARC 21 as a communication format allows us to share records between systems, resulting in less duplication of effort on the part of the catalogers. In cataloging these resources, catalogers are also providing a selection function by choosing to catalog higher-quality resources and leaving behind ephemeral ones. In some cases, catalogers are using existing records, often at a high or collection level of description, to point to a digitized form of that original item. Because library systems are widely deployed in many types of libraries, a large percentage of digital resources of all types fall into the purview of a library, so this activity fits into what we've been doing for many years. Using MARC 21 in our library catalogs leverages the skill and experience of a highly trained workforce of librarians and information professionals to describe these Internet resources.

The investigations into extending MARC and AACR2 to better accommodate the description of and access to Internet resources began in 1991. The MARC Advisory Committee considered proposals that resulted in a number of revisions to MARC, for example, adding descriptive terms for the type of resource and, most important, adding the field 856 to enable the linking from the bibliographic record to the resource itself. In addition, changes were made to the definition of computer file in the Leader/06 (Type of record), also known as the content vs. carrier issue. Changes have also been made to the format to accommodate records for online systems and services. An experiment initiated by OCLC, the InterCAT project, was a proof of concept for whether we can use MARC and AACR2 to adequately describe and have access to Internet resources.

Over the past several years a number of changes were introduced into MARC to accommodate other non-library-centric metadata schemes. In 1994 Proposal No. 94-17 (Changes to the USMARC Bibliographic Format to Accommodate the Content Standards for Digital Geospatial Metadata) was approved by the MARC Advisory Committee. In addition, the committee discussed how to identify that the record used a metadata standard other than AACR2 and others defined in the format. This included some discussion of GILS (Government Information Locator Service) and the ability to use MARC to describe government resources. For both GILS and Dublin Core, codes were added in field 042 (Authentication code) to identify the record as using the elements and content defined by those alternate metadata standards. Another change for accommodating Dublin Core–type descriptions was the addition of field 720 (Added entry—Uncontrolled name) and 856 $q (Electronic format type). This facilitated crosswalking between Dublin Core and MARC.

DUBLIN CORE

The Dublin Core Metadata Element Set (DCMES) is a data element set consisting of fifteen elements with their semantics or definitions. It includes some suggested encodings for specific applications, but it does not mandate on any particular syntax. Thus, it can be expressed in different syntaxes, since it is only an element set. Nor is it a system or a format, so additional structure is required to use it. DCMES does not define content rules, that is, one cannot predict what type of value may be used in a particular element. For instance, in the Creator element one cannot be sure that the data will be expressed as last name before first name.

The Dublin Core has evolved over the last five years, since the initial consensus was formed on the elements in 1995. The Warwick Framework was developed during the second Dublin Core workshop in 1996. It is a conceptual framework for the coexistence of many types of metadata and includes the notion that metadata packages may exist independently and may be linked together. It is a precursor to the Resource Description Framework (RDF), an initiative of the World Wide Web Consortium, which emerged a few years later. There have been seven Dublin Core workshops in five countries, with a broad range of participants from different disciplines and different countries. Since its early development, Dublin Core has shown a tension between simplicity and complexity, which continues today with the emergence of qualifiers for the basic element set. However, it allows for the flexibility of choosing the simple Dublin Core element set or the more complex approach with qualifiers.

The Dublin Core Metadata Initiative[1] (DCMI), the broader body that has developed and maintains the element set, is seeking endorsement of standards bodies—from NISO (Z39.85: Dublin Core Metadata Set went out to ballot in July 2000), from CEN (the European Commission for Standardization), and from IETF (the Internet Engineering Task Force). The Dublin Core process has become more formalized with the formation of the Dublin Core Metadata Initiative (DCMI) and the Dublin Core Advisory Committee.

MARC and Dublin Core have been evolving in parallel. MARC has adapted to a changing world of information by adding elements where needed and allowing for record content from a variety of metadata content standards. Dublin Core began simply and now is becoming more complex with the addition of qualifiers. Many of the goals are similar, particularly that of resource discovery (to search and retrieve resources). MARC, however, supports much more complex and precise searching than Dublin Core does, and libraries use MARC's broad functionality in systems that take advantage of the richness of content designation. An example of this ability is executing a fielded search and limiting by language, country of publication, and so on.

METADATA CROSSWALKS

The purpose of metadata crosswalks is to agree on semantics and to determine equivalence between diverse standards. Metadata crosswalks are very important when considering how various metadata schemes may coexist, because they allow for the capability to work with the same data in different structures. They maximize the usefulness of metadata to the widest community of users. It is essential that the mappings[2] are standardized so that different schemes can interoperate.

Metadata can exist in one of two forms. It can be embedded in the resource such as in meta tags in the header of a Web document, or metadata can reside independently of the resource.

A crosswalk shows the relatedness of the different metadata schemes and provides an element-to-element mapping, in which case those elements that do not fit into the other scheme do not map. In some cases, there may be a more general list of elements in one scheme that is a subset of the more specific scheme. For instance, Dublin Core elements can be mapped to MARC 21 fields and considered a subset of the larger scheme. Since Dublin Core does not insist on a syntax, Dublin Core elements can be encoded in MARC 21 using a crosswalk.

Various metadata crosswalks have been established—Dublin Core to MARC, Dublin Core to GILS, Dublin Core to FGDC (Federal Geographic Data Committee), FGDC to MARC, GILS to MARC, MARC to SGML, and so on. However, problems arise with converted records, particularly when a complex scheme is mapped to a simple one. Some data may be lost, and there may be differences in semantics for the elements. What is meant in one scheme may have a different meaning in another. In addition, the content standards and vocabulary used may vary. Properties may be different, such as repeatability or optionality. For example, in Dublin Core, every element is repeatable and optional, but in MARC 21 not all fields are repeatable and some are mandatory.

A number of projects use the MARC/Dublin Core crosswalk developed by the Library of Congress's Network Development and MARC Standards Office. One is the Nordic Metadata Projects,[3] which allows for the creation, searching, and harvesting of metadata. Metadata for electronic resources is input into a template and becomes a part of the header in meta tags. A MARC converter is available through the project's Web site, which converts the elements and values encoded, using the Dublin Core Element Set into a choice of either UNIMARC, MARC 21, or NORMARC. The resulting record may be used as the basis for the catalog record. The National Library of the Netherlands participates in the Project BIBLINK,[4] which is a European cooperative effort between publishers and libraries, in which the publishers provide the metadata in Dublin Core. The data is then converted and used as the basis for reports to the national bibliography.

CORC (Cooperative Online Resource Catalog) is a large-scale system developed by OCLC. In CORC, data is entered either in a MARC or Dublin Core view and may be output in either format. The Library of Congress is cooperating with OCLC on the crosswalk between Dublin Core elements and CORC elements, also coordinating with the Dublin Core/MARC crosswalk. The CORC crosswalk has influenced the discussions about Dublin Core qualifiers by providing concrete examples and discussions about Dublin Core qualifiers useful for the library domain and may result in the future of additions or changes to MARC elements. It is important to remember that CORC is one implementation of Dublin Core. Some qualifiers used in CORC are Dublin Core qualifiers that have been approved, and some are qualifiers used only in CORC. The CORC project is an important example showing the intersection between these two metadata standards.

The DC Libraries Working Group[5] was formed at the last Dublin Core meeting, partly as a result of discussions concerning CORC and Dublin Core. The group's charter includes the following goals:

- To foster increased operability between Dublin Core and traditional library metadata
- To keep the library community informed of Dublin Core developments
- To analyze qualifiers that are being considered in the Dublin Core community from a library perspective
- To investigate links to library database records to make use of these metadata
- To register existing MARC-controlled elements for use with Dublin Core descriptions

In any discussion of metadata interoperability, crosswalks are a very important factor in how different metadata schemes complement each other. Standards are very important to support interoperability. Descriptive metadata does not serve all needs, and it is necessary to have packages of different types of metadata that fit together (the Warwick Framework idea). This may include descriptive metadata in various formats, administrative and structural metadata, and rights information.

The "lego model" (see figure 7.1) shows the concept of modular extensibility, that is, the idea of complementary packages of metadata and additional elements that support different needs, including local or discipline-specific requirements. In this model, some pieces (building blocks) overlap, and others are used in conjunction with one an-

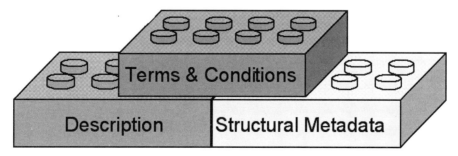

Figure 7.1   Lego model.

other. The description may partially overlap with structural metadata, and terms and conditions may also complement the other blocks.

FUTURE OPPORTUNITIES

Future directions include the further development of Dublin Core and investigations into how Dublin Core records will interoperate with MARC records. Possible MARC modifications may be necessary to accommodate the DC/MARC mapping now that Dublin Core qualifiers have been approved. MARC will coexist with other metadata schemes rather than compete. MARC record descriptions may be one of the building blocks in the lego model.

New opportunities are on the horizon. Library-developed schemes that are used more widely, such as subject headings and classification, could be registered in the Dublin Core Metadata Initiative's registry as possible content standards to be used with Dublin Core elements. ISSN, ISBN, and SICI identifiers exist in library catalog records and could be used as identifiers with the Relation element. How to express properties of agents (i.e., Creator, Contributor, and Publisher elements) is under discussion in the Dublin Core community. This may involve defining a Dublin Core authority element set, which will probably resemble a subset of MARC authority fields. This is an acknowledgment that "agent" information (information about the name) should not be embedded in the record for the resource. In addition, other controlled lists developed by the library community are likely to be registered as part of a Dublin Core registry. Classification and subject schemes (LCSH, MeSH, DDC, LCC, UDC) and language codes (the new ISO 639-2 standard is based on MARC language codes) are some under consideration. A subset of the MARC Code List for relators is being considered to be used to indicate the roles of the Dublin Core elements Creator, Contributor, and Publisher. It is likely that MARC records will be linked to from various sources; this reuse of MARC records could be possible with persistent identifiers as pointers to MARC bibliographic and name authority records.

CONCLUSION

The longevity of MARC shows its ability to evolve over time. There may someday be a replacement, but it is not likely to happen in the immediate future. Large complex systems with complex functionality are built around MARC. Metadata schemes do not have to compete with one another but rather complement each other. The Dublin Core Metadata Element Set can be used in a MARC framework, in which we can benefit both from the MARC structure and its high level of standardization and from the simplicity of Dublin Core. Finally, the fully developed standards in the library community and in MARC are being recognized in the larger community, and they will be used and registered as content standards.

NOTES

1. Dublin Core Metadata Initiative, http://www.oclc.org/oclc/research/projects/core/.
2. "MARC Mappings," MARC 21 Documentation, http://lcweb.loc.gov/marc/marcdocz.html.
3. Nordic Metadata Projects, http://linnea.helsinki.fi/meta/.
4. BIBLINK, http://hosted.ukoln.ac.uk/biblink/.
5. Dublin Core Metadata Initiative, Libraries Working Group, http://www.oclc.org/oclc/research/projects/core/groups/libraries.htm.

III

CATALOGING THE WEB:
OTHER APPROACHES, OTHER STANDARDS

8

Visionary or Lunatic:
One CORC Participant's Psychiatric Evaluation

Norm Medeiros[1]

INTRODUCTION

OCLC's Cooperative Online Resource Catalog (CORC) utilizes existing and emerging metadata standards in an attempt to increase scholarly information retrieval on the Internet. Like other OCLC projects, CORC relies on participants to build the database. Although contributing to this collaborative effort was a motivating factor for the New York University School of Medicine's participation, the chief catalyst was the opportunity to use it as a means to enhance the library's existing "Biomedical Sites by Subject" area, pages consisting of links to biomedical Web sites. CORC has helped the Ehrman Medical Library streamline its efforts to providing access to these quality Internet resources.

BIOMEDICAL SITES BY SUBJECT

The proliferation of scholarly, freely available information on the Internet is staggering. To help provide access to these resources, the Ehrman Medical Library Web Team maintains a "Biomedical Sites by Subject" area devoted to promoting this genre of material. The categories are divided according to National Library of Medicine subject headings, specifically those used within the *List of Journals Indexed*. This authority is the same used to classify e-journals and e-texts within the library's Web site. Resources included within "Biomedical Sites by Subject" pages include:

- Home pages of professional societies
- Major sections from a professional society Web site that offers considerable content
- Pages from professionals with established credentials
- Pages that offer cases, transcripts of cases, protocols, guidelines, and other resources in the field

Resources excluded from consideration include:

- Lists of links
- E-journals, e-texts, and databases, since these are already available on the library's Web site
- Sites for which the credentials of those responsible cannot be established
- Sites the library cannot access due to payment requirements
- Sites of local interest only (exceptions are made for NYU pages)

Prior to joining the CORC project, selected Web pages, in excess of one hundred in total, were maintained entirely by the Web Team. Because the scope of this resource area is enormous, the ability to maintain up-to-date pages was impossible for three librarians. As a result, "Biomedical Sites by Subject" pages (see figure 8.1) were used sparingly by patrons and quickly grew stale.

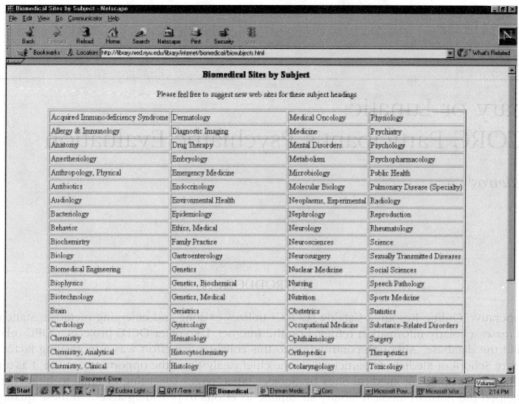

Figure 8.1   Biomedical sites by subject Web page.

CORC PATHFINDERS

The CORC project offers libraries many incentives for involvement. In the case of the Ehrman Medical Library, the chief motivating factor was to further enrich the "Biomedical Sites by Subject" area of the library Web site, replacing these pages with CORC pathfinders. In order to achieve this goal, the process by which Internet resources were identified needed to change, as well as the overall process by which subject-specific pages were created. To this end, the following workflow was instituted:

1. Subject bibliographers identify quality Web sites. The range of biomedical subject areas as dictated by NLM's List of Journals Indexed was divided by the professional staff, making each librarian responsible for approximately seven to ten disciplines.
2. Bibliographers complete "Biomedical Web Site Form" (see figure 8.2). This form allows bibliographers to easily paste and/or type information about the resource into a Web form, which is then sent to the CORC Cataloging Team (CCT).
3. CORC Cataloging Team harvests Web site. The CCT, comprised of staff from the Bibliographic Control Department, enters the resource's URL into the CORC harvester, which creates a rudimentary record for the resource.
4. The CCT uses the bibliographer's form to supplement the extracted metadata. The "Biomedical Web Site Form," completed by the bibliographer, is used to supplement the harvested metadata. Information such as description and subject headings is especially significant, since the description appears on the pathfinder and the subject terms are key access points within the CORC database. It is at this point that the CCT performs authority control on the names and subjects used in the CORC record.
5. The bibliographer creates the CORC pathfinder. After all records for a particular subject have been entered, the bibliographer returns to CORC and creates the subject-specific pathfinder. The resulting pathfinder URL is sent to the Web Team.
6. The Web Team links the pathfinder. The Web Team places the link to the CORC pathfinder into the category for which the pathfinder was created. This in effect replaces access to the original "Biomedical Sites by Subject" page. Although not yet in place, periodic maintenance will be performed on these pathfinders in order to keep their content fresh (see figure 8.3).

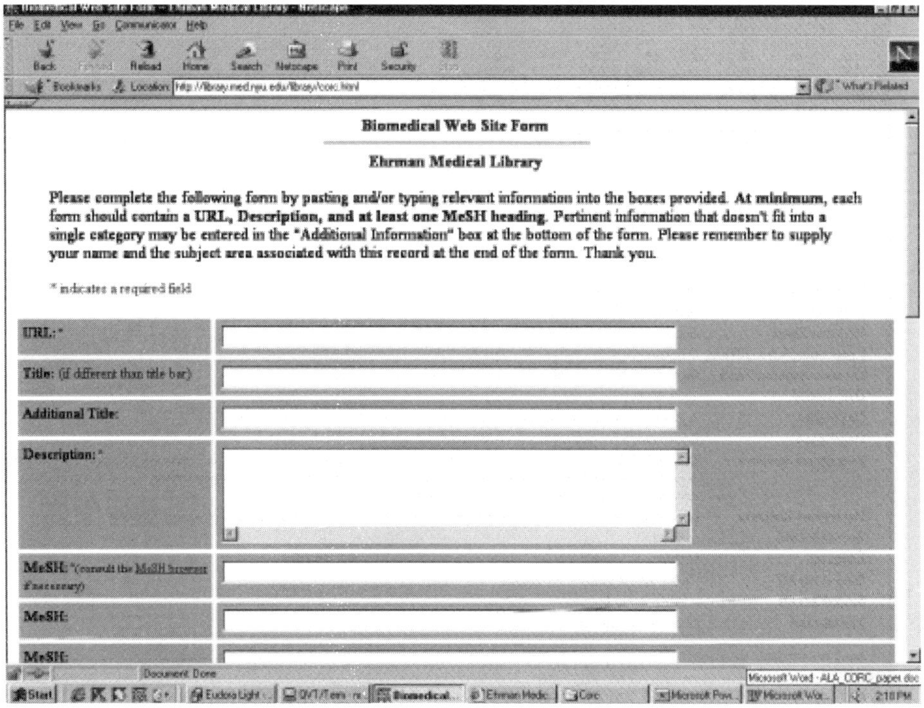

Biomedical Web Site Form

Ehrman Medical Library

Please complete the following form by pasting and/or typing relevant information into the boxes provided. At minimum, each form should contain a URL, Description, and at least one MeSH heading. Pertinent information that doesn't fit into a single category may be entered in the "Additional Information" box at the bottom of the form. Please remember to supply your name and the subject area associated with this record at the end of the form. Thank you.

* indicates a required field

URL: *

Title: (if different than title bar)

Additional Title:

Description: *

MeSH: * (consult the MeSH browser if necessary)

MeSH:

MeSH:

Figure 8.2   Biomedical Web site form as it appears to subject bibliographers.

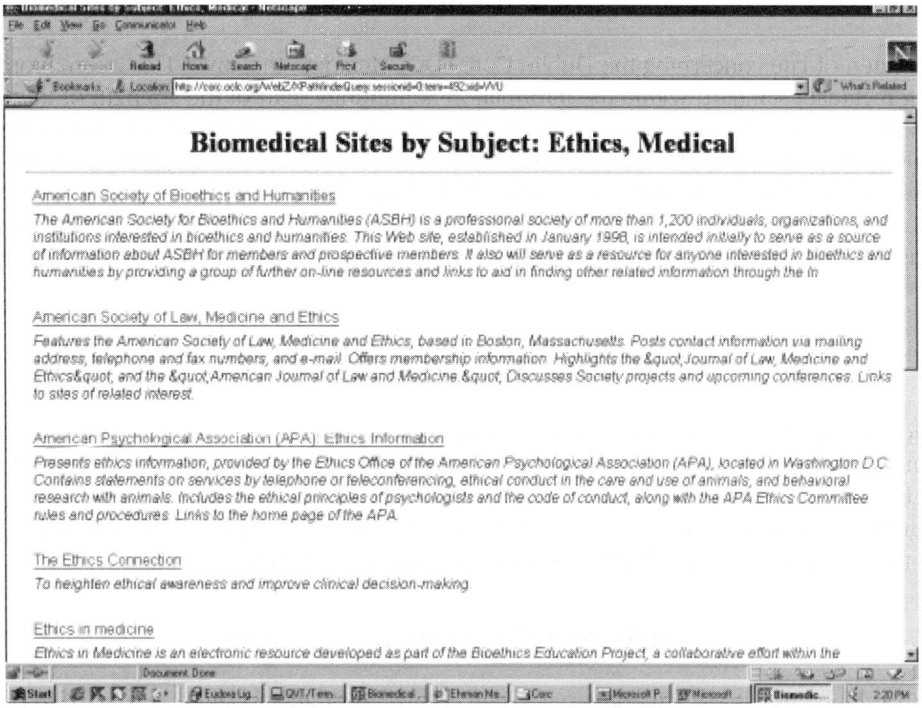

Biomedical Sites by Subject: Ethics, Medical

American Society of Bioethics and Humanities

The American Society for Bioethics and Humanities (ASBH) is a professional society of more than 1,200 individuals, organizations, and institutions interested in bioethics and humanities. This Web site, established in January 1998, is intended initially to serve as a source of information about ASBH for members and prospective members. It also will serve as a resource for anyone interested in bioethics and humanities by providing a group of further on-line resources and links to aid in finding other related information through the In

American Society of Law, Medicine and Ethics

Features the American Society of Law, Medicine and Ethics, based in Boston, Massachusetts. Posts contact information via mailing address, telephone and fax numbers, and e-mail. Offers membership information. Highlights the "Journal of Law, Medicine and Ethics" and the "American Journal of Law and Medicine." Discusses Society projects and upcoming conferences. Links to sites of related interest.

American Psychological Association (APA): Ethics Information

Presents ethics information, provided by the Ethics Office of the American Psychological Association (APA), located in Washington D.C. Contains statements on services by telephone or teleconferencing, ethical conduct in the care and use of animals, and behavioral research with animals. Includes the ethical principles of psychologists and the code of conduct, along with the APA Ethics Committee rules and procedures. Links to the home page of the APA.

The Ethics Connection

To heighten ethical awareness and improve clinical decision-making.

Ethics in medicine

Ethics in Medicine is an electronic resource developed as part of the Bioethics Education Project, a collaborative effort within the

Figure 8.3   CORC pathfinder as it displays to library users.

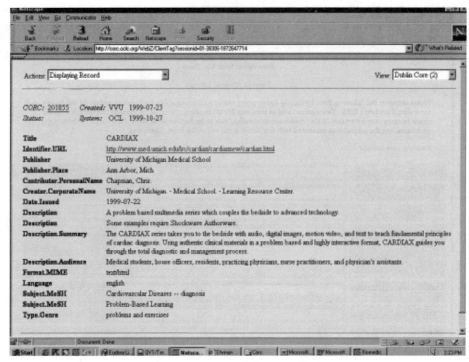

Figure 8.4   Dublin Core record for the Internet resource CARDIAX.

WHY DUBLIN CORE?

Much has been written of late concerning the Dublin Core (DC) Metadata Initiative. This international development has become a leading metadata standard within the information community. Part of the strength of the CORC project is that it allows for both MARC and DC record import and export. This offers great flexibility for users who may want to enter individual records in their library OPACs or, like the Ehrman Medical Library, simply link to HTML documents for use on their Web sites. We decided to create records using DC because it is less strict than MARC (see figure 8.4).

Dublin Core calls for less training of CCT personnel, yet the element set offers sufficient description for CORC pathfinders. Using DC has hastened the record-creation process and broadened the pool of staff capable of contributing to this effort.

BENEFITS OF CORC INVOLVEMENT

CORC participation has allowed the Ehrman Medical Library to provide access to quality Internet resources in a more thorough and timely manner. The workflow involves the entire professional staff, whereby levels of expertise in all subject areas are realized through division of labor. CORC pathfinders are easily updated. Resources can be added and removed without great effort since the resource is stored remotely. The ability to have URL checking on the CORC server also contributed to the Ehrman Library decision to store pathfinders remotely.

DRAWBACKS TO CORC INVOLVEMENT

CORC is not perfect, nor is the library's workflow. Quality control in CORC is lacking in regard to duplicate records. Although the harvester checks against an entered URL, the initial seeding of the system has resulted in a dismaying number of duplicate records, which may not be immediately recognizable to a searcher. Another downfall to the system as it currently exists involves competing vocabularies. CORC's international flavor and the Dublin Core Metadata Initiative in general support any subject scheme. Although Ehrman Medical Library pathfinders are based on the National Library of Medicine's Medical Subject Headings (MeSH), many records are entered in the CORC system with a different subject vocabulary applied, chiefly that of the Library of Congress (LC). Subject bibliographers querying CORC using a MeSH-specific term will not retrieve worthy records that use LC subject headings. A good example of this is the MeSH heading "Substance-Related Disorders." When performing a subject search on this term in CORC, one retrieves 19 hits. A subject search on the LC heading "Substance Abuse" yields 177 hits. An additional search on the related LC heading "Drug Abuse" results in 244 records. At present, no authority control is in place to reconcile these conflicts. Although work has begun on this problem,[2] it may not be easily resolved.

FUTURE CONSIDERATIONS

Prophesying about the future of Web development is risky business. Changes occur too fast and often without warning. However, the Ehrman Medical Library has some short-term goals in mind for CORC utilization:

MyLibrary customization. Individual CORC records are slated for inclusion within the library's Web efforts. MyLibrary, a software tool available from the North Carolina State University Libraries,[3] will allow users to place links to individual CORC pathfinder entries through their personalized library homepage. Such utilization allows for a Web portal such as those now popular with some commercial sites.

NYU School of Medicine resources in CORC. Identifying the best NYU School of Medicine Internet resources and placing records for these in CORC will contribute greatly to the entire CORC community, especially the medical community. Not only will these resources be available through Ehrman Medical Library subject-specific pathfinders, but the Dublin Core metadata can be extracted and entered into the source document, thus allowing metadata-enabled search engines to target these terms. In this manner, the library could become the School of Medicine's hub of metadata development.

Subject-based crosslinks. CORC pathfinders allow sufficient flexibility to allow cross-linking to Ehrman-specific electronic resources within the same subject area. For instance, a CORC pathfinder on cardiology could offer links to electronic journals and texts available on that subject. In addition, linking into the online catalog, MEDCat, or into PubMed citations on a particular subject makes CORC pathfinders that much more useful.

IN SUMMARY

The Cooperative Online Resource Catalog has opened the door to better selection of Internet resources in the biomedical sciences for the Ehrman Medical Library. The NYU School of Medicine community has benefited, as has the entire CORC community. This innovative OCLC project showcases the power of cooperation in taming the Web behemoth.

NOTES

1. The author would like to thank Paul Wrynn and Mary Jo Dorsey, Ehrman Medical Library Web Team colleagues, for their assistance in inspiring this paper.

2. The Metadata and Subject Analysis Committee within ALA's Association for Library Collections and Technical Services is currently exploring this issue.

3. Information on MyLibrary is available at http://my.lib.ncsu.edu/.

9

Working toward a Standard TEI Header for Libraries

Lynn Marko

Libraries are, among many other things, repositories for data. Those data support the information, scholarly, research, teaching, learning, entertainment, and cultural heritage transmission roles for our society, among many others. In support of these roles, librarians, long before computers, developed standards or rules for the representation of the data content in their repositories.

Rules for description and access continue to play an important role in the lives of libraries today. The library-based metadata schemes AACR2 and MARC provide content rules and a formalized communication exchange format among libraries that are stable, mature, well developed, maintained, and, at least among libraries, commonly understood. Some of the content rules are embedded in the MARC format, so it is useful to think of them as together providing data coherence for the library community. We need to expand the library vision of metadata applications beyond our native schema and to become informed about and perhaps subsequently take advantage of the detailed object descriptions prepared by other scholarly and information-rich communities.

One of those opportunities is the Text Encoding Initiative (TEI) developed and used by humanities scholars. The Text Encoding Initiative is an effort that grew out of technology applications to textual analysis employed by the humanities scholarly community. It began in 1988 as a joint project of the Association of Computers in the Humanities, the Association of Computational Linguistics, and the Association for Literary and Linguistic Computing. Prior to 1999, this effort was supported by grant funding. The outcome of this work was the publication of the *TEI Guidelines,*[1] edited by Michael Sperberg-McQueen, then of the University of Illinois at Chicago, and Lou Burnard of Oxford University, who remain the TEI editors today. In 1999, the Text Encoding Initiative moved from grant- to consortium-based support, centered at four primary institutions: the University of Bergen in Norway, Oxford University, the University of Virginia, and Brown University.

The TEI is a consortial effort to develop and maintain encoding standards for textual materials in electronic form for research purposes. The *TEI Guidelines* present specified subsets of SGML, the Standard Generalized Mark-Up Language, in outlines of Document Type Definitions that specify a core tag set. In addition, base tag sets that represent encoding for prose, verse, drama, spoken text, dictionaries, and other genres are also specified. The TEI Header precedes the text and provides the opportunity for the text editor to provide information about the provenance as well as the creation of the electronic text.

Some general characteristics of the TEI tag set include human legibility in a formalized specification. It is a commonly understood transfer mechanism developed for the humanities scholarly community that is international in scope. It has a consortial maintenance agency dedicated to the support and extension of the TEI as an encoding standard benefiting the scholarly community. As a subset of SGML, it is XML compliant.

In its present form, scholars have a rich resource from which to develop tag sets that apply to their particular projects or material. However, in the future as scholarly analysis moves to the Web, the focus of the standard undoubtedly will move toward more general representations of particular genre forms to facilitate scholarly exchange. It is possible that as pressure for Web-based interchange becomes stronger, type definitions will become more standardized.

Scholarly exchange is an important objective of the Initiative. However, a second important objective is to enhance the communication of e-texts, within and between large repositories that are commonly within libraries or in library-based e-text centers. Prominent examples include the University of Virginia[2] and the University of Michigan.[3]

```
<TEIHEADER><FILEDESC>
<TITLESTMT>
<TITLE TYPE="245">History of the peace: being a history of England from 1816 to 1854. With an introduc-
tion 1800 to 1815. By Harriet Martineau.</TITLE>
<AUTHOR>Martineau, Harriet, 1802–1876.</AUTHOR>
<AUTHOR>Craik, George Lillie, 1798–1866.</AUTHOR>
<AUTHOR>Knight, Charles, 1791–1873.</AUTHOR>
</TITLESTMT>
<EXTENT> 600dpi TIFF G4 page images</EXTENT>
<PUBLICATIONSTMT>
<PUBLISHER>University of Michigan, Digital Library Production Service</PUBLISHER><PUBPLACE>
Ann Arbor, Michigan</PUBPLACE>
<DATE>2000</DATE>
<IDNO TYPE="dlps">AAM1569.0001.001</IDNO>
</PUBLICATIONSTMT>
```
Figure 9.1   TEI header.

For those scholars and text creators who found that they did not need the level of detail called for in the *TEI Guide-lines,* a smaller tag set or subset was created, TEI Lite, which has about 150 tag elements. In both of these formats, the document creator provides descriptive information about the subsequent text in a preceding header. The TEI header was designed with bibliographic descriptive principles in mind. However, it is not perfectly aligned with a MARC-based bibliographic record. The following examples show the close relationship between a common TEI header (figure 9.1) and a MARC structured bibliographic record (figure 9.2).

There has been communication between the two communities, often facilitated by e-text centers, partially because much of the text-creation activity is developed in conjunction with and collected by academic libraries. Due to these common interests, the Library of Congress has prepared a MARC to SGML crosswalk.[4] The UK Office for Library and Information Networking Metadata site provides links to mappings of various metadata schemas, including the TEI Header to MARC 21,[5] which is based on the TEI Lite DTD from the University of Virginia, Electronic Text Center.[6]

In order to foster this communication between the scholarly and library communities, the Library of Congress and the Digital Library Federation supported a workshop, TEI and XML in Digital Libraries, held at the Library of Congress, June 30 through July 1, 1998.[7]

There were many positive outcomes from the workshop, including the follow-up reports focusing on best practices for MARC and the TEI.[8] This was a joint effort by Judy Ahronheim of the University of Michigan and Jackie Shieh, then of the University of Virginia. It outlines a common header practice based on the header preparation documents published on the Web from both the United States and the UK. In addition, it offers suggestions for guidelines on how each community could represent data to the advantage of the other. Second, "TEI Text Encoding in Libraries" was prepared under the leadership of Perry Willet of Indiana University.[9] These cooperative efforts demonstrate the growing role of

100 1	$a Martineau, Harriet, $d 1802–1876.
245 10	$a History of the peace : $b being a history of England from 1816 to 1854: with an introduction 1800 to 1815 / $c by Harriet Martineau.
260	$a Boston : $b Walker, Wise, and Company, $c 1865–66.
300	$a 4 v. ; $c 21 cm.
500	$a Book 1 (215 p.) was begun by Charles Knight and completed by G. L. Craik.
500	$a Vols. 3-4 published by Walker, Fuller & Company.
651 0	$a Great Britain $x History $y 19th century.
700 1	$a Craik, George Lillie, $d 1798–1866.
700 1	$a Knight, Charles, $d 1791–1873.

Figure 9.2   MARC record.

libraries as creators and partners in important digital projects. Other well-known examples include: the Kolb Proust Archive at the University of Illinois at Urbana-Champaign, and the Victorian Women Writers Project at Indiana University. Recently, the Center for Institutional Cooperation (CIC) announced a cooperative three-year project to digitize the works in the Lyle Wright Bibliography of American Fiction, 1851–1875.[10] This will be an important addition to the growing digital library of nineteenth-century Americana. This project will digitize microfilmed versions of American fiction listed in the Wright bibliography and use Text Encoding Initiative Guidelines to create encoded text from page images. This work will be shared among nine partner libraries, and it is estimated that it will take three years to complete.

With data formats so closely aligned and maintained by actively engaged practitioners, it would seem that both communities have a wonderful opportunity to assist one another in providing description and access for textual materials. There are several advantages. A formalized alignment between the two communities would foster data exchange through the standardized crosswalk and mapping conventions that could be developed and maintained. Possibilities exist for managing authoritative name forms over time in both metadata formats. For libraries, the advantages are even greater. Considering the high degree of granularity contained in these data formats, it seems likely that developing standardized mapping for MARC between the two would enable analytic cataloging to appear in the national utilities and in libraries without the great expense of original cataloging.

In summary, as pressure for a standardized XML-compliant TEI exchange format grows, libraries can take advantage in many ways. It would be possible for scholarly data to be re-purposed through machine manipulation into MARC records. Content standards as represented in libraries by AACR2 could be fostered and maintained over time and shared between the communities. Finally, metadata exchange could support communication between librarians and scholars. It is possible to look forward to new initiatives such as the Wright American Fiction Project, a cooperative effort between scholars and libraries, to influence the development of common standards and provide more and better access for all.

NOTES

1. *The TEI Guidelines,* http://www.uic.edu/orgs/tei/p3/.

2. University of Virginia Library, Electronic Text Center, *TEI Guidelines for Electronic Text Encoding and Interchange (P3),* http://etext.lib.virginia.edu/tci/.

3. University of Michigan, Humanities Text Initiative, http://hti.umich.edu/.

4. Library of Congress, Network Development and MARC Standards Office, *MARC SGML,* http://lcweb.loc.gov/marc/marcsgml.html.

5. Michael Day, *Metadata: Mapping between Metadata Formats,* http://www.ukoln.ac.uk/metadata/interoperability/.

6. University of Virginia Library, Electronic Text Center, *TEI2MARC Mapping Based on TEILITE.DTD,* http://etext.lib.virginia.edu/~ejs7y/tei-marc.html.

7. "TEI and XML in Digital Libraries," http://www.hti.umich.edu/misc/ssp/workshops/teidlf/.

8. Jackie Shieh, *Description of Text Encoding Initiatives (TEI) Header Elements and Corresponding USMARC Fields,* http://etext.lib.virginia.edu/~ejs7y/tei-usmarc.html. Appendix to *TEI/MARC Best Practices,* http://henry.ugl.lib.umich.edu/libhome/ocu/teiguide.html.

9. Perry Willet, *TEI Text Encoding in Libraries: Draft Guidelines for Best Encoding Practices,* http://www.indiana.edu/~letrs/tei/.

10. Indiana University, CIC Wright American Fiction 1851–1875 Project, http://www.indiana.edu/~letrs/wright/.

10

Libraries and the Future of the Semantic Web: RDF, XML, and Alphabet Soup

Eric Miller and Diane Hillmann, transcribed by Mary S. Woodley

It is important that libraries investigate technologies, standards, and acronyms such as XML (eXtensible Markup Language) and RDF (Resource Description Framework) and the role they will play in the library community.[1,2] The goal of this paper is to provide an understanding of the standards and technologies being produced and how they address the issues of metadata content on the Web: its organization, selection, and management. These technologies apply to the Web across domains and across disciplines; they are based on concepts the library community takes for granted. It is interesting that these kinds of technologies, which are becoming mainstream, are actually the bread and butter of what we do in libraries.

We begin by taking a few steps back to Tim Berners-Lee's early proposal at CERN (Conseil européen pour la recherche nucléaire—European Laboratory for Nuclear Research), which evolved into what is now called the World Wide Web.[3] One can extract two key components from the brief document he wrote asking CERN to fund and support him to develop this project. The first is to foster the ability to use computers to support human communication through the shared exchange of knowledge and information. The second is the exploitation of the computer to facilitate the day-to-day activities of humans and to allow machines to work for us as tools to make our lives easier. These two components are fundamental to the work done by the World Wide Web Consortium (W3C), which is the standards organization behind Web activities, including HTML, PICS, XML, and RDF.[4] These are the standards that allow exchange of information on the Web.

Currently, we have three major tiers, or layers, to solve aspects of various problems. HTML has given us an idea of what we can achieve collaboratively by developing a simple set of tags and sharing documents based on these tags. There are limitations with HTML, especially when people take their rich information and map it into these simple tags. XML, the second tier, is designed to be more open. It does not define tags; instead, it allows a richer exchange of documents. The cultural aspects of this open exchange of information have encouraged development of open-source solutions and promoted products with the ability to cross operating systems—for example, exporting Microsoft Word into HTML and using an XML/HTML editor in Linux. RDF can be viewed as the third tier, or layer, in the movement from a set of distributed documents to a globally shared information environment that would serve as the basis of what is coined by Tim Berners-Lee as the semantic Web.[5]

The current Web can be described by a simple diagram (see figure 10.1), in which each blue circle represents a resource that can be identified by a URL. Documents can relate to other documents based on anchors. Each anchor can point to another resource, but it does not describe the relationship between the documents. Is the anchor pointing to a favorite image, to a document that contains scholarly work, or to a document I dislike? We have no way of understanding the nature of the relationship between these objects; all we know from HTML is anchors. In figure 10.1 we can infer that anchors in http objects 2, 3, and 4 have a relationship, since all refer to http object 1. Search engines like Google and Alexa have the ability to use this basic information, but the exact nature of the relationships remains undefined.

The next tier will simply layer onto the existing infrastructure of the Web and provide mechanisms and standards to support the semantics or context of how objects in the Web relate to one another (see figure 10.2). For example, the author of an article can also be identified as a person who is part of a group. The illustration for the current Web still applies, but now additional semantics are layered to help express how these objects relate to one another. The semantics provide humans and machines with the ability to perform new forms of analysis and to use more enhanced

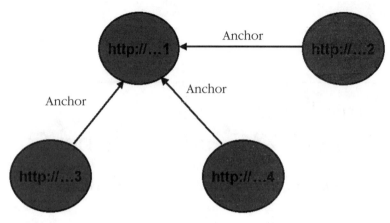

Figure 10.1   The current Web.

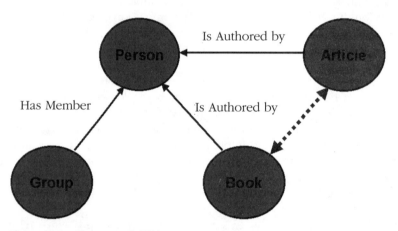

Figure 10.2   The semantic Web.

forms of organization and management. For example, we can draw additional inferences that this person is the author of both this article and that book, and therefore some relationship must exist between the article and the book. This "semantic Web," in essence, provides a layer of understanding on the existing Web.

The transition of the Web into a richer information space, a type of global database, forces us to recognize a blurring of traditional information barriers. By replacing the simple anchor with semantic Web ideas, we are able to share information and link to richer data sets in a new way, creating broad semantic relationships. We now have the ability to point into data sets of other domains (archives, museums, and geospatial data) and to link together data in new and powerful ways. As such, this breaks down traditional boundaries between libraries, archives, and museums. It is a challenge for us technically and socially to make this work.

In the current Web structure, the primary consumers are humans. In the future semantic Web, the primary consumers will be both humans and machines. Machines will be consuming this information, making deductions and organizing information to help people perform their daily tasks. What are the mechanisms needed to make this possible? It is difficult to resolve these issues effectively when those involved in developing the standards for the Web come from many different backgrounds, with diverse experiences and viewpoints on information.

We can identify three key architectural components:

1. Semantics: the meaning of concepts, understanding the concepts within the angle brackets—does a concept mean the same to everyone?
2. Structure: how these concepts or semantics relate to each other; how they are organized
3. Syntax: how these concepts and relations are communicated or transmitted across the wire (includes encoding conventions: the formal grammar to convey semantics and structure)

The first component is the domain of the various resource description communities; RDF provides the means for the second; and XML provides the means for the third.

WHAT IS XML? WHAT IS IT NOT?

XML syntax has been formally adopted by the World Wide Web Consortium. XML is a markup language, a mechanism to define tags and the structural relationship between components in documents. It is considered extensible because the semantics are not defined; that is, there is no precoordination of tags. In HTML, for example, the tags are precoordinated—it is easy to distinguish an HTML document from one that is not encoded using that standard because you know a priori which tags are defined by HTML and which are not. XML does not define a priori sets of tags but rather provides the means for communities to define tags as they see fit. According to Tim Bray, "the right way to think about XML is just like a next generation of ASCII."[6]

XML, however, is not a programming language. It does not replace word-processing software like Microsoft Word, nor is it an ANSI, NISO, CEN, or ISO standard.[7] And XML is not currently a formal means of expressing semantics. XML is about syntax.

An XML processor treats <booktitle>, <author>, <B>, and <I> equally and does not assign meaning to the information within. It is all just tags. As humans, we may think we understand the concepts within the angle brackets, but we can guarantee that the XML processor does not. Solving the problem of shared semantics is not the domain of XML; its task is only to establish rules and standard specifications defining how to declare an element and how to place elements in context with other elements. In order for computing solutions to be interoperable globally, common conventions for how these elements are structured and their corresponding semantics need to exist (for example, what a "person" is or what "authorship" means). XML is the ASCII of the future, and ASCII has never been enough to support general data integration.

In order to communicate across communities, common models for representing semantics and describing resources are necessary.

As a simple example, we might simply want to say, "The author of a particular document is Eric." There are a variety of XML representations of this concept: following are three ways different communities could express the same idea:

1. <document href = http://doc author = "Eric"/>
2. <author> <url> http://doc/ </url> <name> Eric </name> </author>
3. <document> <author> <name> Eric </name> </author> <url> http://doc </url></document>

These different representations reflect very different structures. The very nature of having different syntactic representations representing the same semantic concept makes it increasingly difficult to integrate and exchange information.

RESOURCE DESCRIPTION FRAMEWORK (RDF)

Enter another component, another layer: RDF. The World Wide Web Consortium decided a few years ago that metadata was a major issue. RDF is a substantiation of the Warwick Framework, a concept developed several years ago in conjunction with work on the Dublin Core.[8] It is designed to be the metadata framework for the Web. In RDF, a resource is defined as anything that can be identified: a book, a person, and even a relation that may exist between these—for example, "is authored by." The Resource Description Framework is designed as an enabling technology to support the characterization and organization of resources.

RDF is broken down into two key components: a data model and a schema. The data model supports a "web" of named relationships connecting uniquely identified things, or resources. An XML representation of this model is provided that supports the transmission of the model across applications. The schema enables resource description communities, such as museums, libraries, or e-commerce businesses, to define and relate semantics.

The RDF model is simply a statement that is comprised of three parts: two resources and a corresponding relationship. Figure 10.3 illustrates a simple RDF statement previously discussed: "the document is authored by Eric." In this figure, "Document" is a resource that has a property (e.g., "bib:author"), whose value is another resource, "Eric." In RDF, a special kind of "terminal" resource is a literal. A literal is basically a string value.

In figure 10.4, a "Document" has a property "bib:author," whose value is a literal string of "Eric." The XML representing this statement is included as part of this illustration. Each part of the statement has a URL (Universal Resource Locator), thus the relationship "bib:author" can be de-referenced to find out information about it. For example, we may associate multiple human-readable labels for different applications, such as "Author," "Name," or "100$a" (MARC field tag). Different communities and applications may simply define different human-readable labels or representations for the same semantic concept. The fact that this concept, however, has the same unique identifier is an indication to applications that this is indeed the same semantic. This powerful way to uniquely identify a concept, and then associate any human-readable label in any language to it, enables communities to share machine-readable tokens and to locally define human-readable labels to present the information to users.

One way RDF is designed to layer onto the existing Web is simply by admitting what the Web does: relate resources to other resources. For example, we have a description of a presentation (see figure 10.5): it has a "dc:title" and a "dc:creator"; the value of "dc:title" is a literal "ALA presentation"; and the value of "dc:creator" is a literal "Diane Hillmann." "Diane Hillmann" is a fairly uncommon name, but other authors may possess the same name, so there may be

- ## RDF statement

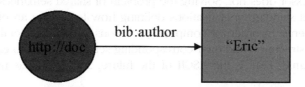

<rdf:Description rdf:about = "http://doc">
    <bib:author> Eric </bib:author>
</rdf:Description>

Figure 10.3   The RDF model.

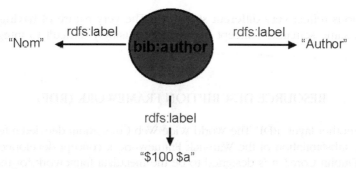

Figure 10.4   The RDF schema.

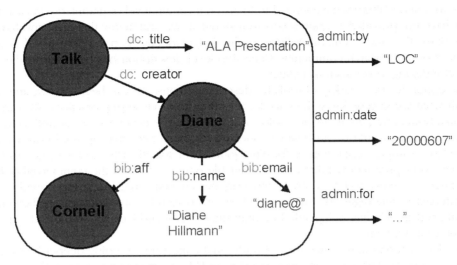

Figure 10.5   An RDF example of a presentation.

a need for a name authority to uniquely identify her. The Web has not yet caught on to the concept of name authority. Uniquely identifying people, places, and subjects is a fairly new concept everywhere except in libraries. In RDF, what we want to do is to replace "Diane" with a pointer to a name authority file, whose declaration in turn may have additional information such as e-mail address and affiliation. "Affiliation" itself could be another resource that may also point to an authority, which distinguishes one "Cornell" from another "Cornell."

One can view the whole description as a resource that can provide additional information: when the page was created, why, and by whom. This additional layer of data can be described as well. This is a powerful paradigm, especially when people can describe *anything* for any reason. The reliability of the descriptions is always dependent on who makes them.

The model for the enabling technologies is in place. XML provides a flexible syntax and RDF provides a common data model for representation and declaration mechanisms that communities may use to declare semantics. However, neither standard prescribes what these semantics should be. The technologies push these issues back to the communities to agree on organizational and descriptive practices and reuse of vocabularies. Communities are now coming together and trying to identify common semantics that will help them share information. The library community is far ahead of other information communities currently tackling the need for cooperation and the problems of sharing data. In a world where anyone can describe anything and describe the same resource for completely different purposes, trust becomes the issue. But whom do you trust to give you the most accurate description, the description that satisfies your information needs? The answer is: people you know, people you relate to, and people who share your values.

LIBRARIES' ROLE IN THE INFORMATION COMMUNITY

Libraries have a rich history in providing access to information that can be shared. The library community has a highly developed legacy syntax and structure (MARC) and rule-based semantics (AACR2 and MARC). It has a tradition of authority control, experience linking to a variety of vocabularies, and has learned to work with a variety of materials and formats.

Most libraries have a Web OPAC (online public access catalog) or will be moving to a Web interface soon. At Cornell University, we have already learned how to integrate data from a variety of sources. Within the OPAC, there are links to aggregator databases and links to article-level information (abstracts), and from there, links to local holdings. We have gone beyond strictly MARC data and now integrate a variety of resources for use by our community. We have learned over the years to add value to self-describing resources. That is what cataloging is about and, as an OCLC-enhancing library, this is what we have been doing with CIP (Cataloging-in-Publication). We have been adding value to metadata by adding richer description and by the process of selection, collection, organization, preservation, and improved access.

Where do we go from here? Libraries have tended to focus on a certain level of granularity in catalogs, that is: books and serial titles. We have not provided as good access to material above and below that level and have instead left that job to other communities. To some extent, this reflects a value judgment based on the print world. It is also a reflection of the perceived focus of the research community. Collection-level description has been left to the archives community, and article-level indexing to commercial entities.

Libraries have the option to use a variety of tools for describing things; we can beg, borrow, and steal an approach and combine it with what we already know how to do, selecting from our legacy practices. We can stretch ourselves beyond our traditional boundaries, go above and below our traditional levels of access, as well as look to the margins at either side. Some examples would be article-level indexing for those titles that up until now were not considered commercially viable (for example, digital images for older journals in specific areas). Other journals have not been indexed except through older print indexes that are not available online—most of the commercial online indexes have been prospective rather than retrospective. Cornell University has created some indexes to provide access beyond author and title to materials locally digitized. Faculty members at universities and colleges are becoming interested in courseware and multimedia, including being able to mount their syllabi and lectures on the Web and share their work with colleagues at other institutions.

Other options involve materials at the "margins" of traditional collections or going deeper in the description of resources than has been done traditionally. One project I (Diane Hillmann) worked on recently was a group of sound recordings of lectures given by visiting celebrities or scholars. In order to access the contents of the recordings, I wrote the specifications to move information from a locally maintained, non-MARC database to a MARC record that could be loaded into our catalog. If I were to do the project again, say in six months or a year from now, I might choose to do it differently—perhaps making use of another metadata alternative rather than adding the information to a MARC record. Most libraries contain material that has been cataloged as a collection for a MARC database, while the individual pieces are indexed elsewhere, perhaps using database software on personal computers. This was not an uncommon solution when money was not available for full MARC cataloging or the material was not deemed suitable for inclusion in the library's catalog. But these databases are often stored on floppy disks, and the disks are often stored in someone's desk drawer and later rediscovered. What happens when you no longer have that version of the database software or a machine to run the format? The information is virtually lost. Libraries need strategies to present such resources to their users and to manage the metadata for those resources without necessarily incurring the overhead of traditional cataloging.

Another potential avenue for using new tools is to provide for the access to and description of Internet resources, including sites that provide research-level materials of interest to library patrons. Government bodies and learned societies are mounting their publications on the Web, along with their print publications or in lieu of print. Professional presentations at conferences are sometimes available on the Web.

Figure 10.6 shows how XML/RDF works for such marginal materials—it describes the presentation on which this chapter is based. At the top of the example are links to namespaces defining semantics used in the record:

xml	eXtensible Markup Language
dc	Dublin Core
vcard	Virtual Business Card
lcnaf	Library of Congress Name Authority
lcsh	Library of Congress Subject Headings

In the first line, <rdf:Description rdf:about=http://purl.org/net/eric/talks/alphasoup> is the URL where the presentation will live on the Web. There are two Dublin Core creator elements. The first author is Eric and he is identified by a link to a <vcard> description. The second creator, Diane Hillmann, is identified by a link to an lcnaf record (which is spurious—it doesn't yet exist in the Library of Congress Name Authority file). The idea of having the author described in two different ways is perhaps unsettling, but it parallels using subject terms/phrases from different vocabularies in the same record (for example, Library of Congress Subject Headings (LCSH) and Medical Subject Headings (MeSH) on the same record). There is also a link to the LCSH record number so that we can link to that vocabulary for cross-references, scope, and other related headings.

To reiterate the point, metadata integration does not require a single database. It is not an either/or decision, a choice between MARC and XML.[9] We can have more than one tool in our toolbox. The challenge is making the data and the information from these various sources work together for the benefit of our patrons while managing the data effectively. If the library community does not take up this challenge, someone else will, and will do it badly.

```
<?xml version= "1.0"?>
<rdf:RDF
xmlns:rdf= "http://www.w3.org/1999/02/22-rdf-syntax#"
xmlns:dc="http://purl.org/dc/elements/1.0/"
xmlns:ac="http://purl.org/dc/agent/1.0/"
xmlns:vcard="http://www.imc.org/pdi/vCard/"
xmlns:lcnaf="http://lcweb.loc.gov/marc/authority/lcnaf/"
xmlns:lcsh="http://lcweb.loc.gov/marc/subject/lcsh/">

<rdf:Description rdf:about="http://purl.org/net/eric/talks/alphasoup">
    <dc:title>Libraries and the Future of the Semantic Web: RDF, XML and
Alphabet Soup</dc:title>
    <dc:creator>
        <ac:Person>
            <vcard:fn>Eric Miller</vcard:fn>
            <vcard:org>OCLC Online Computer Library Center, Office of Research</vcard:org>
            <vcard:email>emiller@oclc.org</vcard:email>
            <vcard:tel-work> 614 764 6109</vcard:tel-work>
            <vcard:url>http://purl.oclc.org/net/eric </vcard:url>
        </ac:Person>
    </dc:creator>
    <dc:creator>
        <ac:Person>
            <lcnaf:100>Hillmann, Diane I., (Diane Ileana), 1948-</lcnaf:100>
            <lcnaf:400>Hillmann, Diane Ileana, 1948-</lcnaf:400>
            <lcnaf:010>nafr00034512</lcnaf:010>
        </ac:Person>
    </dc:creator>
    <dc:subject>RDF (Resource Description Framework)</dc:subject>
    <dc:subject>Libraries</dc:subject>
    <dc:subject>Semantic Web</dc:subject>
    <dc:subject>
        <lcsh:Heading>
            <lcsh:150>XML (Document markup language)</lcsh:150>
            <lcsh:010>sh 97007825</lcsh:010>
        </lcsh:Heading>
    </dc:subject>
    <dc:description>An introduction to XML (Extensible Markup Language) and RDF (Resource Description
Framework), and their potential in a library setting.</dc:description>
    <dc:date>2000-07-06</dc:date>
    <dc:format>text/html</dc:format>
</rdf:Description>
</rdf:RDF>
```

Figure 10.6   XML/RDF example.

CROSSWALKS

Crosswalks can be viewed in two different ways: (1) a way to move your data from one kind of representation to another; (2) a mechanism that allows different kinds of data to be searched and displayed together in a manner transparent to users but stored separately. Crosswalks are eminently useful but also limiting—loss of data invariably occurs. If we perceive XML and RDF as just another way to present traditionally cataloged library materials to our patrons, we've missed the point. We need to learn about these new technologies and exploit their strengths in our context.

We can move forward with some enthusiasm. We conquered MARC numeric tags and we can learn how to deal with the angle brackets. It is time to extend ourselves and to learn and experiment. The library community can contribute a great deal to this effort. We have an understanding of bibliographic structure and indexing. We have insights into user behavior and experience managing "big data."

After I worked for five years in the Dublin Core community, it has become obvious that librarians have a great deal of knowledge to share about how to manage growing data over time. As the Web has grown from something small and specialized that could be searched effectively by a primitive search engine to a monster eggplant that threatens to eat the entire world (not just Chicago), our skills are much in demand. If not us, then who?

NOTES

1. W3C, "Extensible Markup Language (XML)," http://www.w3.org/XML/.

2. W3C, "Resource Description Framework (RDF)," http://www.w3.org/RDF/. For an explanation of RDF, see: Eric Miller, "An Introduction to the Resource Description Framework," *D-Lib Magazine,* May 1998, http://www.dlib.org/dlib/may98/miller/05miller.html.

3. Tim Berners-Lee, "Information Management: A Proposal," March 1989, http://www.w3.org/History/1989/proposal.html.

4. HTML (HyperText Markup Language); PICS (Platform for Internet Content Selection); XML (eXtensible Markup Language), and RDF (Resource Description Framework).

5. Tim Berners-Lee, "Semantic Web Road Map," September 1998, http://www.w3.org/DesignIssues/Semantic.html.

6. Tim Bray, "XML—Extensible Markup Language," interview by Philippe Lourier, April 24, 1998, http://technetcast.com/hz-show-980424.html.

7. ANSI (American National Standards Institute), NISO (National Information Standards Organization), CEN (Conseil européen pour la normalisation), and ISO (International Standards Organization).

8. Carl Lagoze, Clifford A. Lynch, and Ron Daniel Jr., "The Warwick Framework: A Container Architecture for Aggregating Sets of Metadata," June 21, 1996, http://cs-tr.cs.cornell.edu:80/Dienst/UI/2.0/Describe/ncstrl.cornell/TR96-1593.

9. Tim Bray, "RDF and Metadata," June 8, 1998, http://www.xml.com/pub/98/06/rdf.html.

11

Archival Finding Aids as Metadata: Encoded Archival Description

Kris Kiesling

The descriptive apparatus known as archival finding aids (or inventories and registers), having lived in card files, binders, and file cabinets for decades, is now finding a comfortable home on the Web via Encoded Archival Description (EAD).[1] EAD is an SGML/XML–based document type definition developed by the archival community as a mechanism for stable data storage and sophisticated retrieval of the information contained in finding aids. It has been endorsed by the Society of American Archivists as a descriptive standard. Due to its wide-ranging appeal, flexible data structure, and basis in the General International Standard Archival Description (ISAD[G])[2] of the International Council on Archives, EAD has been implemented in numerous repositories in the United States, Canada, the United Kingdom, Australia, and several other countries in Europe.

Finding aids describe archival materials, which can comprise anything from letters and diaries to photographs, sound recordings, and electronic data files. The materials are treated "archivally" rather than "bibliographically," in that they are described as a collectivity sharing a common origin, not as individual objects. Furthermore, the records generated by a government agency in the course of carrying out its functions or the personal papers created by an individual in the course of a career or an avocation rarely have the self-identifying mechanisms that published materials have, so alternate descriptive practices are needed. For an archivist, the relationships between the materials in the collection[3] generally are more important than the individual items themselves. Photographs taken in the late 1800s of a shipwreck in the Arctic, while evocative by themselves, are much more powerful when studied along with the narrative written by one of the ship's surviving crew members. Archival descriptive practices capture those relationships. Finding aids can be used to describe any body of materials for which detailed individual records are not necessary or feasible.

Archival materials are inherently hierarchical. Collections are divided into logical intellectual groupings, which may be further subdivided into smaller and smaller "chunks," ultimately reaching the file or even item level. For example, the dean of a university department may organize her files by subject and within each of those subjects subdivide chronologically or by subtopic or document type. There may be a file for speeches and within that file, copies of individual presentations. To reflect that hierarchy, archival description is essentially multilevel, that is, description proceeds from the general to the specific. A typical finding aid will contain a general description of the entire collection and information about the context of its creation in a scope and content note and a biographical sketch or agency history. This general description may be followed by more detailed descriptions of the collection's component parts, usually subgroups or "series," and finally by a list of containers, files, and/or items that describe the materials in even greater detail. The latter is used by a researcher to request access to the materials but also serves the repository as a representation of the intellectual organization of the materials. In fact, the finding aid can and should draw together related intellectual components of the collection even if the materials are not in that same order on the shelf.

The finding aid, then, functions as metadata about the collection, similar to the way a catalog record functions as metadata for a book, serial, map, or sound recording. However, in addition to serving as a point of access to the materials, the finding aid reflects their intellectual order.

EAD represents for finding aids what MARC 21 represents for catalog records—a communication format and data structure standard. EAD has a basic set of about twenty-five structural elements that can be used in a repeating hierarchy to describe archival materials at the collection level, item level, and any level in between. At the top of this hierarchy are three elements: the EAD Header <eadheader>, which describes the electronic finding aid; Front Matter <frontmatter>, which supports the creation of title pages, introductions, and other formal publication structures; and Archival Description

<archdesc>, which contains the text of the finding aid itself. The following discussion will focus on limited aspects of <eadheader> and <archdesc>, the metadata embedded therein, and relationships with other metadata standards.

EAD contains a block of elements that functions as metadata about the encoded finding aid. These elements are contained within the <eadheader>, which is patterned after the Text Encoding Initiative (TEI) Header.[4] Figure 11.1 shows the basic structure of and some of the elements within the header.

The File Description <filedesc> sub-elements permit the encoding of a formal title for the finding aid, as well as the name of its author and information about the repository as publisher. EAD ID <eadid> contains a unique identifier for the encoded file, while the Profile Description <profiledesc> sub-elements contain information about the encoding—who performed it and when—and specifies the language in which the finding aid is written. The header also allows for version control of the file via Revision Description <revisiondesc>.

The <eadheader> sub-elements should permit Web search engines to identify encoded finding aids and the collections they describe. The Title Statement element, for example, ideally will contain a formal title for the finding aid that incorporates the name of the collection and the name of the holding repository—for example, Robert Lowell, an Inventory of His Papers at the Harry Ransom Humanities Research Center. The *EAD Application Guidelines*[5] provide an extensive discussion of the importance of the <eadheader>, which contains most of the elements that are required by the document type definition (DTD) for an encoded finding aid to parse or "validate."

The Archival Description element <archdesc> holds the text of the finding aid itself (see figure 11.2 for a list of the primary structural elements in <archdesc>).

```
<eadheader>
    <eadid>  EAD ID
    <filedesc>  File Description
        < >  Title Statement
        <titleproper>
        <subtitle>
        <author>
        <publicationstmt>  Publication Statement
        <publisher>
        <address>
        <date>
    <profiledesc>  Profile Description (encoding)
        <creation>
        <date>
        <langusage>
        <language>
    <revisiondesc>  Revision Description
        <change>
        <date>
        <item>
```

Figure 11.1 Partial list of sub-elements in the EAD header.

```
<archdesc>  Archival Description
    <did>  Descriptive Identification
    <bioghist>  Biography or History
    <scopecontent>  Scope and Content
    <admininfo>  Administrative Information
    <controlaccess>  Controlled Access Headings
    <dsc>  Description of Subordinate Components
        <c01>  Component (first level)
            <did>
            <bioghist>
            <scopecontent>
            <admininfo>
            <controlaccess>
            <c02>
```

Figure 11.2 Partial list of structural elements within an archival description.

```
<archdesc>
    <did>  Descriptive Identification
        <repository>
        <origination>  Creator or Collector
        <unittitle>  Title of the Unit being described
        <unitdate>  Date(s) of the Unit being described
        <physdesc>  Physical Description
        <unitid>  Unique Identifier
        <abstract>
        <physloc>  Physical Location
        <container>
```

Figure 11.3   Partial list of sub-elements in the descriptive identification.

It has a required Descriptive Identification sub-element <did> that, at the highest or most general level of description, contains metadata about the collection, including the name of the holding repository <repository>, the name of the creator or collector of the materials <origination>, the title of the collection <unittitle> and its date span <unitdate>, how much material there is <physdesc>, a unique identifier <unitid> (frequently an accession number), and an abstract of the collection's content . Figure 11.3 lists some of the data elements within <did>.

These same elements are used in EAD to encode information for the component parts of the collection. At a lower or more detailed level of description, for example, a file, the <did> sub-elements within Components <c> identify the title of the file <unittitle>, its date(s) <unitdate>, a shelving location <physloc> and <container>, a unique identifier <unitid>, and perhaps an abstract of its content . The use of the <SC>LEVEL</SC> attribute on <archdesc> and <c> elements allows the encoder and the computer to keep track of the hierarchy by specifying whether the particular element is describing the entirety of the materials or some specific part, such as a series, file, or item.

The <archdesc> element and its sub-elements, then, serve as a second layer of metadata, that for the collection materials themselves. The addition of digitized images of the collection materials, which can be embedded in the finding aid or linked to from the finding aid, complicates matters. The images will have their own metadata, most likely a title and date, name of the creator of the original, and perhaps some subject access. EAD directly supports this metadata (in the Digital Archival Object element <dao>) but not metadata for date and method of capture, image resolution, and file format for the digitized image. Instead, these latter may be maintained via a database, a very robust example of which has been developed by the Making of America II project.[6]

Virtually all of the structural and nominal EAD elements carry an attribute through which the archivist can specify a corollary element in another encoding scheme. The <SC>RELATEDENCODING</SC> attribute can be set once for the entire encoded finding aid in the <ead> element. Alternately, the header elements could be mapped to Dublin Core, while the archival description elements are mapped to MARC 21. Then, within <eadheader> sub-elements, the appropriate DC tag would be specified, for example, the Dublin Core Title element within the EAD <titleproper> (the following examples do not include all required elements):

```
<eadheader relatedencoding = "Dublin Core">
    <filedesc>
        <titlestmt>
<titleproper encodinganalog = "Title">Robert Lowell, an Inventory of His
Papers at the Harry Ransom Humanities Research Center</titleproper>
        </titlestmt>
    </filedesc>
</eadheader>
```

Similarly, within the <unittitle> element in <archdesc><did>, the MARC 21 245 field could be specified:

```
<archdesc level = "collection" relatedencoding = "MARC21">
    <did>
        <unittitle encodinganalog = "245">Robert Lowell Papers, 1845–
1988</unittitle>
    </did>
</archdesc>
```

Alternately, the related encoding scheme can be declared in each element as desired:

```
<archdesc level = "collection">
   <did>
<unittitle encodinganalog = "MARC21 245">Robert Lowell Papers,
1845–1988</unittitle>
   </did>
</archdesc>
```

EAD supports the encoding of controlled vocabulary terms in several ways. Terms can be defined as a block of access points in the Controlled Access <controlaccess> element (similar to the way one would segregate them in a MARC record), they can be used within the narrative text of a Paragraph <p>, or they can be encoded within other elements, such as <repository> or <origination>. Figure 11.4 shows the <controlaccess> sub-elements, which comprise the elements used to identify controlled vocabulary terms.

Each of these elements has a host of attributes that enhance the encoding, such as normal, source, encodinganalog, and role. So, for example, if one wanted to embed within a paragraph the authority form of a name, identify the controlled vocabulary list from which it was taken, map the element to a MARC tag, and specify the role the individual plays within the collection without disturbing the natural language in the paragraph, the encoding might look something like this:

```
<p> . . . correspondence from Lowell's second wife, <persname
normal = "Hardwick, Elizabeth, 1916– " source = "lcnaf" encodinganalog
= "MARC21 700" role = "correspondent">Elizabeth Hardwick
</persname> dominates the series. . . . </p>
```

Embedding these encoding analogs in the EAD markup facilitates reuse of the data for multiple purposes—for example, the export of a partial MARC record from the finding aid, and identifying Dublin Core elements for Web cataloging and searching purposes. Other encoding schemes could be specified instead. A number of European repositories designate ISAD(G) data elements rather than MARC 21 and use EAD to generate ISAD-compliant descriptions (and vice versa). It is worth noting that in transforming EAD-encoded finding aids to HTML, data specified in the <controlaccess> sub-elements can be automatically converted to meta tags in the HTML <head>, thereby increasing the chances that a Web search service will locate the finding aids (which, after all, is the purpose of putting them on the Web in the first place). This is also true of encoding analogs in other EAD elements, such as <unittitle> (see previous examples). The following example illustrates the necessary EAD encoding and the resulting HTML transformation. The obvious benefit is that both a MARC 21 100 field and an HTML meta tag can be generated from the same markup, since there is a direct relationship between the 100 field and the Dublin Core Author field.

```
<origination><persname encodinganalog = "MARC21
   100">Lowell, Robert, 1917–1977 </persname></origination>
   <meta name = "dc.author" content = "Lowell, Robert, 1917–
   1977">
```

Given that EAD finding aids contain various types of metadata, the question for Web catalogers and search engines is, what does the top-level metadata point to? Does the metadata point to the finding aid itself (i.e., using the <eadheader>

```
<controlaccess>
   <corpname>
   <famname>
   <function>
   <genreform>
   <geoname>
   <name>
   <occupation>
   <persname>
   <subject>
   <title>
```

Figure 11.4   Partial list of sub-elements in a controlled access.

elements), or does it point to the collection? Can it point to both without confusing the Web crawler or the end user? The *EAD Application Guidelines* contain a mapping between EAD elements and Dublin Core.[7] Theoretically, the metadata in the <eadheader> would incorporate some of the same information as the high-level <did>, such as the name of the repository and some clue as to the title of the collection, which should include the name of the creator of the materials being described. As the mapping in the *Guidelines* illustrates, however, there is not a full one-to-one relationship between Dublin Core and either the <eadheader> or <archdesc> sub-elements. For example, there is currently no way to specify a subject in <eadheader>, so direct correlation to the DC <subject> element is lacking.

Several avenues exist on the Web through which one can locate archival finding aids and the resources they describe. At this point in time, serendipity plays a substantial role. One logical starting place is to conduct a search in a library OPAC. Most online catalogs are Web-enabled, and using the MARC 21 856 field (and soon the 555 field[8]) repositories that create catalog records for their archival materials can link the MARC record directly to its corresponding finding aid for a given collection. Users who begin their search for library resources in their local OPAC, should they retrieve a record for archival materials, can move via links from the MARC record to the finding aid and potentially from the finding aid to images of the collection materials as well.

More advanced users of libraries and archives may go directly to a known repository's Web site to determine if specific archival materials are held by that institution. Many archival repositories have Web pages that list finding aids available in HTML, SGML, or XML. Occasionally, collection descriptions are grouped by topic rather than being listed alphabetically by the name of the creator of the materials. Some repositories have search engines that will allow a user to search across the finding aids at their site. An extension of this scenario is the growing number of multiple-repository Web sites, the products of consortial EAD implementation projects, an example of which is the Online Archive of California.[9] Other consortial projects, including the Online Archive of New Mexico, the Texas Archival Resources Online, and others developing in North Carolina and Virginia, soon will have Web sites available. While these consortial sites typically begin as a partnership between a few institutions, they are intended to be extensible.

A slightly different approach is being taken by the Research Libraries Group through its Archival Resources database.[10] Long a supporter of archival cataloging, RLG has created a search utility that simultaneously searches indexes built from the MARC records in the AMC (Archival and Mixed Collections) file of its international RLIN database and from finding aids, in either EAD or HTML, submitted to the service. The finding aids in a user's search result may be housed on RLG's server or more likely on the server of the repository, but that fact is fairly transparent to the user. This service has the advantage of allowing a user to search collection information from repositories across the United States, Canada, Great Britain, and Europe. Repositories need not be members of RLG to add catalog records or finding aids to the service.

Finally, a Web surfer has some chance of retrieving archival finding aids using search services such as Yahoo!, AltaVista, or HotBot. Results are spotty at best, however, because, frequently, individual finding aids will be buried several layers down in an institution's Web site, easily overlooked by search services. The chances of locating the finding aid for the Robert Lowell papers at the Ransom Center are significantly better using AltaVista, though, than of locating a copy of his *The Dolphin* in the university's online catalog using the same search technique.

As are MARC 21 and Dublin Core, EAD is and probably always will be a work in progress. The EAD Working Group[11] will begin to consider changes to the document type definition in the coming months, most likely looking at Dublin Core, the new version of ISAD(G),[12] and other metadata standards for ways to strengthen the links between them. However, the structure of EAD will continue to serve first and foremost archivists and users of archives, whether they be seasoned researchers who simply want to download the finding aid prior to a trip to the repository or grade-school children looking for images of the "real stuff" on the Web.

NOTES

1. Information about EAD is available at the official EAD Web site maintained by the Library of Congress, http://lcweb.loc.gov/ead/, and the Society of American Archivists EAD Roundtable Help Pages, http://jefferson.village.virginia.edu/ead/. Technical documentation is available from SAA: the *Encoded Archival Description Tag Library: Version 1.0* (Chicago: SAA, 1998) and the *Encoded Archival Description Application Guidelines: Version 1.0* (Chicago: SAA, 1999).

2. ISAD(G) is the descriptive standard adopted by the International Council on Archives in 1993. Information is available at http://www.ica.org/. A copy of ISAD(G) can be downloaded from http://www.ica.org/cgi-bin/ica.pl?04_e.

3. The term *collection* is used throughout this chapter to refer to all types of archival materials, whether they are organizational, corporate, or government records (traditionally known as archives) or personal papers (traditionally known as manuscripts).

4. Information about TEI, an international humanities-based text-encoding effort, is available at: http://www.tei-c.org/.

5. Encoded Archival Description Working Group, *Encoded Archival Description Application Guidelines,* 114–120.

6. The MoA II testbed was "designed to provide a means for the Digital Library Federation to investigate, refine, and recommend metadata elements and encodings used to discover, display, and navigate digital archival objects" (Bernard J. Hurley et al., *The Making of America II Testbed Project: A Digital Library Service Model* [Washington: Council on Library and Information Resources, 1999, 3]).

7. There are also mappings from EAD to ISAD(G) and MARC 21, 235–242.

8. MARBI approved the addition of the URL/URN linking subfield ($u) to the 555 Finding Aids Note field at the June 1999 ALA Annual Meeting.

9. Information about the OAC, which contains finding aids from, at the time of this writing, thirty-five repositories in California, including all of the UC campuses, can be found at http://sunsite2.Berkeley.EDU/oac/.

10. Information about RLG's Archival Resources is available at http://www.rlg.org/arr/index.html. Access to the service itself is available by subscription.

11. The EADWG is the body within the Society of American Archivists responsible for the continued development and maintenance of EAD. It was formed in 1995 and currently has membership from the United States, Canada, UK, and Australia.

12. ISAD(G) has been revised; the new version was to be voted on by the International Council on Archives membership in September 2000.

12

ISO Standards Development for Metadata

Carlen Ruschoff, transcribed by Sally C. Tseng

Technological developments available today have created an environment of high demand and great expectations in the information world. Rising to the challenge, librarians and other "information entrepreneurs" have developed an array of new ideas and schemas for describing, organizing, and in general providing access to electronic information. The problem that this explosion presents is that many of these innovative schemas are not interchangeable. They are usually developed for one discipline or a narrowly defined group of resources and are created in isolation from one another. Between individual schemas, the meaning and the use of terms may be different, the descriptive elements are likely to be inconsistent, and the content descriptors or tags are unlikely to translate from one environment to another. These differences make searching across different databases cumbersome, if not impossible. As we move forward in developing new information products and services, it becomes increasingly important to establish and implement universal standards. These standards ensure that computer hardware and software components work together efficiently and cost effectively. The growing environment in which metadata schemas are employed is no exception. Both metadata developers and consumers are counting on standards to pave the way for economical retrieval and interpretation of information across disciplines and databases.

This chapter presents some of the standards that are applicable to metadata enterprises that have been developed and endorsed by the International Organization for Standardization (ISO), as well as a few that have been promulgated by the National Information Standards Organization (NISO) in the United States.

Before I turn to standards for metadata, I would like to provide a general overview of the standards development process at the international level.

THE ISO STANDARDS ENVIRONMENT

ISO-ANSI-NISO Relationship

Much of the worldwide standards development is carried out by the International Organization for Standardization. The organization is a federation of national standards bodies. Its mission is to promote standards that facilitate the international exchange of goods and services, including areas of intellectual, scientific, and technological activity. To accomplish its mission, ISO has established over two hundred technical committees, each devoted to the development of a specific group of standards. The Committee on Information and Documentation, known as Technical Committee 46 (TC 46), is the group that conducts the work that is of particular interest to libraries, as well as other information entities such as information and documentation centers, indexing and abstracting services, archives, information science, and publishing. Technical Committee 46 is further subdivided into seven subcommittees, each assigned a broad scope of standards to oversee. Attached to the subcommittees are working groups, which are given standards on specific topics to develop (see figure 12.1).

The participants on these committees and working groups are appointed from the ISO membership. Members are usually representatives from standards institutes in various countries. The American National Standards Institute (ANSI) is the United States' official representative to ISO. U.S. standards developers are able to participate in ISO activities as ANSI's representatives. For example, the National Information Standards Organization has been selected by ANSI to

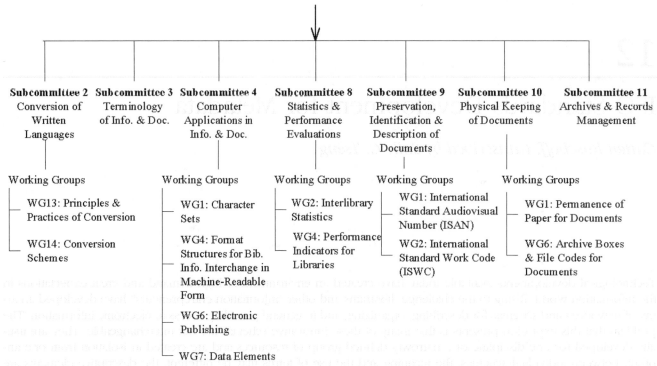

Figure 12.1   Structure of ISO Technical Committee 46: Information and Documentation.

represent the United States on Technical Committee 46 because of its role in promulgating standards for the information industry in the United States. NISO has the responsibility to provide representation to TC 46 meetings, to review all draft standards, and to recommend to ANSI the United States' position on these standards.

NISO is itself a membership organization that is responsible for developing and promoting many of the standards in the United States in the areas of: information retrieval (Z39.50), Information Interchange format (Z39.2), and scientific and technical reports (Z39.18). Both NISO and ISO draft standards are circulated to NISO members for review and comment prior to becoming final. The American Library Association is a NISO member and therefore has the opportunity to review, comment, and vote on national and international standards.

From Proposal to Accepted Standard

An idea for information standards development is presented as a "new work initiative" to the appropriate ISO technical committee for review. These new work initiatives often stem from standards that have been developed within countries that are members of ISO. When the committee determines that a proposal is appropriate to be developed into a standard, the proposal is accepted and assigned a number for identification. This number will remain the same through all stages of review and development. A prefix is added to the number, which changes as the proposal progresses through the review and approval process. Figure 12.2 shows the various stages of a proposed standard and the associated prefixes.

An approved work initiative is assigned a number with the prefix of "WD," signifying that the document is a working draft, and the draft is forwarded to the appropriate working group for development. After the working group has reworked and approved the proposed standard, the draft is relabeled "CD," or committee draft, and forwarded up to its parent subcommittee. A committee draft may be circulated to ISO members for comment while it is under discussion at the subcommittee level. Changes recommended are incorporated into the draft standard. The revised draft standard is then registered as a Draft International Standard and the prefix becomes "DIS." The Draft International Standard is circulated to ISO members, including appropriate national standards bodies, such as ANSI and NISO, for review and ballot. Each of these national standards groups in turn circulates the DIS to its membership. At this point, appropriate draft standards would be made available to the American Library Association for review and comment. After the vote closes and the proposal has received the required number of affirmatives, the standard is registered with ISO as a Final Draft International Standard (FDIS). The FDIS is circulated for two months for a final ballot. Within two months of the final approval, the standard is published as an ISO document.

New Work Initiative
Submitted to Technical Committee for
standards development

↓

Working Draft
Approved New Work Initiative is forwarded to the appropriate Working Group
(WD *nnnn*)

↓

Committee Draft
Approved Working Draft is sent to the appropriate Subcommittee for ballot
(CD *nnnn*)

↓

Draft International Standard
Approved Committee Draft is circulated to ISO members for ballot
(DIS *nnnn*)

↓

Final Draft International Standard
Draft International Standard is circulated for 2
months for final ballot   (FDIS *nnnn*)

↓

ISO Standard
Standard is published within 2 months of final ballot
(ISO *nnnn*)

Figure 12.2   New ISO standard proposal path (simplified).

It is important to note that the path of a standard may not be as simple as described here. ISO standards are developed by consensus and therefore a draft standard may have to be revised, recirculated, and balloted more than one time at any stage in the process in order to achieve consensus.

APPLICABLE STANDARDS TO THE METADATA ENVIRONMENT

Many standards have been developed through the procedure described previously that are suitable for metadata enterprises. The ISO standards, as well as some NISO standards that are most appropriate to library applications, are discussed further on. They have been divided into five broad categories: data elements and content, identifiers, codes, character sets and transliteration of nonroman scripts, and formats and protocols. A list of applicable standards available at the time this article was written is found in appendix A, at the end of this chapter.

Data Elements and Content

One of the most familiar is: *Format for Information Exchange, ISO 2709.* This is the standard upon which the MARC format is based. It provides a basic framework in which to communicate bibliographic descriptions of materials in all forms.

The newest standard on the scene is: *Data Elements for the Exchange of Cataloguing and Metadata.* It is part 5 of ISO/DIS 8459 that provides standards for data elements for acquisitions, ILL, circulation, and holdings statements. This standard is intended to support terminal-to-computer or computer-to-computer communications by providing an official list of data elements used in cataloging systems, as well as a basic structure of that data. This list represents the data elements in four columns: the numeric tag, the element name, the definition of the data element, and a brief description of how to represent the content of the data element. The standard is also intended to support both batch and interactive cataloging transactions. This standard was distributed worldwide for ballot in the summer of 2000.

ISO/IEC 11179, *Specification and Standardization of Data Elements,* is a standard that has been jointly developed by ISO and the International Electrotechnical Commission. This standard presents a framework that assures consistency of data content between information repositories and Computer-Aided Software Engineering (CASE) tools. The standard is being used currently to create registries of metadata element sets that include information that is necessary to describe, inventory, analyze, and classify data. Put simply, these registries provide the information needed for mappings that aid in the interchange of metadata between systems.

While many metadata element sets have been developed for specific purposes or disciplines, few have been proposed for adoption as an ISO standard. A metadata element set is a group of attributes that forms a formal description of an entity. Thus far, most of the ISO standards work on data element sets has been done for the geospatial community by ISO Technical Committee 211, Geographic Information/Geomatics. The Federal Geographic Data Committee (FGDC) has worked closely with ISO TC 211 on the development of these standards and is committed to harmonizing its own data element set, *Content Standard for Digital Geospatial Metadata* (CSDGM, FGDC-STD-001-1998), with the ISO standards.

The Dublin Core Metadata Set has been submitted to NISO as a proposed standard. The set presents fifteen data elements. The proposal is currently under review by a NISO Committee and is now being circulated for ballot to NISO members as draft Z39.85.

Identifiers

A number of standards have been developed to aid in the unique identification of particular works or objects. These standards provide guidance in developing unique character strings called "identifiers." Identifiers are numbers that can be used for linking and rights management. Standards for identifiers require descriptive information such as a cataloging record or metadata that describes the entity and assists in retrieval. Such standards include the International Standard Book Number (ISBN), the International Standard Serial Number (ISSN), the International Standard Recording Code (ISRC), and the International Standard Music Number (ISMN).

NISO has developed two new standards for identifiers. They are the Serial Item and Contribution Identifier (SICI or ANSI/NISO Z39.56-1996), and the Digital Object Identifier (DOI or Z39.84-2000). A third standard, the Book Item and Component Identifier (BICI), is in development. These standards allow identifiers to be assigned to entities within a larger body, such as individual articles in serials, chapters in books, a scene in a movie, or an article or object on a Web site.

Codes

ISO has developed standards for codes that are often required in metadata and cataloging records. These standards provide uniform codes to represent information such as languages, country codes, or names of libraries. They are: ISO 639-2:1998 Codes for the Representation of Name of Languages, Part 2, Alpha-3 Code, ISO 3166:1998 Codes for the Representation of Names of Countries, and ISO/DIS 1511 (ISIL) International Standard Identifier for Libraries and Related Organizations. These codes may be used in data elements that call for descriptive information, such as the language or languages of text or its country of origin. The same codes in a different data element may be used to describe the content of the work, such as work about a country, region, or city.

Character Sets and Transliteration of Nonroman Scripts

Character sets determine how the bytes that represent the characters and symbols within that set are stored and translated to readable characters. ISO has developed standard tables for several character sets for both roman and nonroman alphabets, as well as graphic code sets. These standard character sets include: Latin, Cyrillic, Greek, and many others (see appendix A), as well as mathematical symbols. Use of these standards assures consistent coding of characters within a single system, as well as in exchange of data between systems.

Individual character sets, however, can sometimes be incompatible with one another, causing chaos when working in a multiple-character-set environment. Mixing character sets makes searching, sorting, and other operations very difficult, if not impossible. ISO/IEC 10646:1993 Universal Multiple-Octet Coded Character Set (UCS), more commonly known as Unicode, defines a superset of all established character sets. It is a single universal character set that facilitates the exchange of text files between databases and between computers. ISO Technical Committee 46, Subcommittee 4, Working Group 1, is currently working on mapping characters in individual character sets to equivalent characters in Unicode. Thus far, characters from the Latin alphabet set (ISO 5426), Extended Cyrillic (ISO 5427), African (ISO 6436), Armenian (ISO 10585), Georgian (ISO 10586), Extended Arabic (ISO 11822), Greek (ISO 5428), and mathematical characters (ISO 6862) have been fully mapped to the Unicode standard. The other character sets will be mapped to the standard in the future.

To address the eye-readable nonroman scripts, ISO has developed tables for transliterating nonroman scripts into Latin characters. These tables provide consistency in description and improved accuracy in discovery of entities in all formats. ISO provides tables for Arabic, Chinese, Cyrillic, Greek, Hebrew, and Japanese Kana script.

Formats and Protocols

The standards that have been discussed thus far relate to building metadata sets and providing consistency in structure, representation, and content. The standards that are listed in the last section of appendix A are related, in that they provide the applications for communications and information retrieval. It is important to be aware of these standards because they provide the specifications that transport and resolve metadata.

CONCLUSION

As libraries and other information brokers worldwide progress into the realm of metadata to capitalize on its capacity to "mine" information, international standards will be essential. Enterprises that employ standards that are accepted and used internationally will find more opportunities for partnerships in the exchange of information. At the same time, librarians, as information access developers and consumers, need to ensure that the products and databases we design and purchase are based on accepted standards so that our digital libraries are able to provide consistent and economical access to a wide variety of electronic information.

APPENDIX A: ISO AND NISO STANDARDS APPLICABLE TO METADATA ENTERPRISES

The following descriptions are from the NISO Web site, http://www.niso.org.

Data Elements

ISO 2709:1996 Format for Information Exchange. Specifies the requirements for a generalized exchange format that will accommodate records describing all forms of material capable of bibliographic description, as well as other types of records. This generalized structure is a framework designed especially for communications between data processing systems. It is not for use as a processing format within systems.

ISO/DIS 8459, Part 5: Data Elements for the Exchange of Cataloguing and Metadata. Dictionary of elements and element groups required for the interchange of data between computer systems.

ISO 8601:1988 Information and Interchange—Representation of Dates and Times. Specifies the representation of dates in the Gregorian calendar, and times and representations of periods of time.

ISO 10324:1997 Holdings Statements—Summary Levels. Specifies the representation of holding statements for bibliographic items in all physical formats.

ISO/IEC 11179 Information Technology—Specification and Standardization of Data Elements. A framework that assures consistency of data content between information repositories and Computer Aided Software Engineering (CASE) tools.

NISO Z39.85: Dublin Core Metadata Set [in development]. Defines a set of simple data elements that could be used to describe electronic resource objects in support of discovery (searching) activities.

Identifiers

ANSI/NISO Z39.56:1996 Serial Item and Contribution Identifier (SICI). Specifies a variable length code that can be used to identify contributions for serial publications (e.g., articles) in both the print and electronic environment.

ANSI/NISO Z39.84:2000 Standard Syntax for the Digital Object Identifier (DOI). Specifies the alpha/numeric string that identifies the object being pointed to within the DOI system and the rights holder of the object.

ISO 2108:1997 International Standard Book Number (ISBN).
ISO 3297:1998 International Standard Serial Number (ISSN).
ISO 3901:1986 International Standard Recording Code (ISRC).
ISO 10957:1993 International Standard Music Number (ISMN).

Under Development by NISO

Book Item and Component Identifier: BICI. Specifies the alpha/numeric string that identifies contributions for non-serial items (e.g., chapters of books, indexes) in both the print and electronic environment.

Proposed ISO Standard

International Standard Textual Work Code (ISTC). This standard will be a numbering system that will be assigned to individual textual works to uniquely identify them.

Codes

ISO 639-2:1998 Codes for the Representation of Names of Languages, Part 2, Alpha-3 Code. Defines two sets of three-letter alphabetic codes for the representation of names of 464 languages, one for terminology applications and the other for bibliographic applications.

ISO 3166:1998 Codes for the Representation of Names of Countries. This standard establishes the two- and three-character and numeric codes assigned to countries and other geopolitical entities of the world; it has been adopted in the United States as NISO/ANSI/ISO 3166.

ISO/DIS 15511 (ISIL) International Standard Identifier for Libraries and Related Organisations: Defines a variable length code containing up to twelve characters for the unique identification of libraries and related organizations.

Character Sets

ISO/IEC 10646:1993 Universal Multiple-Octet Coded Character Set (UCS). A character coding system designed to support the interchange, processing, and display of the written texts of the diverse languages. Commonly known as Unicode.

ISO 5426:1983 Extension of the Latin Alphabet Coded Character Set for Bibliographic Information Interchange. Contains a set of 76 graphic characters with their coded representations. It includes a code table and a legend showing each graphic, its name and use, and explanatory notes. Primarily intended for information interchange among data processing systems and within message transmission systems, this character set is designed to handle information in 39 specified languages, as well as transliterated or romanized forms of an additional 32 languages. These characters, together with the characters in the international reference version of ISO 646 (ISO escape sequence ESC 2/8 4/0), constitute a character set for the international interchange of bibliographic citations, including their annotations, in the Latin alphabet.

ISO 5426-2:1996 Extension of the Latin Alphabet Coded Character Set for Bibliographic Information Interchange, Part 2, Latin Characters Used in Minor European Languages and Obsolete Typography. Contains a set of 70 graphic characters and their coded representations. These characters form a supplement to those provided in ISO 5426 by addressing less common and obsolete languages that use the Latin script and obsolete printing conventions. Included is a code table and a legend showing each graphic, its name and use, and explanatory notes. This character set is primarily intended for information interchange among data processing systems and within message transmission systems. These characters, together with the characters from ISO 646/IEC and ISO 5426, are intended to handle information in the following languages: Anglo-Saxon, Greenlandic, Lappish, Latin, Latvian (older forms), and Maltese. They are also intended to cover printing conventions associated with older books—in particular, marks associated with binding signatures.

ISO 5427:1984 Extension of the Cyrillic Alphabet Coded Character Set for Bibliographic Information Interchange. Contains a set of 42 graphic characters with their coded representations. It includes a code table and a legend showing each graphic, its name and use, and explanatory notes. These characters, together with characters in the basic Cyrillic set for bibliographic use registered as number 37 in the ISO International Register, constitute a character set for the international interchange of bibliographic citations, including their annotations, in the Cyrillic alphabet. This character set is designed to handle information in the following languages: Belorussian, Bulgarian, Macedonian, Russian, Serbo Croatian (Cyrillic), and Ukrainian.

ISO 5428:1984 Greek Alphabet Coded Character Set for Bibliographic Information Interchange. Contains a set of 73 graphic characters with their coded representations. It includes a code table and a legend showing each graphic, its name and use, and explanatory notes. These characters, together with the characters in the international reference version of ISO 646 (ISO escape sequence ESC 2/8 4/0), constitute a character set for the international interchange of bibliographic citations, including their annotations, in the Greek alphabet.

ISO 10754:1996 Extension of the Cyrillic Alphabet Coded Character Set for Non-Slavic Languages for Bibliographic Information Interchange. Contains a set of 93 graphic characters with their coded representations. It includes a code table and a legend showing each graphic, its name and use, and explanatory notes. These characters, together with characters in the basic Cyrillic set (number 37 in the ISO international register), constitute a character set for the international interchange of bibliographic citations, including their annotations, in the non-Slavic Cyrillic alphabets for sixty specified languages.

ISO 6438:1983 African Coded Character Set for Bibliographic Information Interchange. Contains a set of sixty African graphic characters with their coded representations. It includes a code table and a legend showing each graphic, its name and use, and explanatory notes. Special characters that are peculiar to African languages in Latin script are contained in this standard. This set, together with the characters in the international reference version of ISO 646 (ISO escape sequence ESC 2/8 4/0), constitute a character set for the international interchange of bibliographic citations, including their annotations, in African language alphabets. (See ISO 5426 for definitions of special characters, including accents and diacritical marks, used by other languages with Latin orthography that may occur in African languages as well.)

ISO 6861:1996 *Glagolitic Alphabet Coded Character Sets for Bibliographic Information Interchange.*

ISO 8957:1996 *Hebrew Alphabet Coded Character Set for Bibliographic Information Interchange.*

ISO 10585:1996 *Armenian Alphabet Coded Character Set for Bibliographic Information Interchange.*

ISO 10586:1996 *Georgian Alphabet Coded Character Set for Bibliographic Information Interchange.*

ISO 11822:1996 *Extension of the Arabic Alphabet Coded Character Set for Bibliographic Information Interchange.*

ISO 6862:1996 Mathematical Coded Character Set for Bibliographic Information Interchange: Contains a set of graphic characters with their representations. It includes a code table and a legend showing each graphic, its name and use, and explanatory notes. This set is used for the international interchange of bibliographic citations for maps.

ISO 6630:1986 Bibliographic Control Characters: Contains a set of fifteen bibliographic control characters for use in cataloging rules, filing rules, and indexing rules of the countries and language groups of the bibliographic community. It includes a code table and legend specifying each bibliographic control character and indicating its code position. Explanatory notes describe the functional characteristics of individual control characters in detail. This bibliographic control character set is an extension of the basic control character set defined by ISO 646 (ISO escape sequence ESC 2/1 4/0) and is primarily intended for the interchange of bibliographic information.

Transliteration of Nonroman Scripts

ISO 9:1995 *Transliteration of Cyrillic Characters into Latin Characters—Slavic and Non-Slavic Languages.*

ISO 233:1984 *Transliteration of Arabic Characters into Latin Characters.*

ISO 259:1984 *Transliteration of Hebrew Characters into Latin Characters.*

ISO 843:1997 *Conversion of Greek Characters into Latin Characters.*

ISO 3202:1989 *Romanization of Japanese (Kana Script).*

ISO 7098:1991 *Romanization of Chinese.*

Formats and Protocols

ISO/IEC 10027 Information Resource Dictionary System (IRDS) Framework. Defines an architecture for creating a shareable repository that contains information resources relevant to all or part of an enterprise or project. The repository may include: (a) data needed by the enterprise; (b) the computerized and possibly noncomputerized processes that are available for presenting and maintaining such data; (c) the available physical hardware environment on which such data can be represented; (d) the organization of human and physical resources that can make use of the information; (e) the human resources responsible for generating that information.

ISO 23950:1998 Information Retrieval (Z39.50) Application Service Definition and Protocol Specification. Specifies a client/server–based protocol for information retrieval. It specifies procedures and structures for a client to (a) search a database provided by a server, (b) retrieve database records identified by a search, (c) scan a term list, and (d) sort a result set. It also specifies access control, resource control, extended services, and a "help" facility. The protocol addresses communication between the client and server (which may reside on different computers); it does not address interaction between the client and the end-user. This standard is identical to ANSI/NISO Z39.50-1995. The Maintenance Agency and Registration Authority for this standard is the Library of Congress (USA).

   Union Catalogue Profile. International registered profile to be used with ISO 23950. See http://www.nla.gov. au/ucp/.

IV

TOOLS FOR CATALOGING THE WEB

13

MARCit Magic: Abracadabra!
From a Web Site to a MARC Record

Laura Bayard

The innovation of the 856 field in MARC records allowing hyperlinked URLs (Uniform Resource Locators) and the trend toward Web-based library catalogs create a universe of possibilities. Library patrons, perceiving that qualitative judgments have been made about materials found through their libraries' catalogs, demand similar access to Web resources. Librarians perceive not only the opportunities to enrich local collections but also the benefits of "one-stop-shopping," that is, single, subject-oriented searches that retrieve materials in all formats when Web resources are included in the catalog.[1]

Systematic efforts to provide access to Web resources through library online catalogs, however, are daunting. Librarians are cognizant of the dark side of Web resources, and therefore they make serious evaluations of costs and benefits. The labor-intensive activities required to select and catalog Web sites and then maintain their URLs are compared to the value added to the catalog and the collection. The Web sites' dark side includes their vanishing or changing URLs; varying content quality because of a lack of uniform standards; organizational and archival difficulties; perceived ephemeral nature because they are free; and their overwhelmingly proliferating numbers.[2] If the interest expressed in articles and presentations about systematic inclusion of Web sites in library catalogs is any measure, then librarians are determined to conjure ways to provide the desired access to Web resources. The hope may be for magical solutions, but technology provides real opportunities through new cataloging tools that transform existing metadata into records for the online catalog—a technological alchemy.

IT AIN'T MAGIC, BUT IT'S A CLOSE APPROXIMATION

Tools that automate Web site cataloging seem to be magical, but behind the illusion is a metadata crosswalk. No, this isn't an incantation. A metadata crosswalk is a mapping from data about data in one format to another format. At the Metadata Institute in May 1998 Rebecca Guenther described metadata crosswalks as characteristically having a "fluid capability to work with [the] same data in different structures."[3] Crosswalks map metadata in the header of an HTML document to a MARC and/or Dublin Core format—a metadata standard influenced by MARC but composed of fifteen elements in a labeled form developed for Web site creators and authors to use.[4] Moreover, the mappings can occur in either direction. For example, metadata in Dublin Core format can be pasted into a Web site's header and is capable of attracting Web browsers for resource retrieval.

A metadata crosswalk, therefore, maps metadata found in a particular part of a Web site in a format recognized by Web browsers to a particular field in a MARC record and vice versa. Specifically, a Web site's invisible metadata residing in the title header in the HTML source file can be inserted automatically through a metadata crosswalk into the field for the title proper (245 subfield *a*) in a MARC record, a format accepted by library catalogs. Abracadabra! Technological alchemy.

Of course, mapping metadata information to the title-proper field is most useful when the information in the Web site's title header actually is a recognizable title descriptive of the site's content. Unrecognizable symbols or words representing a working title used by the creator of the Web site's structural, technical form will require editing in the MARC record. For better or worse, the titles from the internal sources many times are different from the title-frame titles or other prominent eye-readable titles on the Web site. Remember, too, that a crosswalk cannot map what is not there. No matter how sophisticated the mappings might be in a crosswalk, if data were omitted from the Web site header, then no information will appear magically in the resulting MARC record. These problems arise from resource creators' lack of uniform acceptance and use of metadata standards. Although bibliographic input standards for MARC formats are quite well developed and accepted, further refinement of definitions and development of guidelines are underway in a study by the CAPC (Cataloging Policy Committee) Subcommittee on Source of Title Note for Internet Resources of OLAC (Online Audiovisual Catalogers). The subcommittee called for comments in hopes of eventually clarifying murky terms that tend to be applied differently by cataloging agencies. Under consideration are terms that describe the Web page or a specific place on the page, as well as terms from internal sources.[5] Meanwhile, cataloging wizards must continue to judge which form of title among several is the "most complete or fullest" and then, as needed, edit the title fields in the magically created records.

Tools for automated Web site cataloging contain a labeled form with boxes where information can be keyed or pasted, opening opportunities for subject wizards to become also cataloging wizards. In one workflow scenario, collection development librarians using their knowledge of the sites' subject content could invoke a cataloging tool at the time a Web site is selected and complete the labeled form. Records could be enhanced later by catalogers adding call numbers and controlled-vocabulary subject headings. In an era of diminishing cataloging resources, diversifying at least some portions of the cataloging activities to selectors simultaneously signals the importance of the selected Web site for the collection and creates partnerships to accomplish mutual goals.

This chapter will look closely at MARCit, a commercially available crosswalk and automated cataloging tool, so that we may gain an understanding of how the magic occurs. A brief overview of a couple of tools now in test mode follows, showing the hopes for the future.

MARCIT: A MAGIC WAND

MARCit, a tool to assist in cataloging Web sites, was announced at the American Library Association 1998 Mid-Winter Meeting. Developed by Nichols Advanced Technologies (now Sagebrush Technologies), MARCit continues to be relevant three years later, an eon in technology's life-terms. In 1999 MARCit received an award for innovative educational technology from *Media & Methods Magazine*.[6]

To evaluate MARCit, begin at its Web site.[7] As long as the hardware and software requirements listed on the site are met, a copy of MARCit can be downloaded for cataloging trials for up to ten Web sites.[8] A *Quick Start Guide* is available from the site and MARCit technical support is an e-mail message away. The CD-ROM version and a complete instruction manual are included in the purchase price of $49.95 for one workstation.[9]

With the Web site to be cataloged visible on the monitor, double-click on the desktop icon to invoke MARCit. A floating MARCit icon and a blank labeled template appear. Use Tab or Shift-Tab, or click on a field to move around the MARCit templates. Help is available through buttons on the template's tool bar and within each window. MARCit's mappings are found in two lists in the tool bar Help. One list is arranged by MARC tags with their corresponding sources of data; the other, by sources of data with their corresponding MARC tags.

MARCIT'S MAGIC INGREDIENTS: OPTIONS

In the initial session, a click on Tools/Options yields a window of selections to customize cataloging. The selections made and saved in the Options window remain operational for subsequent records but can be amended as desired in the future. Because the information is selected essentially one time and then used repeatedly, the options and mappings are described in detail in the following paragraphs.

The first option defaults to the vendor-recommended default, "use associated browser," although, if preferred, a path for a different browser could be specified in the box for "use the command line." In the second option, select a call number type from among three choices, Dewey, LC, or Local. The selection indicates which call-number tag will appear in the MARC record, 082, 050, or 090, respectively. Next, specify whether or not the call number will be inserted in an 852 subfield *h* (call number) field of the MARC record.

Each bibliographic record created will contain a MARCit-supplied, sequential control number inserted in an automatically created 001 field. The control number can be seen in the grayed box, indicating that manual changes to the numbers are prevented. Then, in the next box labeled "control number identifier," enter the text to be displayed in the automatically created 003 fields.

The next option requests a three-letter language code, for example, "fre" for French. The code will appear in the element for language in the fixed field (008/35-37). Other MARCit-supplied data appearing in the fixed-field area of the bibliographic record do not appear in templates or in windows. For example, MARCit generates the date that the record is created, using the format YYMMDD (MARC 008/00-05). In addition, a MARCit-created 007 (physical description) field contains values in the mandatory subfields, representing remote computer files ("cr-unu"). Also, the record's leader (MARC LDR/00-23) is system created, including the size of the completed record.

Moving on to the next option, specify the institutional code that will appear in each MARC record's 040 (cataloging source) field to represent the cataloging agency. The next option box asks for a phrase to be entered that relates to the type of computer file or data note, such as "File is in HTML format." The phrase is mapped to the 516 (type of computer or data note) field of each MARC record. Similarly, in the next option, specify a phrase that indicates mode of access, such as "World Wide Web." This phrase is mapped to the MARC 538 (systems details note) field.

MARCit's template provides a 1 (lowest) to 5 (highest) scale for rating the quality of the Web site. If the assessment feature is desired, then in the Options window, in the box labeled "Place assessment in," key "514" (data quality note), or a tag for a preferred field in which to display the assessment. Any tag specified other than 514 will appear at the end of the bibliographic record, rather than in numerical tag sequence. By leaving the box blank, assessment information will not be saved. If the assessment feature is not selected, then skip the next option, which allows for a standardized text string to precede the assessment rating display. Save selections and close the Options window by clicking on the "okay" button. The MARCit blank template reappears. With a click anywhere in the MARCit blank template, the invisible cursor reappears.

MORE MAGIC INGREDIENTS: MARCIT TEMPLATE

With a single click on the floating icon, the selected Web site's URL pops into the blank template's space labeled "URL," mapped to the MARC field 856, and title-header information pops into the space labeled "Title," mapped to the MARC 245 subfield *a* (title proper). An examination of the inserted title is necessary for the reasons stated earlier. The general material designation (245 subfield *b*), "[computer file]," is MARCit-supplied for all records. First indicators are set automatically to a value dependent upon the presence or absence of a main entry (MARC 1XX). Second indicators, which control filing, are set at "0" for all titles, except ones beginning with the words "a," "an," or "the," which are set at "2," "3," or "4," respectively. The template contains a box for specifying a subtitle (mapped to 245 subfield *b*) and a box for specifying an alternate title (mapped to field 246). When more than one alternative title is needed, the MARC records will need to be edited to include them.

MARCit's template provides two boxes for author. If the author is the main entry, then the name heading is inserted in one of the boxes, the one for a personal (field 100) or the one for a corporate (field 110) author main entry. If, however, the name heading is intended to be an added entry, then click on the "add another" button at the end of the appropriate box, selecting either the personal (field 700) or the corporate (field 710) author, and insert the name heading in the new box. The author boxes' sizes are fixed in length. Name headings of more than 50 characters must be completed in the MARC record.

MARCit's template includes a window for assigning subject headings, composed of four boxes. The first box, labeled "first subject," is for terms and names used as subjects and it is mapped to subfield *a*. The drop-down menu for the first box allows "topical," "local," "personal name," "corporate name," or "geographic name" to be selected, thereby specifying the appropriate MARC tag 650, 690, 600, 610, or 651, respectively. The remaining three boxes are used to insert as many as three subdivisions. Each of the subdivision boxes' drop-down menus offer options for the type of data to be inserted: "general," "chronological," or "geographic," which in turn will specify the subfields of *x*, *y*, or *z*, respectively. When the "add another subject" button is clicked, four more boxes labeled "second subject" and "subdivisions" are appended to the template. Up to five subjects may be added in this fashion. Except for the local subject headings (690), MARCit sets the second indicator to "4," indicating that the heading is from a controlled list, but the specific thesaurus is not named. Most people would rather the second indicator be set to "0," indicating that LCSH (Library of Congress Subject Headings) was used, avoiding one more point to edit in the MARC record. Subject wizards using MARCit in a workflow scenario as described previously may be more comfortable using the local subject heading option to insert their own best words to describe the subject of the site. If library catalogs include the MARC 690 fields in keyword searches, then the records are enriched by the keywords. If cataloging wizards subsequently enhance the MARC records, then the keywords' presence could facilitate the work of assigning classification numbers and controlled-vocabulary subject headings.

MARCit does not furnish tags for conferences, uniform titles, or series. The remaining portions of MARCit's template accommodate information about assessment, publication, controlled numbers, and bibliographic notes. The notes window of the template, for example, is devoted to boxes for different kinds of bibliographic notes. Enter the required "source of title note" in the box labeled "general note" (mapped to MARC 500). For a note summarizing the Web site's purpose or content, a box labeled "summary" (mapped to MARC 520) is appropriate to use. Because words can be copied directly from the Web site and pasted into the box, a rather lengthy statement can easily and quickly be entered. Rating the site's "interest level" is possible from a drop-down menu listing established categories. By clicking on a selection from the list, the text representing the category will appear in the 521 field and a single character code representing the selection will be inserted in the fixed field (MARC 008/22). The "public note" box is mapped to the public note subfield of the URL (856 subfield *z*) field. The "description of materials" box is mapped to the URL subfield (856 subfield 3) that allows naming the part of the bibliographic item to which the field applies, such as "Finding aid to the Hesburgh papers."

MARCit does not prevent saving the template just because information is omitted from any boxes. Obviously, the more completely filled out the template is, the closer one is to achieving a fully standard record for the library's catalog.

ABRACADABRA!: FROM A WEB SITE TO A MARC RECORD

When the MARCit template is completed, click on the tool bar icon "Save." The data become a MARC record that is stored in an active file. Rename, empty, or delete the file before saving another completed template; otherwise, the new information will be appended to the data from the previous record. MARCit-created records can be imported into any online catalog that accepts MARC records. How they are imported depends upon a library's automation system. Each library must work with its local systems office to determine the right loader program for importing the records. Perhaps a viable loader program already is in use to import MARC records from a provider, such as MARCIVE, OCLC, or BNA.

Web site access through the library's catalog is desirable for reasons enumerated at the outset. MARCit's early availability to libraries fulfilled a need. It continues to be an important cataloging tool for small- and medium-size libraries, such as school and special libraries. The start-up cost is minimal. The product is reliable. It is easy to use because of its windows and navigation functions. The help information as well as the availability of the technical support are beneficial to librarians. MARCit adheres to MARC standards. The MARCit-generated fixed field and other mandatory data speed the cataloging process, even more than local systems' templates and macros can, because MARCit has the added attraction of the crosswalk feature. Its labeled template allows noncatalogers to participate in cataloging at the point of site selection. Unfortunately, editing the MARC records is necessary to complete lengthy headings, to insert International Standard Book Description (ISBD) punctuation, to add more alternate titles, and to change subject indicators to reflect use of LCSH. The most significant disadvantage is the inability to create records simultaneously for the local catalog and for others' use.

OTHER MAGIC WANDS

OCLC's CORC (Cooperative Online Resource Catalog) project supports shared cataloging: the system went into production in July 2000.[10] CORC offers automated record creation and maintenance, supports MARC and Dublin Core metadata standards, and provides a catalog of Internet resources.[11] Its resource catalog can be searched in conventional ways, and the records can be viewed in either Dublin Core or MARC formats. Bibliographic records are created in a Web environment using CORC-generated data and a crosswalk. The labeled Dublin Core template allows noncatalogers to participate in cataloging activities. CORC supports "dynamic generation of Web pages with resources organized appropriately for integration with libraries' portal pages."[12] Pathfinders can be created by cataloging Web sites in CORC and imbedding the Dublin Core metadata in a local Web site's internal header sources. Pathfinders can also be searched in CORC, yielding links to the Web sites. CORC promises excellent possibilities for automated and reinvented cataloging. For example, research is underway to develop detection and correction features for headings through CORC's links to authority records.[13] Future plans include developing an automatic link-update feature. In addition, CORC incorporates the fruits of another OCLC research project that ended in fall 1999. The Scorpion Project's objective was to develop tools "for automatic subject recognition based on . . . the Dewey Decimal System."[14] CORC suggests Dewey classification numbers and thesaurus subject headings for the resource being cataloged. CORC's more innovative automated features might not be perfected yet, but the investigations surely are shaping the future for organizing Web resources. Abracadabra! Technological alchemy.

Metadata standards created and used by entities in specialized areas, such as archives and government agencies, accommodate specialized data. Many crosswalks exist between and among metadata standards. A list of some of them with their links (slightly out of date now) initially was gathered by Michael Day for the Resource Organisation and Discovery in Subject-Based Services (ROADS) project.[15] Increasingly, metadata standards are mapped to Dublin Core and to MARC to enhance description and thus facilitate retrieval of resources by Internet users, simultaneously according status to Dublin Core and MARC as the emerging "industry standards." In an ongoing digital library research project at the Energy and Environmental Information Resources (EE-IR) Center, FGDC (Federal Geographic Data Committee) geospatial metadata were mapped to Dublin Core and MARC as a response to studies showing that the likelihood is high that users retrieve zero hits when searching the FGDC Clearinghouse database.[16] Machine conversion of FGDC metadata to Dublin Core and MARC is available for testing at the EE-IR Center's Website, which intends to include its records in OCLC's CORC and WorldCat.[17]

HOCUS POCUS—NOT

Libraries with the goal to provide access to Web resources through the online catalog face a lot of work that strains available resources. Our magical solutions are the cataloging tools that automate as much of the cataloging activities as possible and provide ways for cataloging wizards and subject wizards alike to participate in the goal. Both MARCit and CORC are viable magic wands. MARCit is excellent for small- and medium-size libraries that want an economical, speedy, and easy way to create MARC records for their catalogs. For libraries dedicated to the principle of cooperative cataloging environments and perhaps already using OCLC, CORC is an excellent choice. Libraries that create Web sites will be able to embed CORC's Dublin Core metadata in their headers and create pathfinders. In addition, CORC is exploring exciting innovations to address otherwise expensive but beneficial activities, such as automated creation of classification numbers and controlled-vocabulary subject headings, automated heading detection and correction, and automated link update. Conquering the Web's dark side may be too much to expect, but taming it seems possible with technological alchemy. Abracadabra!

NOTES

1. G. Margaret Porter and Laura Bayard, "Including Websites in the Online Catalog: Implications for Cataloging, Collection Development, and Access," *Journal of Academic Librarianship* 25, no. 5 (1999): 390–394. The article is a description and analysis of a small pilot project to catalog Web sites for the online catalog during February–April 1998 at the University of Notre Dame Libraries. MARCit was examined for possible use in the project, before it was decided to keep it in a cooperative cataloging environment.

2. Laura Bayard, *Including Web Sites in the Online Catalog: Selecting and Cataloging Resources for the Next Century* (paper presented at the ILF 2000 Annual Conference, Indianapolis, Ind., March 14, 2000), slide 5, http://www.nd.edu/~lbayard/ALAmetadata/ ALA0700_files/v3_document.htm. The Porter/Bayard article formed the basis of the presentation, expanded to include updated information, including more coverage of MARCit.

3. Rebecca Guenther, "Metadata Standards: MARC" (paper presented at ALCTS/LITA Institute's Managing Metadata for the Digital Library, Washington, D.C., May 4–5, 1998), slide 8.

4. "Dublin Core Metadata Initiative," http://purl.org/DC/.

5. Online Audiovisual Catalogers, Cataloging Policy Committee, Subcommittee on Source of Title Notes for Internet Resources, *Terms Used in Source of Title Note: Report and Call for Comments (First Draft)*, http://ublib.buffalo.edu/libraries/units/cts/olac/ capc/draft1.html.

6. "MARCit, the Internet Cataloging Tool, Receives *Media & Methods Magazine* 1999 Portfolio Award," *MARCit News*, April 30, 1999, http://www.marcit.com/news/pr19990430.html.

7. "MARCit, Cataloging the Internet," http://www.marcit.com/index.html.

8. "[MARCit] Hardware Requirements," http://www.marcit.com/hardware.html. Minimally, computers must run either Windows 95 or NT and have available 5 MB of hard-drive space and 16 MB RAM. An Internet connection and a search engine that is either Netscape Navigator or Microsoft Internet Explorer, version 3.0 or higher, are needed. Downloading time could be 20 to 40 minutes, depending upon the speed of the modem used.

9. "Download MARCit Sample," http://www.marcit.com/download/index.html.

10. "Cooperative Online Resource Catalog," http://www.oclc.org/oclc/corc/.

11. Terry Noreault, "OCLC Research Activities: OCLC CORC Features," (paper presented at American Library Association Mid-Winter Meeting, San Antonio, Texas, January 14–19, 2000), 19.

12. Thomas B. Hickey, "CORC–Cooperative Online Resource Catalog," *Annual Review of OCLC Research, 1998,* http://oclc.org/ clc/research/publications/review98/hickey/corc.htm.

13. Ed O'Neill, "Authority Control for the Internet," *OCLC Newsletter,* May/June 1999, http://www.oclc.org/oclc/new/n239/ feature/06feature.htm.

14. OCLC Office of Research, *The Scorpion Project,* http://orc.rsch.oclc.org:6109/.

15. Michael Day, *Metadata: Mapping between Metadata Formats,* http://www.ukoln.ac.uk/metadata/interoperability/.

16. Adam Chandler, Dan Foley, and Alaaeldin M. Hafez, "Mapping and Converting Essential Federal Geographic Data Committee (FGDC) Metadata into MARC21 and Dublin Core: Towards an Alternative to the FGDC Clearinghouse," *D-Lib Magazine* 6, no. 1 (January 2000), http://www.dlib.org/dlib/january00/chandler/01chandler.html.

17. "EE-IR Center FGDC [to] MARC21 Metadata Converter," http://cuadra.nwrc.gov/converter/. To use the converter, follow the requirements: parse FGDC metadata by using the MP parser, and establish that metadata in both .html and .sgml versions reside in the Web server's same directory. The .sgml version is retrieved by the converter; the MARC record's 856 field points to the .html version on the local server.

14

Anticipating the Deluge:
The INFOMINE Project and Its Approach to Metadata

Juan Carlos Rodriguez

INTRODUCTION

In late 1993 it became evident that there would be not only an explosion of content on the Web but also a growing amount of information that would be useful to the academic community. We realized that librarian-structured metadata projects would prove to be very helpful to the growing number of Internet users having difficulty finding useful, relevant Internet resources. In addition, we realized that traditional collecting criteria, indexing, and subject cataloging could be carried forward and become more valuable in the new medium. However, due to exponential growth of useful Web sites, we realized that these traditions would have to be made simpler and more streamlined. MARC would be important, but full MARC would be a luxury. Thus we created our core approach, somewhere between cataloging and indexing, providing descriptions of the resources and using a minimum number of mostly traditional fields.

HISTORICAL BACKGROUND

In 1993, libraries were just becoming aware of the value of the Internet as an information source. Many libraries had set up Gopher servers that provided information about their libraries and some were providing access to useful Gopher sites via hierarchical subject listings. It was also during this time that the World Wide Web began to gain attention. Although the Web was developed in late 1980s, it wasn't until 1993, with the development of the graphical browser Mosaic, that the Web begin to draw attention from the academic community as a place where information could be stored, accessed, and shared. During the fall of 1993, some libraries (particularly those with the foresight to see the potential of the Web) began to concentrate more on creating library Web sites than on maintaining their existing Gopher sites. Creating Web sites, however, required knowledge of the Hypertext Markup Language (HTML), the language used to format the content displayed on a Web browser. Many viewed HTML as too cumbersome or difficult to learn. However, others took it upon themselves to learn HTML and create these Web pages. Librarians began to create links to useful resources on the Web in a variety of subject disciplines. For example, it was very common to see a list of the library's choice for the ten best sites in physics. Many of these pages were created by reference librarians with some subject expertise in a particular area. The University of California, Riverside (UCR), was one of these libraries. However, we quickly realized that creating such lists was going to be very labor-intensive and also that many libraries were creating similar lists containing the same ten sites. There had to be another approach. We felt that incorporating the power of a database-driven Web site that could produce dynamically created Web pages, as well as facilitate a collaborative approach to resource sharing and collecting, was worth pursuing. Thus, under the coordination of Steve Mitchell, science reference librarian, and Margaret Mooney, head of the Government Publications Department, the idea of INFOMINE[1] was born.

BRIEF HISTORY AND DESCRIPTION OF INFOMINE

The central theme during the construction of INFOMINE was to make it easy to use, as well as adhere to the following guiding principle: to establish a cooperative network to build a finding tool for public domain academic Internet resources that emphasize the creative use of technologies that enable librarians: (1) to extend professional expertise to the world of the Internet; (2) to focus energies on the intellectual work of selecting, evaluating, organizing, describing, and disseminating quality Internet resources of value to the scholarly community; and (3) to share knowledge, effort, and resources while doing this.

It was also important that we incorporate a hypertext database–centered approach to virtual library building. The advantages were that it: (1) eliminates the need to know HTML; (2) includes the ability to dynamically create HTML pages; (3) provides in-depth subject indexing and multiple access points without redundant keyboarding; (4) eases the maintenance and updating of tasks; and (5) facilitates multicampus/multi-library collaborative efforts in content building. INFOMINE's primary mission is to serve as an Internet finding tool for the university community, as well as to help researchers, educators, and students understand and become aware of the value the Internet has for locating research information. We also focus on K–12 educators, students, parents, and members of the community. Our collection goal has been to include resources most relevant to university-level faculty and students. We realized that it would be difficult, if not impossible, to provide a comprehensive list of all useful sites, so instead we have focused our energies on selecting the highest quality and most comprehensive resources.

INFOMINE was released in January 1994, making it one of the first library-originated projects on the Web (see figure 14.1). INFOMINE is organized into nine broad subject categories: (1) Biological, Agricultural, and Medical Sciences; (2) Government Information; (3) Instructional Resources—K–12; (4) Instructional Resources—University; (5) Internet Enabling Tools; (6) Map and Geographical Information Systems (GIS); (7) Physical Sciences, Engineering, Computing, and Mathematics; (8) Social Sciences, Humanities, General Reference, and Business; and (9) Visual and Performing Arts.

Each one has a facilitator or co-facilitator who is responsible for coordinating the collection development efforts for his or her particular category. As of June 2000, INFOMINE contained over 20,000 resources and averaged about one million requests per month during the year 2000. The success and value of a site are determined not only by the amount of traffic it receives, but also by the number of sites that provide links to it. Currently, over 12,000 sites, mostly of an educational or scholarly nature, have created links to INFOMINE.

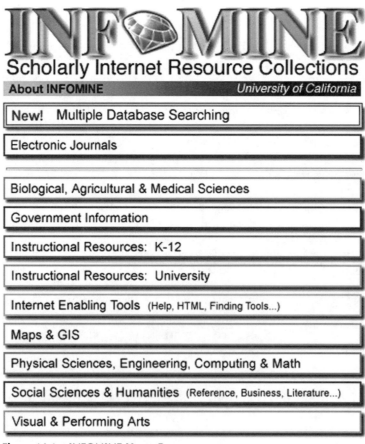

Figure 14.1   INFOMINE Home Page.

The management of the database is made possible via easy-to-use forms. Typically, a new resource can be added in as little as fifteen to twenty minutes. A unique feature includes a URL checker that not only identifies outdated URLs but also suggests possible correct URLs. INFOMINE is funded by the library of the University of California, Riverside; the Fund for the Improvement of Post-Secondary Education (FIPSE, U.S. Department of Education); and the U.S. Institute for Museum and Library Services (IMLS National Leadership Grant).

SEARCHING INFOMINE

Searching INFOMINE is very easy. The user can search all of the categories, some of the categories, or a single category. The user also has the option of searching a variety of fields that include: title, subject, keyword, author, and/or annotation. Searching features include: Boolean, proximity, phrase, and truncation (see figure 14.2).

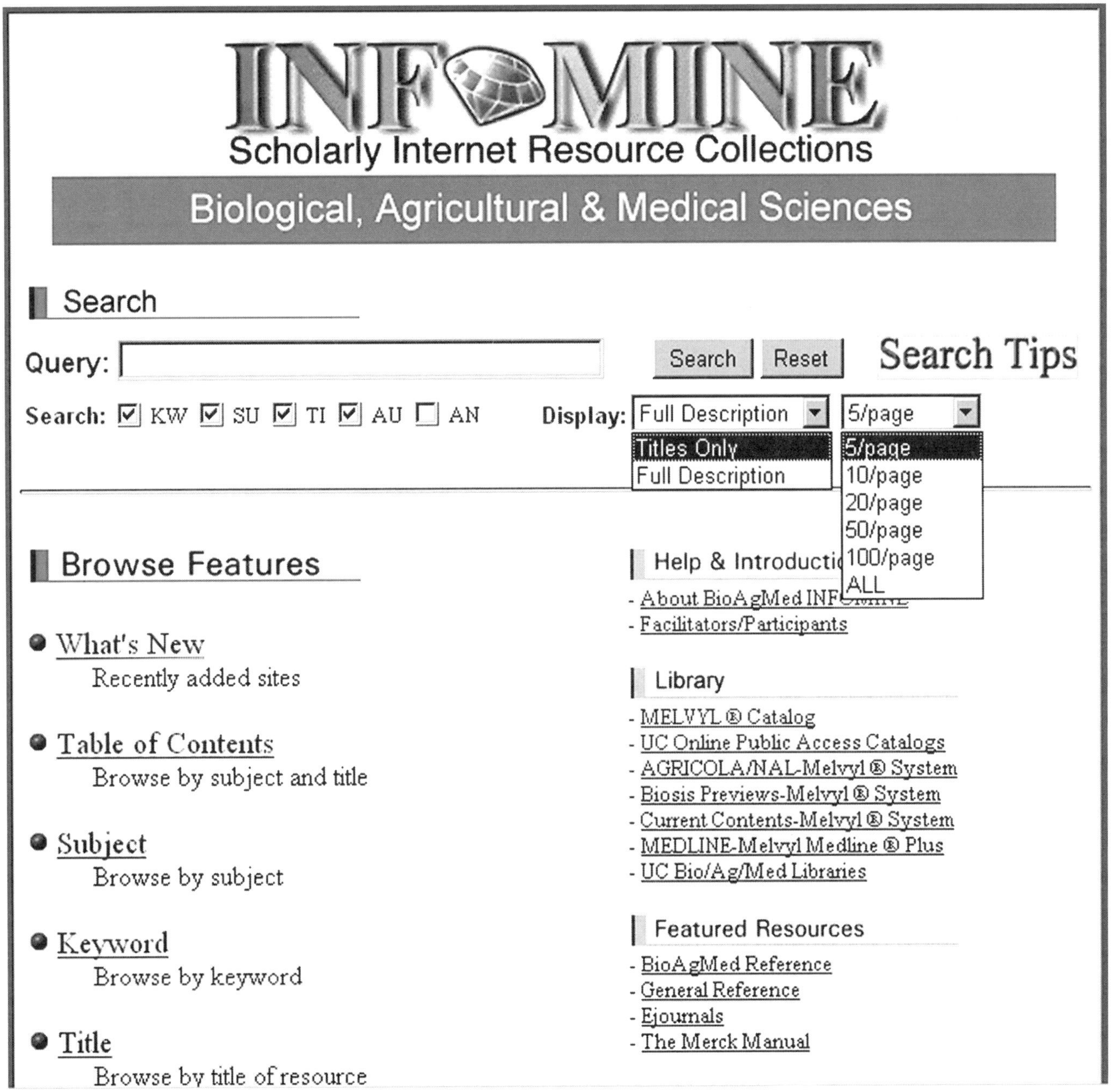

Figure 14.2   INFOMINE biological, agricultural, and medical sciences category.

What's New!

Biological, Agricultural & Medical Sciences

Records added within the last 20 days (since 2000-02-22).
Number of Resources Found: 25

The Agricultural Communications Documentation Center Database
"The Agricultural Communications Documentation Center is a literature collection developed by agricultural communications faculty members at the University of Illinois at Urbana-Champaign. It is offered as a service to students, teachers, researchers, professional communicators and others who are interested in communications related broadly to agriculture, food, natural resources and rural affairs.

More than 16,450 documents now make up the collection. All are available within the Center or in libraries located elsewhere on the Urbana-Champaign campus. The collection involves agriculture-related communications in more than 90 countries and is expanding at the rate of about 100 documents a month.

All documents in this collection deal with communications in connection with agriculture. They emphasize the human and social dimensions of agriculture, not the physical or technical aspects. So you will not find in them literature about how to grow crops or raise livestock, for example. You will find literature about human interaction in agricultural and rural settings, internationally."
[Terms leading to related resources]
URL: http://web.aces.uiuc.edu/agcomdb/docctr.html
Record #: 19615
Created: 2000-03-10

Compendium of Pesticide Common Names
"For purposes of trade, registration and legislation, and for use in popular and scientific publications, pesticides need names that are short, distinctive, non-proprietary and widely-accepted. Systematic chemical names are rarely short and are not convenient for general use, and so common names are assigned by standards bodies. More than 1000 pesticide common names have been assigned by the International Organization for Standardization (ISO)... This Compendium is believed to be the only place where all of the ISO-approved names are listed, and it also includes approved names from national bodies for substances that do not have ISO names.

This electronic compendium is intended to provide details of the status of all pesticide common names, together with their systematic chemical names, molecular formulae and

Figure 14.3   INFOMINE's "what's new" page.

There are several browse features that include table of contents (titles listed by subject), titles, subjects, authors, keywords, and the ability to browse hyperlinked subject and keyword indexing terms embedded within a record. Users can also browse resources that were added the previous twenty days using the "What's New!" feature (see figure 14.3).

In addition, INFOMINE provides a current awareness feature that users can subscribe to. Subscribed users will receive periodic, user-specified e-mail announcements of newly added resources to a particular category.

There are also multiple display options. The user can control the number of resources INFOMINE displays per result screen. Values range from five per page to all returned resources per page. The user can select the full description, which includes the title of the resource, as well as the annotation, and a link to "terms to search for related resources," which will present the user with all of the keywords, title words, authors, and subjects that were used to describe and index the resource (see figure 14.4). The other display option is "Titles Only," which displays only the title of the resource.

COLLECTION-BUILDING APPROACH

The quality of a database is based on many factors, most notably the quality of the resources contained and the level of description of these resources. It was decided early on that traditional collecting criteria, indexing, and subject cataloging could be carried forward to build and maintain databases of Web-based information. However, Web sites that were of academic value began to grow at an exponential rate, and we realized that these traditions would have to be modified, made simpler and more streamlined. It would be too expensive and time-consuming to do otherwise. MARC would be important, but full MARC would be a luxury that could not be afforded. Thus we created our core approach, somewhere between cataloging and indexing, providing descriptions of the resources and using a minimum number of mostly traditional fields (e.g., author, title, subject, keyword). Since then, other similar approaches have been introduced, most notably Dublin Core. We wanted to extend bibliographer/selector expertise to the Internet and provide

Click on terms to search for related resources.

Title:
The Agricultural Communications Documentation Center Database

Related Subjects:
AGRICULTURE -- SOCIAL ASPECTS -- BIBLIOGRAPHY
COMMUNICATION IN AGRICULTURE -- BIBLIOGRAPHY
COMMUNICATION IN RURAL DEVELOPMENT -- BIBLIOGRAPHY

Related Keywords:
BIBLIOGRAPHIC DATABASES
SEARCHABLE

Related Title Words:
AGRICULTURAL COMMUNICATIONS DOCUMENTATION CENTER DATABASE

Related Authors:
ACDC
THE AGRICULTURAL COMMUNICATIONS DOCUMENTATION CENTER
UNIVERSITY OF ILLINOIS AT URBANA-CHAMPAIGN

URL:
http://web.aces.uiuc.edu/agcomdb/docctr.html

Annotation:
"The Agricultural Communications Documentation Center is a literature collection developed by agricultural communications faculty members at the University of Illinois at Urbana-Champaign. It is offered as a service to students, teachers, researchers, professional communicators and others who are interested in communications related broadly to agriculture, food, natural resources and rural affairs.

More than 16,450 documents now make up the collection. All are available within the Center or in libraries located elsewhere on the Urbana-Champaign campus. The collection involves agriculture-related communications in more than 90 countries and is expanding at the rate of about 100 documents a month.

All documents in this collection deal with communications in connection with agriculture. They emphasize the human and social dimensions of agriculture, not the physical or technical aspects. So you will not find in them literature about how to grow crops or raise livestock, for example. You will find literature about human interaction in agricultural and rural settings, internationally." [19615]

Figure 14.4   INFOMINE related resources page.

easy-to-use database-management functions that would allow librarians to participate without extensive training. Subject terminology originates from a standard controlled vocabulary, the *Library of Congress Subject Headings* (LCSH). On average, over five headings are applied per record, while keywords average about eight. The number of indexing terms that is used is generally much larger than the number found in many library or Internet-related databases. This has been a major factor in INFOMINE's value.

ADDING INFOMINE RECORDS

INFOMINE participants are first required to access the database functions page by entering a log-in name and password. Once granted access, participants must identify themselves to the system by entering their initials and campus or organization affiliation. This allows INFOMINE to keep track of who has added and/or edited records and will facilitate the process of identifying records for future exportation (if necessary). Once identified, the participant is presented with several options: the option to add a resource, edit a resource, or fix a URL (see figure 14.5).

The adder page was designed for simplicity, but it is also robust enough to allow for comprehensive indexing. The participant is presented with several fields in which to input URL, title of the resource, author, subject, keyword, and annotation (see figure 14.6).

All the fields can contain multiple entries, which are separated by semicolons. In addition, the participant selects the database category that this resource falls under. Of course, a resource may belong to several categories. For example, the Environmental Protection Agency Web site may be included in both the Government and Bio-Agricultural Medicine categories. The central theme around all management functions is simplicity and efficiency. Keywords that are common among all categories are included as a pop-up window, from which the participant can select from a list of keywords, which are then automatically included in the keyword field. In order to prevent duplicate records, the URL is checked against existing records in INFOMINE. The title is also checked against existing records. To help alleviate the load on high-traffic Web sites, many sites are now served from mirror Web servers that have different URLs. Thus it is now common for the same resource to have two distinct URLs. Also, an annotation or description is included. Many times the annotation is taken directly from the Web site.

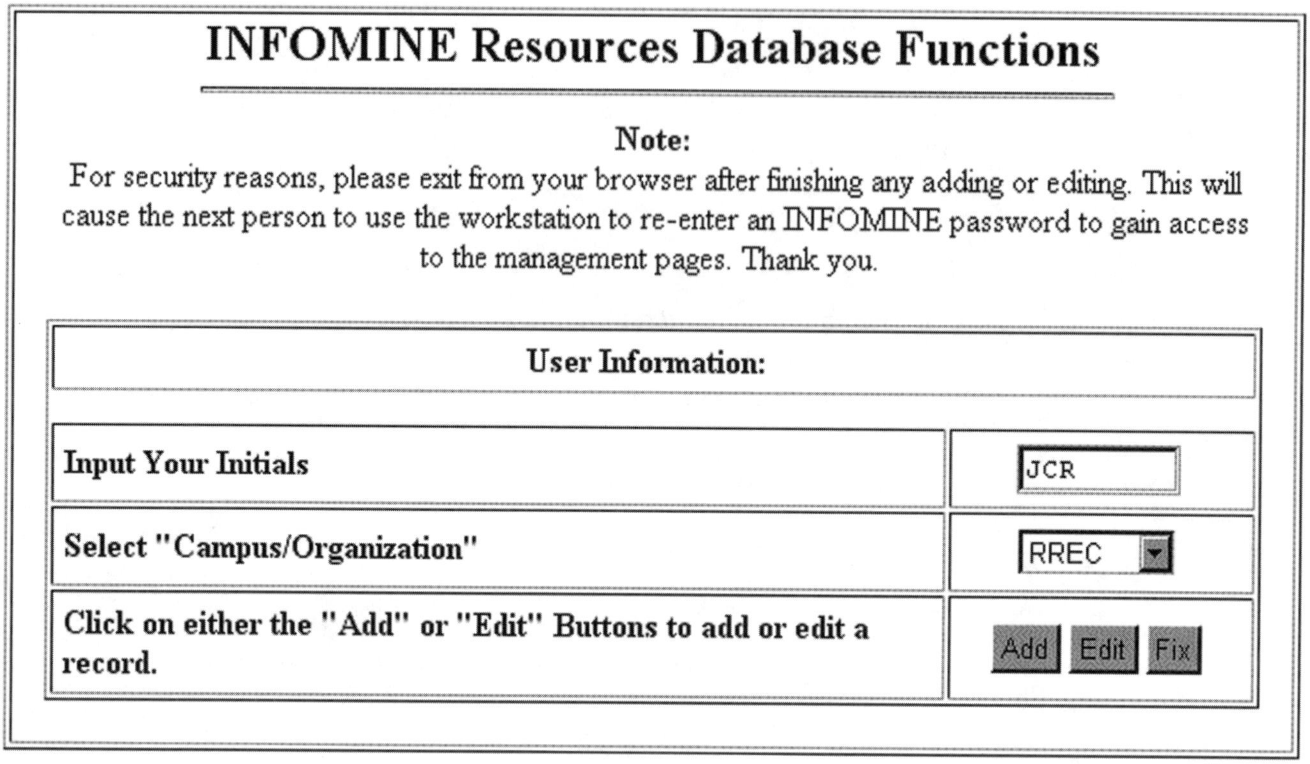

INFOMINE Resources Database Functions

Note:

For security reasons, please exit from your browser after finishing any adding or editing. This will cause the next person to use the workstation to re-enter an INFOMINE password to gain access to the management pages. Thank you.

User Information:	
Input Your Initials	JCR
Select "Campus/Organization"	RREC ▼
Click on either the "Add" or "Edit" Buttons to add or edit a record.	Add Edit Fix

Figure 14.5   INFOMINE resources database functions.

Once all the metadata is entered, the resource is previewed to ensure that all information is accurate. The resource is automatically added to the INFOMINE database, which can then be searched and browsed in the "What's New!" section.

EDITING INFOMINE RECORDS

The process of editing records is also very simple and straightforward. First the resource to be edited is searched using the Editor Record search (see figure 14.7).

The powerful record search allows you to search by record number, date the record was added to INFOMINE, subject words, title words, keywords, URL, author, record creator, record editor, modification date, and document type. Once the record is located, the participant is presented with the INFOMINE Editor page, from which the necessary changes may be made to the record (see figure 14.8).

LOCATING AND FIXING OUTDATED URLS

As we all are aware, Web sites are volatile creatures. Many Web sites, even stable ones, undergo revision and restructuring and sometimes disappear altogether. In order to keep up with the dynamic nature of the Web, INFOMINE has incorporated not only a URL checker but a fixer as well (see figure 14.9).

INFOMINE attempts to connect to all of the sites included in the database several times a month, flagging resources that it is unable to connect to. It also checks to see if the Web site has either moved or been modified. Modified Web sites are important to identify, in that although you may still be able to connect to the resource, it may have changed in content. A change in content can be checked simply by comparing the size of the indexed Web site to the previous size. A better approach, which we are exploring, is to conduct keyword analysis using sophisticated artificial intelligence algorithms.

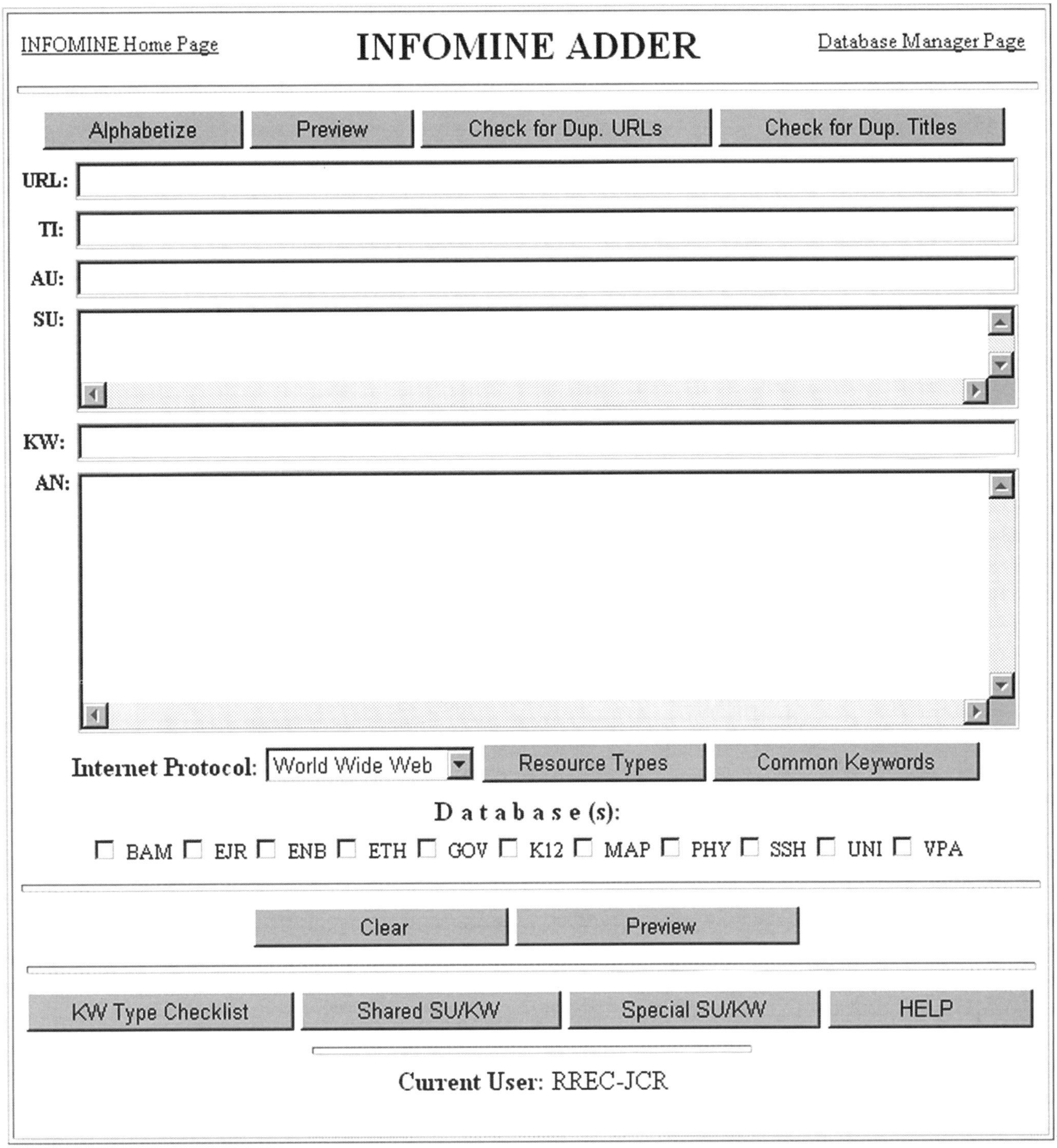
INFOMINE Home Page
INFOMINE ADDER
Database Manager Page
Alphabetize
Preview
Check for Dup. URLs
Check for Dup. Titles
URL:
TI:
AU:
SU:
KW:
AN:
Internet Protocol:
World Wide Web
Resource Types
Common Keywords
Database(s):
BAM EJR ENB ETH GOV K12 MAP PHY SSH UNI VPA
Clear
Preview
KW Type Checklist
Shared SU/KW
Special SU/KW
HELP
Current User: RREC-JCR

Figure 14.6 INFOMINE adder.

ADVANCED FEATURES

In the pursuit of efficiency and speed, INFOMINE has incorporated an automatic keyword extractor that will visit the Web resource being added and suggest keywords that describe it. The participant can then make the decision to add, modify, or remove the suggested keywords. This capability is automatically activated when the URL is entered. It first recommends additional URLs for the keyword crawler to search (see figure 14.10).

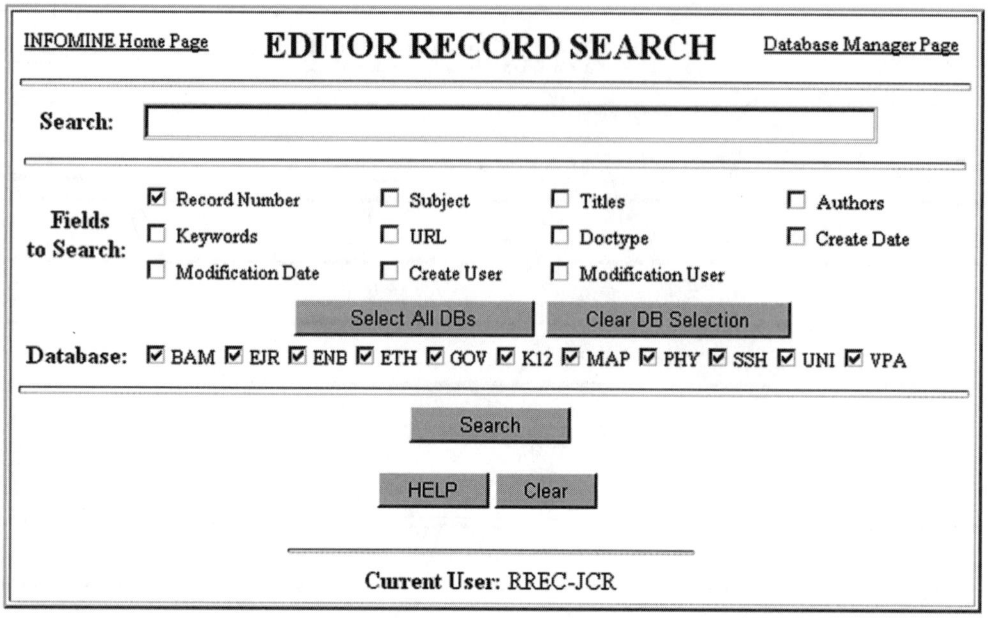

Figure 14.7 INFOMINE editor record search.

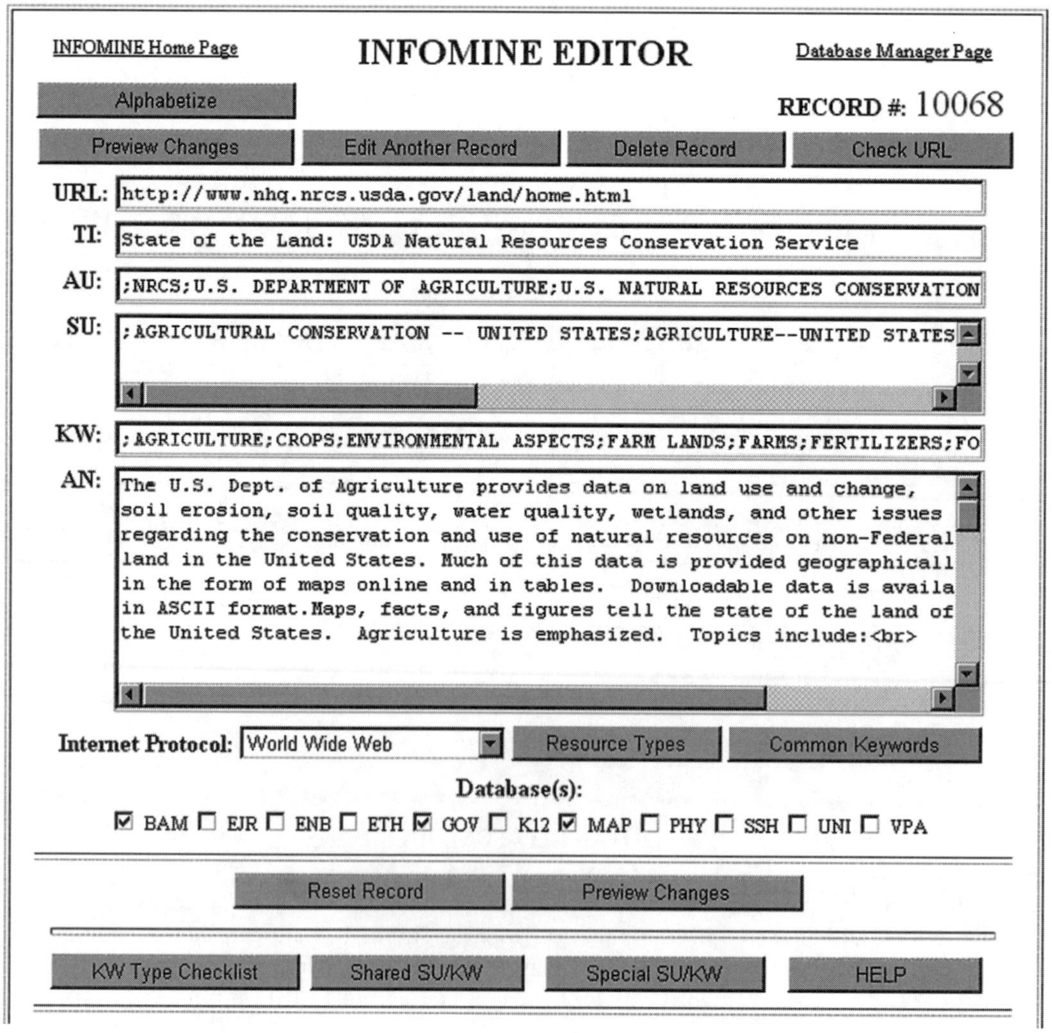

Figure 14.8 INFOMINE editor page.

Error [Types]:	☑ FAIL ☑ R-FAIL ☑ SNTX ☑ R-SNTX ☑ MV ☑ R-MV ☑ MD ☑ R-MD
Database:	☑ BAM ☑ EJR ☑ ENB ☑ ETH ☑ GOV ☑ K12 ☑ MAP ☑ PHY ☑ SSH ☑ UNI ☑ VPA ☑ BLANK
Records to return: [10 ▾]	View [Reset] Clear Errors Clear Databases Database Manage Page

Id: 2068	Title:	*Glossary of Soil Microbiology Terms*
Error: MV	Current:	http://www.ifas.ufl.edu/~dmsa/glossary.htm
	Possible:	http://dmsylvia.ifas.ufl.edu

Id: 2794	Title:	*GMDigest : Gypsy Moth*
Error: MV	Current:	http://www.fsl.wvnet.edu/fhp/gm_digest/gmdigest.html
	Possible:	http://fhpr8.srs.fs.fed.us/wv/gmdigest/gmdigest

| Id: 2809 | Title: | *GenomeNet* |
| Error: MD | Current: | http://www.tokyo-center.genome.ad.jp/ |

| Id: 3102 | Title: | *HIV InSite : Gateway to AIDS Knowledge* |
| Error: MD | Current: | http://hivinsite.ucsf.edu/ |

| Id: 5740 | Title: | *International Copper Study Group* |
| Error: FAIL | Current: | http://igm.cnig.pt/copper/copper.html |

| Id: 5992 | Title: | *Counties On-Line* |
| Error: FAIL | Current: | http://govt.net/govtlist/counties.htm |

Figure 14.9   INFOMINE URL checker.

Many times the main page of the resource may not be that useful, and thus a second or third page is necessary to adequately extract appropriate, useful, and accurate keywords. In addition, once the URL is entered, a search for all possible duplicate records is conducted. All possible duplicates are listed in a separate window, where you can clone the keywords or subjects used in the duplicate record. This is useful when you are adding a subsection of a resource with similar content and you want to use the same keywords that were used to describe the original record.

The creation of a hybrid system that achieves a balance between the reach of a search engine and metadata quality typical of human-created virtual libraries will be a challenging endeavor but one that may prove to be most beneficial. This can be achieved through the development of "smart" systems that combine these two approaches. Major advances are being made in the development of machine learning–based "smart" software, which crawls over resources and automatically describes and classifies them.

Although there is great room for improvement in machine learning applications in these areas, we view these techniques as providing assistance that will boost productivity while also saving time and labor. This approach will amplify, not replace, expert effort in content building. The subject and resource description of librarians will remain at the core of INFOMINE's approach, although it will be greatly augmented by this "smart" software.

LIMITED AREA SEARCH ENGINE (LASE)

As of June 2000 the INFOMINE database contained over 20,000 records but did not even come close to being a comprehensive collection of all academically useful sites on the Web. In fact, it would be nearly impossible to manually locate relevant resources and then add them to INFOMINE. In addition, the indexing will never reach the level that we would like in order to provide specific searching. For example, through the use of INFOMINE access log files we found that many users of INFOMINE were searching for very specific terms such as a particular species of spider. Although INFOMINE may include several very good entomology Web sites with information on particular species, our level of indexing may not go deep enough. To better handle this type of query, we are developing a Limited Area Search Engine, or LASE, that will provide many useful enhancements not only to the end-user's searching but also to the management of resources within INFOMINE. These enhancements include the following:

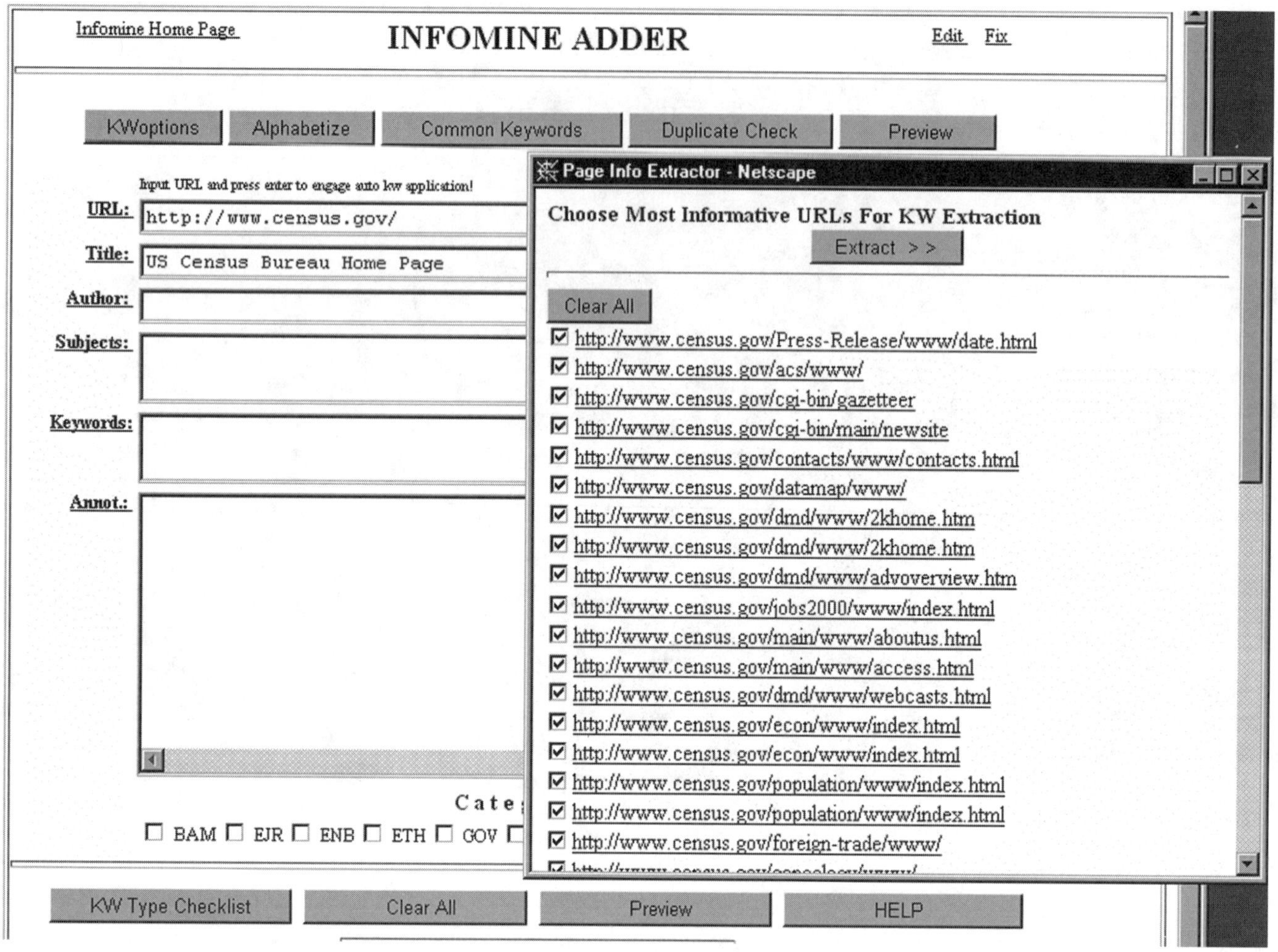

Figure 14.10   INFOMINE keyword crawler.

Enhanced Searching

Full-text searching will be achieved through the development of a LASE. Using the base URLs included in the INFOMINE database, a crawler will automatically harvest and index the full text of the Web resources included in IN-FOMINE. This provides the user with more expansive, comprehensive searching in a much larger collection, as well as user choice of high precision and/or high recall, which will provide greater user control of amount and quality of information. This approach combines the best of two worlds of Internet finding tools: the quality of an expert-created virtual library and the reach of a focused and guided search engine. As a result, the records contained in INFOMINE will be, on the whole, of much higher quality and much more relevant to researchers and students than those typically seen in the large search engines.

Record Creation

LASE will also assist with the task of record creation by automatically entering data into many fields, as well as suggesting data for other fields. This approach has been implemented in the keyword extraction function, previously discussed. Machine-assisted indexing can also be carried forward to include annotations as well as subjects. This functionality is currently being explored and will be implemented in future versions of INFOMINE.

Approval Plan for the Web

Creating metadata for the resources to be included in INFOMINE is only one of two important tasks that are involved in creating virtual libraries. The other is the identification of resources to be included. The majority of the attention has been in the application of metadata to valuable resources. Very little has been written or discussed regarding the process of identifying these resources. How is this done? Is it also done manually, possibly through the use of popular search engines? However, we can do better through the use of automatic preselection—in a sense, an approval plan for the Web.

Through the use of the LASE, the crawler will automatically harvest additional linked sites for librarian review, as well as evaluate additional high-quality resources for librarian review through significant keyword occurrence, linkage analysis, and user statistics. The idea is to help preselect quality resources. This will allow librarians to better use their intellect and expertise through reduction of redundant, mundane, and costly tasks.

INFOMINE will continue to feature tens of thousands of expert-created records, while augmenting these with millions of records created by the crawling system. Both these kinds of records will feature fielded indexing, as well as near full-text indexing and retrieval. The expert-created records will be of an increasingly more important, general, and reference-oriented nature, while the crawling-system records will provide the specificity necessary to enable the detailed searching often absent in virtual libraries.

MAKE INFOMINE YOURS

Many libraries have been creating their own specialized subject collections or have been providing their users with links to useful search engines and/or directories. While it's useful to provide these links, many libraries would like to have the ability to incorporate searching abilities into their own Web sites. Many search engines have allowed users to integrate search forms into their own Web pages by providing them with the HTML source code necessary to create this functionality. INFOMINE also provides this functionality using the OurINFOMINE approach. Through the use of OurINFOMINE, libraries will be able not only to integrate the search forms into their existing Web sites but also to create hard-coded searches into their Web pages that will automatically query the INFOMINE database using preselected query terms. This can be achieved via links on a page or through the use of pull-down menus. We have made the creation of these hard-coded searches very simple through the implementation of a hard-coded HTML Generator. You just enter the INFOMINE query you would like hard-coded, and the HTML Generator will create the HTML code to be used. In addition, the search results page can also be modified to include a header and footer of your choice, thus maintaining your library Web site's "look and feel."

COLLABORATIVE COLLECTION BUILDING

Although the introduction of machine-assisted collection has improved the ability to build collections, there still remains the need for human intervention. As of February 2000, it is estimated that over one billion Web sites are on the Internet,[2] and of those only a small fraction are academically useful. The Web will continue to grow at an ever-accelerating pace. At current levels of growth, the total content of the community of academic virtual libraries will represent an increasingly smaller portion of the total number of worthwhile Internet resources. Many libraries are not able to keep up as they were able to a few years ago. In addition, many libraries do not have the systems in place to create and support large Internet collection projects. While there is room for many good library-based Internet finding tools, perhaps not every library or library system can afford to do this work well by itself or needs to duplicate, sometimes from scratch, such a service. Many libraries are creating very similar, extensive Internet resource collections at considerable costs. It should be possible for libraries to pool their resources to build a better, more comprehensive tool.

INFOMINE is beginning to work with selected colleges and universities to methodically and systematically develop a national cooperative network of content and system builders. This effort is known as National NetGain. By working together, we will create a better tool, distribute tasks in a way that will continue to make large virtual libraries thrive, eliminate redundant (and expensive) content-building systems, and generally provide a far better Internet finding tool service than we could by working individually. There are several levels of participation. The easiest way is by suggesting resources to be added to INFOMINE. This is done via a "Suggest a Resource" link that can be found at the bottom of any INFOMINE page. Individuals are also encouraged to participate. The benefits of participation include the satisfaction that your expertise is benefiting users who are looking for useful, relevant academic information on the Internet. All of the records that individuals create are owned by the creator and can be exported as brief MARC records that can then be imported to a local OPAC or other database. In addition, all participants have the opportunity to get involved with the decision-making process as new features or collection-development policies are being discussed and implemented. Institutions can also participate by providing managing and/or associate editors. Institutional participants will have the opportunity to create customized views of INFOMINE for their institution. Other options include the creation of specialized categories that they could maintain. For example, an institution may want to create a category for business resources only. Together, we could do what librarians do better and save more resources than we could by continuing to work individually. Currently, INFOMINE is partnering with the following organizations: several University of California (UC) campus libraries; several California State University campus libraries; UC/Stanford Internet Government Information Project; UC/Western Association of Map Libraries Map Project; Gallery of Art Research Libraries in California (GARLIC) Project; Project Isaac; the National Library of Agriculture's AgNIC Project; and the California Digital Library Searchlight Project.

FREE OPEN ACCESS

The INFOMINE system and database are being built as an open-source project. Unlimited access to INFOMINE will always be free, whether you participate or not. The goal is that, eventually, the system will be provided as public domain software (GNU General Public License) that will be of use to the virtual library community. Our hope is that we can in a more specialized way contribute to virtual library system development in much the same way that the creators of Linux and Apache have in the development of operating system and Web-server software. A possible future scenario could be the creation of specialized INFOMINE categories that would be created and maintained independently of the main INFOMINE system. They would be created locally and would pass resources back and forth between all of the specialized INFOMINE systems, thus eliminating the need for participants to go through the main INFOMINE system and therefore maintaining local control of the management and display of resources. The potential exists for a large, relevant resource, and it can be achieved through collaborative partnerships, either by sharing resources and expertise and/or by joint collection building.

IMPROVING AND PRESERVING ACCESS

Over the next few years, libraries will be faced with important decisions on how best to provide relevant and accurate access to scholarly Internet resources without having to go through the myriad of search engines on the Web. Our users will demand such services. Libraries are in the logical and pivotal position to meet these challenges. Should libraries continue to depend on the commercial search engines to provide access to Web resources or should they build a better search tool? Many collaborative virtual library projects such as INFOMINE are out there for libraries to become involved with. No longer can one individual library attempt to do this alone. Librarians must not only be reactors to information technologies but must also play a large role in creating or structuring them. We need to work with commercial vendors and computer scientists and demand from them and explain to them our knowledge of information usage and organization. After seven years of experience in creating virtual libraries and spending many reference service hours helping Internet searchers use these tools, we believe strongly in the importance of human-created directories and virtual libraries to the success of locating relevant information. It is noteworthy that many of the major search engines (e.g., Google[3] and AltaVista[4]) now employ some type of directory approach in providing subject categories and browsable interfaces. The obvious major problem with the virtual library approach is that it takes time and human energy to keep up with and to organize and maintain the growing number of useful resources. However, libraries must be willing to devote the time and resources necessary to create these finding tools.

It is likely that the currently free commercial finding tools will begin charging for use or will provide biased search rankings that have been purchased or will increase their advertising to the point of distraction. In the ever-changing landscape that is the Internet, one thing remains constant: the need for the library and university community to have access to objective, high-quality, and effective finding tools that will remain in the public domain. Through participation in collaborative projects such as INFOMINE, this need can be realized.

NOTES

1 INFOMINE: Scholarly Internet Resource Collections, http://infomine.ucr.edu/.

2. Danny Sullivan, "Search Engine Sizes," http://searchenginewatch.internet.com/reports/sizes.html.

3. Google, http://www.google.com/.

4. AltaVista, http://www.altavista.com/.

SELECT BIBLIOGRAPHY

Mason, Julie et al. "INFOMINE: Promising Directions in Virtual Library Development," *First Monday* 5, no. 6 (June 2000), http://firstmonday.dk/issues/issue5_6/mason/index.html.

Mitchell, Steve. *INFOMINE: National Netgain,* http://infomine.ucr.edu/participants/netgain/.

Mitchell, Steve, and Margaret Mooney. "INFOMINE: A Model Web-Based Academic Virtual Library," *Information Technology and Libraries* 15, no. 1 (March 1996), http://infomine.ucr.edu/pubs/italmine.html.

Mooney, Margaret. "Linking Users to Internet Government Information Resources through INFOMINE," *DLA Bulletin* 16, no. 1 (Fall 1996): 31–34.

V

DIGITAL LIBRARIES:
PRACTICAL APPLICATIONS OF THE STANDARDS

15

Interpretive Encoding of Electronic Texts Using TEI Lite

William Fietzer

You often read in the recent literature of academic libraries that new digital technologies such as the Internet promise to foster more collaboration between librarians and faculty.[1] By customizing resources and study materials for individual classroom use, these technologies are expected to enable librarians to play a more primary role in the pedagogical exchange of information. One of the few real-life examples in which these expectations appear on their way to being fulfilled occurs at the University of Minnesota Libraries Electronic Text Research Center (ETRC).

The ETRC's mission is to provide access to a variety of digitized information resources and services in the humanities for students, staff, and faculty at the University of Minnesota. One of its ongoing projects in this regard involves the selective analysis and enrichment of electronic texts using the Text Encoding Initiative (TEI) descriptive markup language.

TEXT ENCODING INITIATIVE

TEI is a subset (HTML is another) of the Standard Generalized Markup Language (SGML) designed specifically to plumb the content and structure of textual documents in new and original ways.[2] TEI documents possess a header-body structure as HTML does, but, unlike HTML, TEI elements are not prescribed. That is, the encoder must define in the header through the use of a Document Type Definition (DTD) what encoding rules are followed in the body of the document. TEI provides rules files to encode and delineate the structure and meaning of the data within entities such as prose, poems, letters, and so on. Once the encoder chooses the proper rules file, elements peculiar to that set of rules can be applied to encode and describe the item.

The basic structure of a document encoded in TEI resembles the display in figure 15.1. If you are familiar with HTML and SGML, you will notice TEI's basic resemblance to the structure and outline of documents encoded in those formats. Tags common to HTML, such as those for paragraphs <p> and for functions such as identification references <id = " ">, apply with equal validity in TEI.

INTERPRETIVE ELEMENTS AND STRUCTURE

One powerful capability that distinguishes TEI (and its simplified form, dubbed TEI Lite) from other brands of SGML concerns the interpretive elements <InterpGrp> and <Interp>, which allow encoders to place analytical codes within the text. Analytical codes within this context refer to any kind of free-floating, semantic, or syntactic interpretation that an encoder wishes to attach to all or part of a text. These interpretations may be familiar linguistic categorizations such as clause or morpheme; characterizations of narrative structure such as theme or reconciliation; or independent values defined and assigned by individual encoders or groups of encoders.

The values that delimit this third group of independently assigned interpretive encoding are placed toward the bottom of the string of encoded text in the "back" section following the body. The structure for such encoding follows the schematic in figure 15.2, which is used for marking instances of unexpected or unusual references to gender in the text.

```
<tei.2>
<teiheader>
<fileDesc>
<titleStmt>
<title></title>
<respStmt>
<resp></resp>
<name></name>
</respStmt>
</titleStmt>
<publicationStmt>
<distributor></distributor>
</publicationStmt>
<sourceDesc>
<bibl></bibl>
</sourceDesc>
</fileDesc>
</teiHeader>
<text>
<body>
<div1 = "chapter">
<p></p><p></p>
</div1>
<div2="chapter">
<p></p><p></p>
</div2>
</body>
<back>
</back>
</text>
<tei.2>
```

**Figure 15.1   The basic structure
of a TEI document.**

```
<text><back>
<div 1 type="Interpretations"><p>
<interpGrp type ="Gender Marking" resp="KR">
<interp value="female" id="gndr-fem">
<interp value="male" id="gndr-male">
<interp value="other" id="gndr-other">
</interpGrp>
</p></div1></back></text>
```

Figure 15.2   Example of gender marking encoding.

As you might imagine, defining and applying such tags proves to be a difficult and controversial undertaking. The connotative and denotative aspects of any term, as well as the need to define the contextual instances in which it can be applied, may daunt any individual encoder. Without a predetermined set of guidelines, no standardized approach to textual encoding is possible. The difficulty and volatility associated with this task require interested parties to convene to discuss and reach consensus on what, where, and how particular analytical concepts should be applied.

PROJECT STRUCTURE, OPERATION, AND THE WTW

Out of these circumstances originated several steering committees comprised of faculty, library staff, and student encoders to address these and other issues associated with the analytical encoding of electronic text done in the ETRC. Facilitated by Professor Miranda Remnek, head of the ETRC, these steering committees determine policy for the following three electronic encoding projects currently under way: the Women's Travel Writing Project (WTW), which covers American women's travel writing from 1830 to 1930; the Early Modern French Women Writers Project (EMFWW), which encodes texts written in France from the fifteenth to eighteenth centuries; and the Early Nineteenth Century Russian Readership and Culture Project (ENCRRC), which is devoted to Russian readership, culture, and press materials from the nineteenth century.

The WTW represents perhaps the best-developed project of the three, with twenty-five different encoded texts that recount the adventures and exploits of women travelers in some of the most exotic regions of the nineteenth-century world. Like the subject areas of the other projects, women's travel writing contains an area of interest common to several university departments. It also reflects the new wave of scholarship that stresses the value of travel narratives as primary sources for understanding women's identities. As such, women's travel writing provides an area of intellectual exploration unencumbered by the weight of scholarly tradition. Like the subject matter in the other projects, the time period under consideration obviates practical concerns over authoritative editions and copyright.

The steering committee for the Women's Travel Writing project devised analytical concepts that fall into four main categories: Ethnicity, Gender Marking, Transportation, and Women's Occupations. These categories subdivide further along a spectrum of complexity, from the simple male-female distinctions involved in gender marking to the panoply of occupations contained under the rubric of Women's Occupations.

CONCEPT APPLICATION

A simple yet flexible set of guidelines is used to apply the categories to the texts themselves. The project manual stipulates that Gender Marking, for example, be applied only in overt references of gender. "Male" applies only when the text contains an obvious instance of male dominance or privilege. "Female" applies only in explicit instances of a woman transgressing gender lines or when the text offers explicit comparisons between men and women. "Other" applies to those circumstances where the narrator encounters a different gender system or where the gender of the person appears ambiguous. When the encoder applies the software to insert the interpretive tag around a particular word or phrase, the marked-up text resembles the following:

<seg>woman</seg>

After the encoder inserts the analytical element attribute relevant to the particular instance, the coded subtext with the software-supplied tags resembles this example:

[Div1] TYPE = "chapter" N = "18"
  [P] N = "18.1"
  [SEG] ANA = "gndr-fem"

The first two lines indicate the location of the interpretive tag. The third line supplies the value of the analytical code applied by the encoder.

Encoders tag only an initial word or two of a particular instance. Displayed in red oversized text when viewed online, the highlighted text alerts the reader to examine the surrounding text more closely to evaluate the particular concept applied. The highlighted text on the Web screen has been supplied as figure 15.3.

USING THE CATEGORIES

Whoever accesses the encoded texts over the World Wide Web employs XML-compliant DynaWeb software that facilitates on-the-fly access through any browser. Each text has four search approaches available on pull-down menus that separate into two groups. The DynaWeb software, with its built-in thesaurus, provides the full-text and expanded search options. The analytic encoding supplied by ETRC staffers enables project and course category searches. Table 15.1 summarizes and distinguishes the different types of searches that are available.

With the in-house analytical encoding that the ETRC provides, the latter two categories can be customized from semester to semester or tailored to the individual class to meet the professor's or instructor's pedagogical needs.

Unlike the full-text and expanded searches that operate on individual words in the text, the project and course category searches retrieve all paragraphs that contain the specific conceptual content, regardless of whether they contain the specific search term used. Thanks to the additional tagging enhancements provided by project encoders, a "Gender-Female" category search, for example, retrieves ninety-three paragraphs in the WTW database that do not

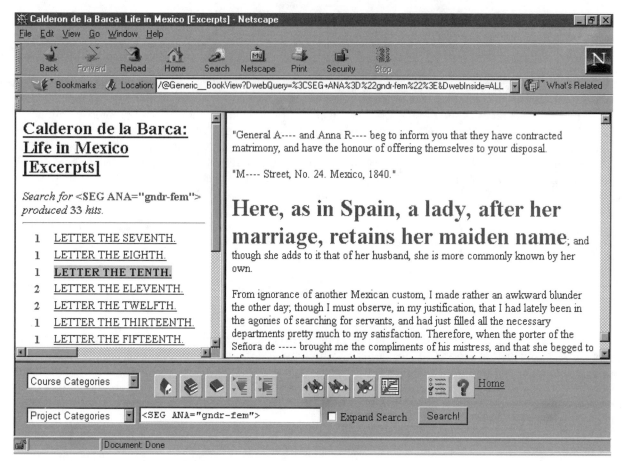

Figure 15.3 DynaWeb software display of gender marking encoding.

Table 15.1 A comparison of search categories.

SEARCH CATEGORY	DESCRIPTION AND FUNCTION
Basic Search	A full-text search that is used to retrieve all instances in the text(s) of the search term or phrase being used. This approach may be used with all our texts, at the collection or individual book level.
Expanded Search	A thesaurus-based search that is used to retrieve not only instances of the search term, but also instances of related words in the text, as defined by in-built DynaWeb thesauri. (The thesauri in question are derived from Houghton-Mifflin thesauri, and are not changed in any way by WTW.) This approach also may be used with all our texts, at the collection or individual book level.
Project Categories Search	An analytical (metadata) search that is used to retrieve additional passages that reflect the content of the search but do not necessarily contain the search terms used. The software looks for analytical metadata tags created using SGML (Standard Generalized Markup Language) that are attached to the texts by our encoders. These tags represent sample research categories identified by our advisory board. This approach will not at present find relevant passages in all our texts (some texts are still being encoded).
Course Categories Search	An analytical (metadata) search that also is used to retrieve additional passages that reflect the content of the search, but do not necessarily contain the search terms used. This search type contains categories developed in connection with individual courses. Taking this approach, users will retrieve passages only in selected texts, that is those encoded for the courses in question. (The user who takes the Project Categories approach will eventually be able to search those categories across all texts in the database.)

contain the word "female" in a cross-document search. The enhanced search capability provided by analytical encoding opens the documents to increased retrieval and deeper analysis.

The encoding facilitates users' ability to compare conceptually relevant passages within and across texts. By alerting them to the anomalies and contradictions within and among these texts, users can evaluate authorial observations and judgments within the context of nineteenth-century European conventions. In doing so, these operational capabilities question the values of the authors being examined, along with the categorization process itself.

EVALUATION AND CRITICISM

Some educators question the quality and/or depth of the concepts being encoded, but the analysis is not intended to be either high-concept or didactic. Even with improved technological capabilities and a consensus approach from all concerned parties, the encoding process itself remains a subjective, labor-intensive activity, subject to human error and misjudgment. Differences in interpretation arise despite the most stringent guidelines.

Despite these concerns, interest in the potential and capabilities of analytical encoding continues to grow. During the 1999–2000 year, students in the University of Minnesota's History 1012 class employed the basic full-text feature of the software to complete their assignments. During 2000–2001, they are asked to use the entire spectrum of analytical categories to perform their examination of these texts. At the same time the History of Science program, in conjunction with the WTW, devised a special taxonomy of natural science categories for its Women and Science course. One course in the French department devised specialized linguistic analytical encoding to examine medieval text in the WTW's companion archive, Early Modern French Women Writers, while another explored the geographic and historical difficulties encountered in reading Flora Tristan's *Peregrinations d'une Paria*. In the fall of 1999 the ETRC hosted its first conference on analytical encoding and women's travel writing, which was attended by scholars and students from all over Minnesota and the upper Midwest.

FUTURE PLANS

The ETRC plans to improve the quality of its analytical encoding feature by installing more powerful software that combines the interpretive coding with character-based search capabilities and holds the results in a buffer for additional analysis. Students now access these texts only through the ETRC Web site; soon they will be able to access the texts directly through the University of Minnesota's online catalog. The ETRC anticipates expanding the bibliographies associated with each author or subject, improving its geographical interface option, increasing quality control, and refining the analytical terms employed by its encoders. Professor Remnek expects the number of encoded texts to increase by one-third and to include narratives in new subject areas such as Cuba and sixteenth- and seventeenth-century France.

All of the analytically encoded texts have been cataloged in OCLC's CORC (Cooperative Online Resource Catalog) database. Having these texts available for access in a national-level database promises to increase their use and further stimulate interest in the analytical encoding of texts for educational purposes. Input from other institutions should expand the discussion and refine the question as to what uses analytical encoding of electronic texts can be applied.

CONCLUSION

When the ETRC began its interpretive encoding projects three years ago, the electronic encoding of texts was in its infancy. Many scholars and researchers questioned the value of placing text online; library administrators wondered whether the time and labor investment would prove worth the expense. The goal for most TEI practitioners involved structurally encoding as many texts as possible and placing them online, but the full potential of TEI and analytical encoding remained untapped. Structurally encoded texts became the foundation of the TEI markup language as it appeared on the Internet.

The time has arrived for deeper applications, such as analytical encoding to unlock all of TEI's pedagogical potential. Through the application of the TEI markup language in its analytical encoding projects, the Electronic Text Research Center demonstrates how interpretive encoding provides a viable means to promote collaboration between faculty and librarians and to further colleges' and universities' missions of developing their resources for the educational benefit of their constituencies.

NOTES

1. Don Tapscott, "Reinventing the University," *NewsScan Exec,* Spring 1998, http://www.newsscan.com/exec/spring1998/reinventing.html.

2. Nancy Ide and Jean Veronis, *The Text Encoding Initiative: Background and Context* (Dordrecht, The Netherlands; Boston: Kluwer Academic Publishers, 1995).

ADDITIONAL READING

C. M. Sperberg-McQueen and Lou Burnard, *Guidelines for Electronic Text Encoding and Interchange* (Chicago: Text Encoding Initiative, 1994).

16

Developing the Use of Metadata at the National Library of Medicine: From Decision-Making to Implementation

Diane Boehr

The concept of adding metadata to Web resources produced by the National Library of Medicine (NLM) has been explored over a period of time. Some individual projects at the library, such as our online *Current Bibliographies in Medicine* and the material in the *Profiles in Science* database, have consistently been issued with imbedded metadata.[1] We are now ready to expand the use of metadata library-wide to internal and external resources. We intend to develop a minimal data set of information that ideally would be included for every online resource issued by NLM and, in addition, that has the ability to be expanded and enhanced to accommodate the needs of various categories of resources. While most people would agree that adding this type of data to a resource has the potential to improve retrieval, the actual mechanisms for implementation have been hampered by concerns about what material should receive metadata, who should supply it, and whether any existing search engines used on NLM Web pages could actually make use of this data.

However, NLM staff members recognize that we have the opportunity to improve access to electronic resources through the addition of metadata. Applying metadata to external as well as internal resources is a natural expansion of our traditional role of identifying and controlling (through indexing and cataloging) quality resources in the biomedical field. NLM hopes that adding to the critical mass of material containing metadata may encourage more search engines to make use of it.

BACKGROUND

In 1999, one of the NLM Associate Fellows, Elizabeth M. Smigielski, did an overall study of metadata use at NLM. She defined metadata as having two required components: (1) Data used to aid the identification, description, and location of networked electronic resources; and (2) Metadata tags encoded into HTML source code. Using this definition, she found seven projects/areas of the library where some metadata were being created. Five of these used an in-house metadata scheme predicated on Ht:/Dig retrieval mechanisms, one used traditional Dublin Core, and the other used Dublin Core with local extensions. One of the projects began in 1992, but most of the others began between 1996 and 1999.

Dropping the second requirement, that is, HTML coding, yields a few additional occurrences of metadata for electronic resources in the library. Certainly, all the existing cataloging records for networked electronic resources in MARC format need to be taken into account. In addition, all the information collected and stored in standardized templates for the MEDLINE*plus* database[2] constitutes another type of metadata. (MEDLINE*plus* is a consumer-oriented service providing access to online information about specific diseases and conditions and also has links to consumer health information from the National Institutes of Health, dictionaries, lists of hospitals and physicians, health information in Spanish and other languages, and clinical trials.)

A variety of different input standards exist in various sections of the library, which include: standardized Dublin Core metadata; minimal system-generated metadata; and nonstandardized, system-defined metadata.

IMPLEMENTATION STRATEGIES

Our main goal is to create a basic and consistent set of metadata for use throughout the library. NLM sees itself as having a three-pronged role in its use of metadata. First, we would like to experiment with extending the Dublin Core set to be more accommodating of diverse or special needs (e.g., recording administrative or management data such as permanence and archiving data), while still maintaining its internal consistency and ease of use. We also want to contribute to the evolution of Dublin Core into a standard that does more to support the creation of consistent metadata by different groups. Second, we would like to supply a critical mass of metadata records in which the level of confidence in the data supplied can be assured, thus encouraging search engines to make use of the data. Third, NLM wishes to extend the use of its standardized vocabulary and classification schemes, which have proved to work well in the tangible resources environment, in order to enhance retrieval of Web resources.

To effect these goals, NLM will develop an input template for library-wide use, using the fifteen Dublin Core elements as a base but extending and redefining these elements for our local needs. Unlike standard Dublin Core, in which all fields are optional, NLM will require the use of certain fields for all metadata records. This basic set should be clearly defined and simple enough to understand, so that the originator of a resource could create the metadata and embed it in the resource. Selected resources will be forwarded to catalogers who will add elements to the basic data, creating an enhanced metadata record with MeSH, NLM classification, and possibly authorized forms of name headings. Some or all of these enhanced records may also be converted to MARC format and added to our library catalog.

Before actually designing our own template, NLM decided to become a participant in the OCLC CORC (Cooperative Online Resource Catalog) project, to see how well our resources could be described using Dublin Core and how easily records could migrate into our integrated library system. This experience will allow us to refine our own data set. However, it is obvious that Dublin Core is really intended to serve only as descriptive metadata (and even for that purpose it has shortcomings). For administrative and management data, libraries/institutions will need to develop their own tags, definitions, and standards. As a national library with a major responsibility for archiving medical resources, NLM is very concerned about recording and storing permanency data for the electronic resources we are making available. The library wants to establish consistent policies and procedures to ensure accessibility of electronic resources to users, as well as communicate to them whether an electronic resource available today will be available in the future, retrievable at the same address, and whether it will be changed or unchanged in content. Assigned permanence levels can also aid in determining which resources should receive enhancement of the basic metadata. While NLM has an initial focus on electronic resources that we create, we recognize that the work done here may provide a model for other publishers of electronic information.

NLM's Working Group on Permanence has proposed that three aspects of permanency be recorded. Exact values and definitions for each field are still being developed.

Identifier Validity (IV). The extent to which a user can be assured that a given name or other identifier will always retrieve the same resource. This may range from "undefined" to "guaranteed."

Resource Availability (RA). The extent to which a given resource is guaranteed to remain available in electronic form. This may range from "no guarantee" to "permanently archived."

Content Invariance (CI). The extent to which the content of a given resource and the links it contains are guaranteed to remain unchanged. This aspect includes whether a resource is expected to grow over time or is fixed in size, as well as whether or not the content is subject to being revised or replaced.

The most logical location for recording and storing these data appears to be as part of the resource's metadata, ideally embedded in the resource itself. From there, permanence data can also be displayed in our catalog if we choose to make traditional MARC records for these resources, or we can extract the data and create a separate database if needed for administrative purposes.

WHAT IS NLM'S LONG-TERM ROLE?

In addition to controlling our own electronic resources, we also intend to search for and identify high-quality biomedical-related sites from other sources and supply metadata for those. From past experience we have learned that it is more effective to review sites by producer/publisher than by topic, and we intend to continue to harvest external resources in that manner.

We then need to compare the metadata being created for outside resources with the requirements we have established for internal resources. Do they match? If not, we will have to determine why and whether we can rationally justify the differences (e.g., are they equivalent to differences in a catalog record vs. a bibliographic citation?). If the differences cannot be justified, one set of standards may need to be modified.

There is an underlying assumption in the CORC project that participants are identifying high-quality resources. Many librarians are willing to trust the judgments being made and will add CORC records created by others to their own databases with little or no further evaluation. This saves much duplication of effort on the part of individual libraries and selectors. It is particularly useful when libraries make their selection criteria available publicly

For example, NLM has the following criteria for resource inclusion outlined on the MEDLINE*plus* Web site:

Quality, Authority, and Accuracy of Content

- The source of the content is established, respected, and dependable. A list of advisory board members or consultants is published on the site.
- The information provided is appropriate to the audience level, well-organized, and easy to use.
- Information is from primary resources (i.e., textual material, abstracts, Web pages).
- Lists of links are evaluated/reviewed/quality-filtered.
- The purpose of the Web page is educational and is not to sell a product or service. Most content is available at no charge.

Availability and Maintenance of the Web Page

- The Web site is consistently available.
- Links from the site are maintained.
- The source for the contents of the Web page(s) and the entity responsible for maintaining the Web site (Webmaster, organization, creator of the content) are clear.
- Information is current or an update date is included.

Special Features

- The site provides unique information to the topic with a minimum of redundancy and overlap between resources.
- The site contains special features such as graphics/diagrams, glossary, or other unique information.
- The content of the site is accessible to persons with disabilities.

Knowing this information, libraries with similar selection criteria might rely on NLM's judgment and not repeat the same decision-making process before including a particular resource in their own database.

Conversely, it might also be valuable to know which sites did not make the cut, and why. Is there a way for NLM and other libraries to identify the sites we've rejected, and the reasons why, in order to keep others from having to go through the same process?

Storing and distributing this type of information raises interesting ethical issues, as libraries do not want to be seen as censoring or blocking access to sites. This is particularly true of libraries such as NLM that are also federal agencies. However, by selectively harvesting particular resources within a topic, we are making quality judgments that are potentially useful for our colleagues. Further discussion is needed in the library community on how and if we should store this type of information. If we do decide to document these decisions, to whom should we make these data available, and how?

SUMMARY

Although many details are still to be resolved, NLM sees the value of adding encoded metadata to electronic resources to enhance searching and retrieval. Initially, we will focus on internally produced resources. While we intend to use Dublin Core as the base for a metadata set, we will implement some local modifications, including requiring certain fields on all records and adding elements for administrative/management purposes, particularly permanency information. We believe the results of our work will be useful in identifying areas in which Dublin Core is weak or inadequate and needs adjustments or additional elements. In addition, NLM will review external resources, searching by particular publishers/producers to identify high-quality biomedical resources, which will be enhanced with NLM-supplied metadata.

NOTES

1. Alexa T. McCray, Marie E. Gallagher, and Michael A. Flannick, "Extending the Role of Metadata in a Digital Library System," in *IEEE Forum on Research and Technology Advances in Digital Libraries: Proceedings, May 19–21, 1999* (Los Alamitos, Calif.: IEEE Computer Society Press, 1999), 190–199.

2. Naomi Miller, Eve-Marie Lacroix, and Joyce E. B. Backus, "MEDLINEplus: Building and Maintaining the National Library of Medicine's Consumer Health Web Service," *Bulletin of the Medical Library Association* 88, no. 1 (January 2000): 11–17.

17

Integrating Bio-Collection Databases: Metadata in Natural History Museums

Stanley Blum, transcribed by Manuel Urrizola

This chapter is about biological collection databases, the most important information resources held by natural history museums, and our efforts to use metadata to develop a query system that integrates our databases across institutions and taxonomic disciplines.

There appear to be many similarities between the library and natural history communities. In particular, I've noticed that many of the same words have special significance, such as *collection, catalog,* and *classification.* It may also be true, however, that we are two peoples divided by a common language. Our respective definitions of these words may have subtle but important differences. These may become apparent as I first attempt to describe what it is we do with biological collections in natural history museums. After sketching our collections and the catalogs that represent them, I'll describe the distributed search and retrieval system we are layering on top of our collection databases to provide integrated access. I'll then talk about what we expect we'll have to do in the future with metadata to make the system scaleable.

One thing I should note at the outset concerns our different perspectives on metadata. One of the first people I met who talked about metadata explained the concept to me functionally as: "data about data that helps with discovery, access, and assessment or interpretation."[1] Much of what I've heard and read from the library community appears to emphasize the discovery and assessment functions of metadata. I come to metadata from a database and systems perspective, and I think we tend to focus more on access and assessment and how we can encode these functions in software that integrates multiple data sources. I've also come to believe that the distinction between data and metadata is not that useful because it's fundamentally a question of perspective; things we consider metadata in one situation become data in another.

Most people think of natural history museums as places to see dinosaur skeletons and stuffed animals. They are unaware that a large proportion of a typical museum's budget and staff are dedicated to systematic biology, the science of discovering, naming, describing, and classifying organisms (a.k.a. taxonomy). The primary research materials of systematic biology are the specimens housed in the biological collections of natural history museums. In a very fundamental way, these collections document life on earth.

The collections in a natural history museum are typically organized and managed according to disciplines based on higher taxonomic groups, such as botany, entomology, and ichthyology. The work of keeping a fish collection is very different from keeping plant or insect collections. Consequently, any fish collection is typically managed more or less independently of the plant, bug, and bird collections in the same institution. There are typically between five and fifteen independent collection management units in any museum, and they don't necessarily talk to each other much. Over the last one hundred plus years, each discipline has developed its own deeply ingrained work practices. The similarities between collections within a discipline are almost always stronger than similarities between collections in a single institution.

The number of specimens in a collection varies widely, from tens of thousands to tens of millions. Globally, natural history museums are estimated to hold about 2.5 billion specimens.[2] The taxonomic diversity contained in a collection also varies widely. Large entomology collections may have specimens representing more than 100,000 species, while the largest mammal collection contains representatives of fewer than 6,000 species. Finally, the geographic scope among collections also varies, from regional to global, though even a global collection always has strengths in particular regions.

Before the advent of computers, many but not all disciplines made paper-based cataloging a part of standard collection management practice; items were cataloged either in ledgers or on cards. Computer-based cataloging began in the 1960s and became widespread by the middle to late 1980s. By 1990 the cataloging of natural history collections had become widely perceived as a database problem, to be solved by the application of off-the-shelf database management systems, from Oracle to dBase. For the last decade, this has meant relational database management systems.

For a variety of reasons almost every collection uses a uniquely developed or at least highly customized cataloging application. So while each collection performs similar activities and keeps roughly the same information, each collection database represents a potentially unique solution to the cataloging problem.

So the question is why do we need to integrate access to all these databases? The answer is relatively simple: Any scientific question that can be answered by data from one collection can be answered better by data from many collections. That is illustrated nicely by the collection localities represented in three fish collections: the University of Michigan Museum of Zoology, the Tulane University Museum of Natural History, and the Florida Museum of Natural History. Michigan has special expertise or history of fieldwork in Mexico, Tulane in the southeastern United States, and Florida in the Caribbean. If you need to know the distribution of a fish in this part of the world, you're going to get a better answer by combining data from all three collections (see figure 17.1).

The question then becomes: How can we do this? How can we create an integrated view from all the different conceptual schemas represented in all these different databases? (See figure 17.2.)

The Association of Systematics Collections (ASC) took the first steps toward such integration in a workshop at Cornell in 1992.[3] This was an effort to use data modeling to reconcile the work practices and data concepts represented in all the discipline-specific databases. The effort met with some success and the result was a single model in which you can see the main elements of every discipline (see figure 17.3).

Put another way, every database tells the same story: Agents go to a locality, perform a collecting event, and generate one or more collection objects (specimens or groups of specimens). These objects can be sorted and broken down into parts and derived objects such as images. Each specimen is identified as being a member of a taxon (e.g., species) and ultimately may even get cited in a reference or publication.

Authors of the model had two hopes: (1) that it would serve as a guideline or template for succeeding generations of collection databases (thereby reducing overall heterogeneity); and (2) that it would serve as a federation schema in a system that implemented the emerging technical ideas about federating databases. With a federation schema in hand,

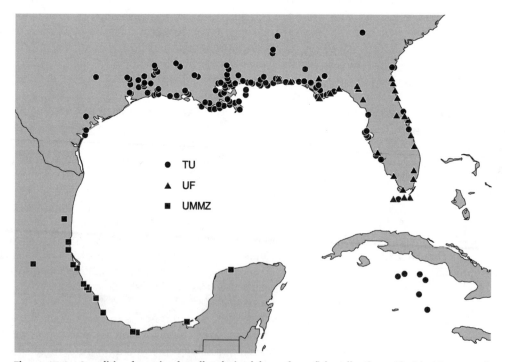

Figure 17.1   Localities for striped mullet derived from three fish collections: Florida Museum of Natural History (triangles), Tulane University Museum of Natural History (circles), and University of Michigan Museum of Zoology (squares).

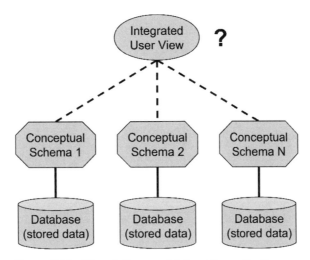

Figure 17.2 The challenge of integrating collection databases.

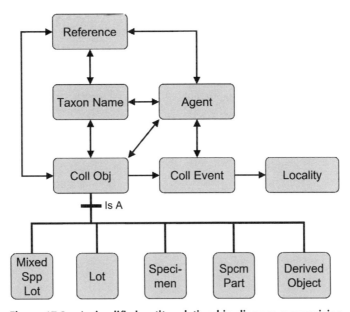

Figure 17.3 A simplified entity-relationship diagram summarizing the information model for biological collections.

we hoped to build tools that would automate query and data transformations and enable us to query all our databases in a seamless fashion.

Since 1993 the ASC model has served as the point of departure in some efforts to build new collection databases, but it was also ignored by others. By either route the result is the same; the "standard" has not significantly reduced the amount of heterogeneity among systems. Most of us are now skeptical that further standards work will change that. Heterogeneity among systems cannot be eliminated—it has to be accommodated.

The ASC model was, in fact, conceived to serve as a federation schema, but dealing with a schema that complicated is still beyond our technical grasp at this point. So, presently, we're trying to achieve useful results with something simpler than the ASC model. What we've done instead is to take the "core" approach and developed what we call (with a nod to a less specialized predecessor) the "Darwin Core." To build our prototype, we combined that with yet another page from the library community: a set of query tools based on the Z39.50 protocol for information retrieval (see figure 17.4).

The Darwin Core consists of 23 elements (see figure 17.5). The first three—institution code, collection code, and catalog number—uniquely identify any record that appears in a result set. Then we have a series of taxonomic fields

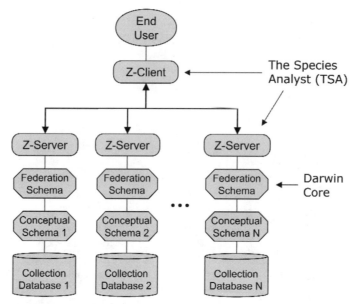

Figure 17.4   High-level system architecture of the Species Analyst.

1. InstitutionCode
2. CollectionCode
3. CatalogNumber
4. ScientificName
5. Kingdom
6. Phylum
7. Class
8. Order
9. Family
10. Genus
11. SpecificEpithet
12. Collector

13. Year*
14. Month*
15. Day*
16. Country
17. StateProvince
18. County
19. Locality
20. Longitude*
21. Latitude*
22. BoundingBox*
23. JulianDay*

Figure 17.5   Elements of the Darwin Core. Elements marked with an asterisk have numeric values. All others are simple text.

that provide taxonomic identification as well as access points, according to scientific classification. These are followed by basic information about the collector, collecting date, and locality. Our guiding principles in shaping the Darwin Core have been simplicity and commonality; to include things that are commonly recorded, things that are commonly requested, and to structure them as simply as possible.

The software that gives life to the Darwin Core is "The Species Analyst"[4] (TSA)—a client-server system, developed by David Vieglais (University of Kansas Natural History Museum), based on Index Data's YAZ toolkit for the Z39.50 protocol.[5] The Z-client can be used as a stand-alone utility or an extension to Windows applications, like Excel or ArcView. The client communicates over the Internet with Z-servers that have been installed at participating institutions. The Z-server receives the query and communicates directly to SQL databases via ODBC (Open Database Connectivity). The Z-client then integrates the results from individual servers into a single data set and passes them directly into the desktop application. More recently, Vieglais has developed a Web-to-Z gateway, which makes the system accessible via a Web browser.[6]

Our results so far indicate that the Species Analyst will provide very powerful information retrieval capabilities to the users of collection data. Performance is adequate now, but the system hasn't been well publicized yet, so we don't have a lot of users. This will change as more data providers (collections) come online. It's currently deployed on about eighteen different collections in the United States, Canada, and Mexico, so only a few collections can be queried in any one discipline. A project called "FishNet" was recently funded and over the next two years will bring about twenty

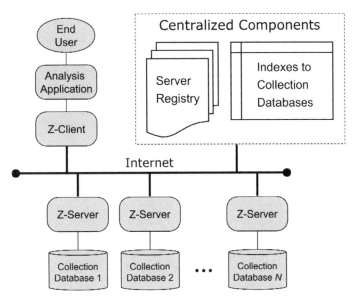

Figure 17.6   High-level system architecture of the Species Analyst, showing centralized components.

fish collections online. Other vertebrate disciplines are developing proposals and could bring another forty or fifty collections online in the United States alone. Collaborations with our European colleagues began in the fall of 2000.

An important question now is whether the current system will scale to accommodate more users and more collections. Does every client need to talk to every server out there to find out if it contains relevant information? Currently, there is a very small centralized component to the system, the server registry, which enables you to find out which servers are connected and functioning (see figure 17.6). Before submitting a query, a user can choose which servers will be queried. But this only enables people to use their a priori knowledge about a server's contents—that a bird collection isn't likely to contain information about butterflies, for example. A user looking for a particular kind of butterfly, or butterflies from a particular region, probably won't know beforehand which of the twenty butterfly servers should be queried. If we can build a centralized profiling system that indexes every collection by taxonomy and by geography (another kind of metadata), the client could first query the central index automatically to find out which collections have items of interest. The result would be a more targeted search, faster response times for users, and a reduced query load on participating servers.

In summary, the information-modeling work we have done in the natural history community has been useful, but its effects have been subtle. The simple "core" approach is producing retrieval and integration results now. And finally, additional metadata about our databases, that is, taxonomic and geographic indices, will be needed to accommodate expected growth.

NOTES

1. Bruce Gritton, "Metadata Comments," in Metadata listserv: metadata@llnl.gov, March 3, 1994, http://www.llnl.gov/liv_comp/metadata/papers/comments-gritton.html.

2. W. Donald Duckworth, Hugh H. Genoways, and Carolyn L. Rose, *Preserving Natural Science Collections: Chronicle of Our Environmental Heritage* (Washington, D.C.: National Institute for the Conservation of Cultural Property, 1993), 14.

3. Biological Collections Data Standards Workshop, *An Information Model for Biological Collections: Report of the Biological Collections Data Standards Workshop, August 18–24, 1992.* (Washington, D.C.): Association of Systematics Collections, 1993. Drafts of the model itself may be found at gopher://www.keil.ukans.edu:70/11/standards/asc.

4. The Species Analyst is a project of the North American Biodiversity Information Network (NABIN) and the University of Kansas Natural History Museum and Biodiversity Research Center. The Species Analyst has been supported by grants from the U.S. National Science Foundation and the North American Commission for Environmental Cooperation.

5. Index Data, "PHP YAZ," http://www.indexdata.com/phpyaz/.

6. "The Species Analyst Web Interface (v2.0b)," http://habanero.nhm.ukans.edu/TSA.

18

The Colorado Digitization Project: An Overview

William Garrison

The Colorado Digitization Project (CDP), begun in the fall of 1998, is a collaborative initiative that involves Colorado's archives, historical societies, libraries, and museums.[1] The CDP will create a digital library-museum that will provide the people of Colorado with access to the rich historical and cultural resources of the state. Institutions participating in the project will be able to contribute content that is "born digital," as well as materials that exist in another format and have been digitized. It is anticipated that the virtual collection will include such resources as letters, diaries, government documents, manuscripts, digital versions of exhibits, artifacts, oral histories, and maps.

To initiate this effort, the Colorado State Library awarded a federal Library Services and Technology Act (LSTA) grant of $71,000 that brought together the partners for the CDP, identified ongoing and planned digitization initiatives, developed guidelines for digitization projects, conducted a pilot project, and identified future funding options. Subsequently, the CDP was awarded a two-year $499,999 grant from the Institute on Museum and Library Services and a second LSTA grant of $107,000. In addition, the Regional Library Systems of Colorado awarded the CDP a $36,000 grant. The grant funds have allowed the expansion of the initial project to include:

- Establishment of four regional scan centers
- Training for Colorado archivists, librarians, and curators in digitization
- Creation of a union catalog of metadata
- Support for 20–25 collaborative digitization initiatives
- Research on key issues
- Creation of 50,000 new digital images

The purposes of the CDP are to ensure public access to the resources in Colorado, to promote the economic and efficient delivery of full text and graphic resources to the people of Colorado, to contribute to the national effort to develop digital libraries and museums, and to work with educators to help meet the Colorado history standards. With these purposes, the goals of the CDP are:

- To create an open, distributed, publicly accessible digital library that documents crucial information for the residents of Colorado
- To expand the collaborative structure among the state's libraries, museums, archives, and historical societies to coordinate and guide the implementation of a virtual digital collection
- To establish criteria and standards to guide the selection of materials for inclusion in the digital library
- To demonstrate the value of libraries/museums in the emerging electronic information environment and their important contribution to the state's development
- To assist libraries, archives, historical societies, and museums in the digitizing of materials and managing digital projects through training programs and consultation
- To emphasize the content and rich resources held by Colorado archives, historical societies, libraries, and museums
- To work with the Colorado K–12 environment to incorporate digital objects that assist teachers, parents, and students in meeting the Colorado history standards

As it is a collaborative effort, the CDP has a variety of working groups with membership from different constituent groups. The groups include: the Steering Committee, the Metadata Working Group, the Website Working Group, the Museum Working Group, the Scanning Centers Working Group, and the Selection/Collection Development Working Group. The Steering Committee is responsible for the general oversight of the grant and project implementation. The Metadata Working Group is responsible for reviewing the options for the description of digital resources and for developing guidelines for metadata to be used by project participants. The Website Working Group was responsible for the development of a Web site for the project. The Museum Working Group will be responsible for advising on the unique requirements of museums, historical societies, and archives that will participate in the CDP. The Scanning Centers Working Group assists in identifying and developing guidelines for scanning that can be used by project participants at the CDP Scan Centers. The Selection/Collection Development Working Group assists in developing guidelines for the virtual collection.

The Web site (http://coloradodigital.coalliance.org) has been available since 1999. In addition to listing resources and information about the project, the Web site presents the standards and guidelines developed by the working groups. Guidelines for metadata, scanning, and collection policy are presented, as well as information about starting a project. Links to digital project resources are provided, as is information on legal issues. The Web site also contains a section on digital collections available in Colorado. Users are able to browse existing collections by media format, by geographic location, or all projects in a single list. This is not the union catalog yet. Projects or collections are included whether actually available (i.e., digital images are accessible) or planned, in which case a link to the host institution site is provided. Also available on the Web site is the pilot project on the Colorado Coal Field Wars that is intended to help K–12 teachers in using digital resources. This project was developed in cooperation with the Colorado Endowment for the Humanities (CEH) and the University of Denver. The initial project is available on the Web site, and the lesson plans that were developed and written by teachers who attended the CEH-sponsored teacher's institute are going to be made available on the site as well.

As mentioned earlier, research on key areas of the project will be conducted during this phase of the CDP. Research into specific issues related to enhanced use of digitization in Colorado's institutions will be done. Among the aspects being researched are exploring the impact of digital images available via the Internet on museum attendance, investigating user satisfaction with various approaches for providing access to digital objects (the interpretive/exhibition approach versus the catalog approach), and evaluating the use of the pilot project Colorado Coal Field Wars site, including teacher use as well as student use.

As part of its mission, the CDP held a Leadership Seminar on Digitization during the fall of 1999. Future plans for the project were discussed, and workshops were held on the standards developed at that point in time. During this phase of the project, workshops are being conducted primarily at the scanning centers that have been established. Thus far, three workshops have been planned. The first is the Introduction to Digitization; the second is the Introduction to Metadata; and the third is the Introduction to Scanning. The Introduction to Digitization workshop is designed to introduce CDP grant participants to the range of issues associated with digitization of primary source materials. The Introduction to Metadata workshop focuses on the creation of metadata for digital objects and introduces participants to the CDP metadata standards and the creation of metadata records using MARC or Dublin Core. Participants in this workshop will also be introduced to the CDP Union Catalog and the record-building capabilities. The Introduction to Scanning workshop will introduce participants to the issues surrounding the scanning of images and objects.

It should be pointed out that the CDP has licensed the OCLC SiteSearch software to build its union catalog for accessing the digital collections in Colorado. The SiteSearch software will allow CDP participants to batch load records into the system and will allow record creation directly. The CDP is working with OCLC on enhancements to the software, as there are currently limitations on the variety of formats handled. It is anticipated that SiteSearch, as implemented by CDP, will enable participants to contribute records in a variety of formats. A loading profile is being developed for the CDP participants. Initially, records may be batch loaded in either MARC format or Dublin Core. The capability to load records in Encoded Archival Description (EAD), as well as records in other formats (e.g., VRA), is being developed. Of course, participants may also create records directly in SiteSearch in either Dublin Core or MARC. For example, records in MARC format and records in Dublin Core are currently stored as separate databases in SiteSearch; however, the user will be able to search across databases without having to know in which database or format a record is stored. The CDP is looking forward to working with OCLC on the development and enhancement of the SiteSearch software.

As this book is devoted to metadata, it seems appropriate to include information about the metadata standards as developed by the CDP. Creators of metadata may include catalogers, curators, archivists, Web site developers, database administrators, authors, editors, volunteers, and librarians. The guidelines developed are intended to promote best practices and consistency in the creation of bibliographic records. This has been done to enhance online search and retrieval accuracy, to improve resource discovery capabilities, and to facilitate and ensure future interoperability. One primary purpose of the CDP is to provide access to unique resources and special collections in digital format. To accomplish this objective, participating institutions must create metadata or cataloging data at a sufficient level to support the needed identification and access. In the past few years, new approaches to the description of digital resources have emerged at the same time that established cataloging standards (e.g., the MARC format and AACR2R) have been applied to digital resources. Participants in the CDP have adopted a variety of approaches to describing digitized resources. Several are using MARC; several have embedded descriptive information in the HTML markup of the digital images; and others are embedding archival finding aids within HTML and linking these citations to the MARC records. Some museums are linking their Web search engines to their databases that were created using commercial database software. Some providing access to government information are using the Visual Resource Association (VRA) Core Description Categories, the RLG Reach Element Set, and Encoded Archival Description.

The Metadata Working Group realized very early on that which standard an institution chooses for the creation of metadata depends on a variety of factors. These factors include the type of materials that is being described and digitized, the purpose of the digitization project (access or preservation), the potential user, the knowledge and expertise of project staff, and the technical infrastructure of the institution. The level of detail for a resource also varies from institution to institution. Information may be proprietary or confidential and may not be distributed or accessible on systems open to public access. Agreement on inclusion of such administrative information is unlikely. As a result, the Metadata Working Group determined that information of this type might better reside on the local site.

As a result, the working group recommended that the CDP create a union catalog of descriptive metadata and cataloging data. Although it is still a developing standard, a recommendation was made to use the Dublin Core as the standard for CDP records. To facilitate the building of the database, the working group developed a minimum set of elements that must be included in a cataloging or metadata record. The core or required elements are a minimum set of elements that must be included in a record and are based on the fifteen Dublin Core elements. The working group recognized that additional elements might be required for particular formats and has accommodated this in its recommendations.

The recommendations of the group for the "core" and "full" record in Dublin Core are as follows:

Mandatory Elements	Optional (Desirable) Elements
Title	Contributor
Creator	Publisher
Subject	Relation
Description	Type
Identifier	Source
Date	Language
Format	Coverage
	Rights

The "mandatory" or "core" elements were designed along the same guidelines as the core records for the Program for Cooperative Cataloging. In addition, the working group recommended that a "qualified" Dublin Core be implemented. This record employs modifiers and schemes for each element as appropriate. For example, a recommendation has been made that subject terms from a recognized thesaurus be used.

Each element of the Dublin Core has been defined. For example, the subject element has a description as follows:

SUBJECT
Label: Subject
MARC Maps: 6XX
Definition: Topic of the digital resources. Typically, subject will be expressed as keywords or phrases that describe the subject content of the resource, or terms related to significant associations of people, places, and events, or other contextual information.
Mandatory: YES
Repeatable: Yes. May enter up to ten subject fields
Scheme: Use established thesaurus: Library of Congress Subject Headings (LCSH), Art and Architecture Thesaurus (AAT), Thesaurus for Graphic Materials (TGM), Medical Subject Headings (MeSH), ICONCLASS, etc.

Input guidelines:

1. Prefer use of most significant or unique words, with more general words used as necessary.
2. Subjects may come from the title or description field or elsewhere in the resource.
3. If the subject is a person or organization, enter as outlined under Creator.

Examples of subject terms/descriptors are also provided. In addition, the working group developed a metadata matrix that provides information on the various formats and fields. This matrix lists by field and format those elements that are mandatory and desirable and includes information on which modifiers and/or schemes may be required or desirable.

The working group realizes that the Dublin Core is a developing standard, and changes to the elements, modifiers, and schemes may occur. The changes will be reflected on the CDP Web site.

NOTE

1. The author wishes to thank Liz Bishoff, CDP Project Director, and the CDP staff for allowing him to use material taken directly from the CDP Web site for this chapter.

19

The Instructional Management System (IMS) Standard: Solutions for Interactive Instructional Software and Dynamic Learning

Brad Eden

The Instructional Management System (IMS) standard was developed by Educom/EDUCAUSE as a result of a common need among educational institutions for nonproprietary, Internet-based strategies for customizing and managing the instructional process and for integrating content from multiple publishers into distributed/virtual learning environments.[1] In November 1994, Educom (now EDUCAUSE) launched a new initiative called the National Learning Infrastructure Initiative (NLII). The association's research focused on these objectives: the development of a substantial body of instructional software, the creation of an online infrastructure for managing access to educational materials and environments, the facilitation of collaborative and authentic educational activities, and the certification of acquired skills and knowledge. The overall objective of the IMS, therefore, can be summarized as "enabling an open architecture for learning."[2]

The formal name of the IMS, as of December 1, 1999, is the IMS Global Learning Consortium, Inc. This consortium is the successor to the IMS/Educom project that was begun in 1994. The entire standard has been called a course management system, a learning server, and even an integrated learning system. IMS is concerned with standards for learning servers, learning content, and even the commercial integration of these capabilities. While the idea for the IMS originated in higher education, it now encompasses corporate and government entities, K–12 interests, and continuing education opportunities. The IMS standard defines technical specifications that developers and creators of educational products and services should incorporate so that they are interoperable. As such, the IMS standard is not a software product but a metadata standard that assists the developers and creators of educational products in the production of interactive, Internet-based "courseware" that is platform independent. Although everything is currently proprietary, the goal of the IMS is to standardize.

THE FIVE IMS SPECIFICATIONS

The three main objectives of the IMS are: to support the inherently collaborative and dynamic nature of learning, to develop standards for locating and operating interactive materials, and to build the structure for developing and sharing content. Five specifications have been developed or are currently under development by the IMS to achieve these objectives:

- The IMS Learning Resources Meta-Data Specification
- The IMS Enterprise Specification
- The IMS Content and Packaging Specification
- The IMS Question and Test Specification
- The IMS Learner Profiles Specification

The IMS Learning Resources Meta-Data Specification was released in August 1999; its purpose is to create a uniform metadata standard for learning resources so that they can be more easily found/discovered, using metadata-aware search tools that reflect the unique needs of users in learning situations.

The IMS Enterprise Specification was released in November 1999; it is aimed at administrative applications and services that need to share data about learners, courses, performance, and so on, across platforms, operating systems, and user interfaces.

The IMS Content and Packaging Specification will be released in two parts. Part 1 was released in February 2000, and part 2 was released in August 2000. This specification makes it easier to create reusable content objects (e.g., educational courseware components) that will be useful in a variety of learning systems.

The IMS Question and Test Specification was released in February 2000 and addresses the need to be able to share test items and other assessment tools across different systems.

Finally, the IMS Learner Profiles Specification was released in 2000, and it will look at ways to organize learner information so that learning systems can be more responsive to the specific needs of each user.

Each of these specifications focuses on a particular provision for delivering and managing effective online materials and learning environments. Some other aspects of the IMS include: procedures for making existing content IMS-enabled; making sure that developmental costs of the standard are free to the public; providing numerous benefits for teachers who use IMS-enabled and IMS-compatible systems; and the fact that the IMS is working with the National Institute of Standards and Technology (NIST) to develop a conformance-testing and certification program. Currently, over two hundred participants are in the IMS Developers Network. These are corporations, universities, publishers, educational software companies, and digital educational libraries under agreement to actively create and implement IMS-compliant materials and environments. Some of the names include IBM, Microsoft, Sun Microsystems, Princeton University Computing and Information Technology, University of California, University of Michigan, Texas A&M University, NetDimensions, the NEEDS project, eCollege, and @learning.

THE IMS AND OTHER METADATA STANDARDS

Groups within NIST, ARIADNE, and the Institute of Electrical and Electronics Engineers (IEEE) have been working together since 1997 with the IMS to develop open, market-based standards for online learning, including specifications for learning content metadata. In 1998, IMS and ARIADNE submitted a joint proposal and specification to IEEE, which forms that basis for the current IEEE Learning Object Metadata (LOM) base document—itself a classification for a pre-draft IEEE Specification. The IEEE LOM Base Document defines a set of metadata elements that can be used to describe learning resources.[3] This includes the element names, data types, field lengths, and definitions. The specification also defines a conceptual structure for the metadata, as well as conformance statements for how metadata documents must be organized and how applications must behave in order to be considered IEEE conforming. The IMS community recommended that a select Core of elements must be identified from this document in order to simplify initial implementation efforts. The IMS developed a representation of the metadata in XML (eXtensible Markup Language) and surveyed its member institutions around the world to identify the Core elements. The IMS Meta-Data Best Practice and Implementation Guide (MBPIG) is the result of this survey.[4] It provides access to four documents that assist in the implementation of the IMS standard. These documents are:

- The IEEE Learning Object Meta-Data Base Document
- The IMS Learning Resource Meta-Data XML Binding Specification
- The IMS Core and Standard Extension Library
- The IMS Taxonomy and Vocabulary Lists

The IMS MBPIG identifies a minimum set of IEEE metadata elements called the IMS Core. The remaining IEEE metadata elements form the IMS Standard Extension Library (SEL). Choosing this smaller set of elements will foster a base level of metadata interoperability and will enable easier implementation of basic metadata capabilities into software vendors' existing products. The IMS MBPIG also provides general guidance about how an application may use the Core and Extended metadata elements, as well as a sample XML representation and document type definition (DTD) of a conforming metadata record to assist developers with their metadata implementations. The nineteen IMS Core metadata elements and the sixty-seven SEL elements are given in table 19.1.

The following four requirements must be met in a metadata instance to conform to LOM:

1. The metadata instance must contain one or more LOM element(s).
2. All LOM elements in the metadata instance are used to describe characteristics as defined by the LOM specification.
3. Values for LOM elements in the metadata instance are structured as defined by the LOM specification, and this structural information is carried within the instance.
4. If the instance contains extensions to the LOM structure, then extension elements do not replace elements in the LOM structure.

Table 19.1 IMS core and SEL metadata elements.

Number	Element Name				IMS _Core_ or SEL
1	**General**				
1.1	Identifier: Reserved				
1.2	Title				
		LangString			
			Language		SEL
			String		Core
1.3	Catalog Entry				
1.3.1		Catalogue			Core
1.3.2		Entry			Core
1.4		Language			Core
1.5	Description				
		LangString			
			Language		SEL
			String		Core
1.6	Keywords				
		LangString			
			Language		SEL
			String		SEL
1.7	Coverage				
		LangString			
			Language		SEL
			String		SEL
1.8	Structure				SEL
1.9	AggregationLevel				SEL
2	**Life Cycle**				
2.1	Version				
		LangString			
			Language		SEL
			String		Core
2.2	Status				SEL
2.3	Contribute				
2.3.1		Role			Core
		Entity			Core
		Date			
			DateTime		Core
			Description		
				LangString	
				Language	SEL
				String	SEL
3	**MetaMetaData**				
3.1	Identifier: Reserved				
3.1	CatalogEntry				
3.2.1		Catalogue			SEL
3.2.2		Entry			SEL
3.2	Contribute				
3.3.1		Role			SEL
3.3.2		Entity			SEL
3.3.3		Date			
			DateTime		SEL
			Description		
				LangString	
				Language	SEL
				String	SEL
3.4	MetadataScheme				Core
3.5	Language				Core

Table 19.1   IMS core and SEL metadata elements. *(continued)*

Number	Element Name			IMS _Core_ or SEL
4	**Technical**			
4.1	Format			_Core_
4.2	Size			SEL
4.3	Location			_Core_
4.4	Requirements			
4.4.1	Type			
		LangString		
			Language	SEL
			String	SEL
4.4.2	Name			
		LangString		
			Language	SEL
			String	SEL
4.4.3	MinimumVersion			SEL
4.4.4	MaximumVersion			SEL
4.5	InstallationRemarks			
	LangString			
		Language		SEL
		String		SEL
4.6	OtherPlatformRequirements			
	LangString			
		Language		SEL
		String		SEL
4.7	Duration			
	DateTime			
	Description			
		LangString		
			Language	SEL
			String	SEL
5	**Educational**			
5.1	InteractivityType			SEL
5.2	LearningResourceType			
		LangString		
			Language	SEL
			String	SEL
5.3	InteractivityLevel			SEL
5.4	SemanticDensity			SEL
5.5	IntendedEndUserRole			SEL
5.6	LearningContent			
		LangString		
			Language	SEL
			String	SEL
5.7	TypicalAgeRange			
		LangString		
			Language	SEL
			String	SEL
5.8	Difficulty			SEL
5.9	TypicalLearningTime			
		DateTime		SEL
		Description		
			LangString	
			Language	SEL
			String	SEL
5.10	Description			SEL
		LangString		
			Language	SEL
			String	SEL
5.11	Language			SEL

Table 19.1　IMS core and SEL metadata elements. *(continued)*

Number	Element Name			IMS <u>Core</u> or SEL
6	**Rights**			
6.1	<u>Cost</u>			<u>Core</u>
6.2	<u>CopyrightandOtherRestrictions</u>			<u>Core</u>
6.3	<u>Description</u>			
		<u>LangString</u>		
			Language	SEL
			<u>String</u>	<u>Core</u>
7	**Relation**			
7.1	Kind			
		LangString		
			Language	SEL
			String	SEL
7.2	Resource			
7.2.1	Identifier: Reserved			
7.2.2	Description			
		LangString		
			Language	SEL
			String	SEL
8	**Annotation**			
8.1	Person			SEL
8.2	Date			
		DateTime		SEL
		Description		
			LangString	
			Language	SEL
			String	SEL
8.3	Description			
		LangString		
			Language	SEL
			String	SEL
9	**Classification**			
9.1	<u>Purpose</u>			
		<u>LangString</u>		
			Language	SEL
			<u>String</u>	<u>Core</u>
9.1	TaxonPath			
9.2.1	Source			SEL
9.2.2	Taxon			
9.2.2.1			ID	SEL
9.2.2.2			Entry	SEL
9.3	<u>Description</u>			
		<u>LangString</u>		
			Language	SEL
			<u>String</u>	<u>Core</u>
9.4	<u>Keywords</u>			
		<u>LangString</u>		
			Language	SEL
			<u>String</u>	<u>Core</u>

A metadata application conforms to LOM if it satisfies the following two requirements:

1. A LOM-conforming application must be able to process at least one LOM element.
2. If an application receives a conforming LOM metadata instance, stores it, and then transmits it, then the application preserves the original metadata instance during transmission.

The IEEE LOM specification has been mapped to the Dublin Core Metadata Element set, but an established crosswalk has yet to be compiled. Figure 19.1 illustrates the basic components of this mapping.

AN EXAMPLE IMS CASE SCENARIO

A practical application of the use of the IMS standard can be constructed. A medical instructor needs to create a computer courseware module to provide access to a tutorial and quiz for a class in pediatrics. Use of IMS-compliant software will enable the construction of the source code and vocabulary needed to provide platform-independent access via the Internet worldwide. For instance, description of the resource may incorporate Dublin Core elements in the areas of Creator, Title, and Description, while the Subject element would provide access to the MeSH thesaurus. In addition, the IMS metadata vocabulary would define the Learning Level, Educational Objectives, Pedagogy, and Prerequisites elements. IMS-based products would then allow the delivery system to manage various vocabularies and metadata content. For the instructor, all of this underlying metadata would be invisible and transparent. The practical consequence of all this would be that searching and browsing across IMS-content collections would result in higher recall and precision, and content creators would spend less time trying to find supporting materials for their own courseware development.

A CURRENT IMS SUPPORTER/DEVELOPER: NEEDS

One project that has been involved early on in the development and delivery of computer courseware elements in higher education has been the National Engineering Education Delivery System (NEEDS). This National Science Foundation grant project, originally begun in 1992, was part of the Synthesis Coalition, a group of eight universities across the country, whose purpose was to reform and renew undergraduate engineering education.[5] The NEEDS database involved the construction of computer courseware modules in undergraduate engineering that would challenge engineering students to work collectively and collaboratively to solve problems and design simple engineering structures. These courseware modules would be cataloged into a database, which would then be available to anyone worldwide for use in instruction and education.

I was lucky enough to work as the NEEDS cataloger during 1995–1996. It was an innovative project not only in its direction and content, but also in its allowing me to work as a remote cataloger on the project from my home in Houston, Texas. The ability to catalog computer courseware modules from anywhere in the world enabled me to experience the remote work environment, while still being able to participate in meetings at host university sites such as the University of California at Berkeley, Iowa State University, Cornell University, and California Polytechnic State University at San Luis Obispo.[6] It was a wonderful example of the future collaborations possible between information management and technology initiatives.

NEEDS has recently joined both the National Digital Library initiative and the IMS Developers community. The NEEDS database contains educational courseware modules that are ideal for integration into the IMS standard. Many projects similar to NEEDS are currently under development, and the IMS standard will assist in the cross-integration, delivery, and access required for users to acquire this material without special software or hardware requirements.

CONCLUSION

The Instructional Management System metadata standard originally developed in the higher education community to assist in the construction, description, and delivery of and access to computer courseware applications. In its most recent newsletter, IMS announced that it is seeking incorporation in the state of Delaware and that its mission is "Defining the Internet Architecture for Learning."[7] IMS developers continue to discuss, release drafts, and revise implementations of the five specifications that are the core of the project. Support for the Learning Resource Interchange, the first commercial implementation of the IMS Content and Management Systems specification, has recently been announced by Microsoft Corporation and others in the IMS Developers Network. Educators, instructors, and teachers will be actively incorporating IMS-compliant technology in the development of interactive courseware modules in any number of educational fields and practices in the near future. For most of us, that may mean becoming an implementer of the IMS, actively using the IMS standard as a creator of instructional courseware, or even searching IMS-compatible software as a user. It would appear that the IMS metadata standard is well on its way to providing platform-independent

Dublin Core #	Dublin Core Name	Dublin Core Label	IEEE Learning Object Meta-data
1	Title	TITLE	General.Title

The name given to the resource by the CREATOR or PUBLISHER

| 2 | Author or Creator | CREATOR | LifeCycle.Contribute when LifeCycle.Contribute.Role has a value of "Author". |

The person or organization primarily responsible for creating the intellectual content of the resource. For example, authors in the case of written documents, artists, photographers, or illustrators in the case of visual resources.

| 3 | Subject and Keywords | SUBJECT | General.Keywords. For those wishing more specificity of Subject, a category of Classification can be used with a Purpose of "Subject". Classification has elements for Description, Keywords, and Taxonpath(s) that are specific for the Purpose. |

The topic of the resource. Typically, subject will be expressed as keywords or phrases that describe the subject or content of the resource. The use of controlled vocabularies and formal classification schemas is encouraged.

| 4 | Description | DESCRIPTION | General.Description |

A textual description of the content of the resource, including abstracts in the case of document-like objects or content descriptions in the case of visual resources.

| 5 | Publisher | PUBLISHER | LifeCycle.Contribute when LifeCycle.Contribute.Role has a value of "Publisher". |

The entity primarily responsible for making the resource available in its present form, such as a publishing house, a university department, or a corporate entity.

| 6 | Other Contributor | CONTRIBUTOR | LifeCycle.Contribute with the type of contribution specified in LifeCycle.Contribute.Role. LifeCycle.Contribute can be repeated. |

A person or organization not specified in a CREATOR element who has made significant intellectual contributions to the resource but whose contribution is secondary to any person or organization specified in a CREATOR element (for example, editor, transcriber, and illustrator).

| 7 | Date | DATE | LifeCycle.Contribute.Date when LifeCycle.Contribute.Role has a value of "Publisher". |

The date the resource was made available in its present form. Recommended best practice is an eight digit number in the form YYYY-MM-DD as defined in http://www.w3.org/TR/NOTE-datetime, a profile of ISO 8601. In this scheme, the date element 1999-09-26 corresponds to September 26, 1999. Many other schema are possible, but if used, they should be identified in an unambiguous manner.

| 8 | Resource Type | TYPE | Educational.LearningResourceType |

The category of the resource, such as home page, novel, poem, technical report, dictionary, etc. For the sake of interoperability, TYPE should be selected from an enumerated list that is under development in the workshop series at the time of publication of this document. See http://sunsite.berkeley.edu/Metadata/types.html for current thinking on the application of this element.

| 9 | Format | FORMAT | Technical.Format |

The data format of the resource, used to identify the software and possibly hardware that might be needed to display or operate the resource. For the sake of interoperability, FORMAT should be selected from an enumerated list that is under development in the workshop series at the time of publication of this document.

| 10 | Resource Identifier | IDENTIFIER | General.CatalogEntry. General.Identifier is currently a RESERVED term, as there is no specified method for creation of a GUID. |

String or number used to uniquely identify the resource. Examples for networked resources include URLs and URNs (when implemented). Other globally-unique identifiers, such as International Standard Book Numbers (ISBN) or other formal names would also be candidates for this element in the case of off-line resources.

| 11 | Source | SOURCE | Relation.Resource when the value of Relation.Kind is "IsBasedOn". This reduction is currently under consideration within the Dublin Core community. |

A string or number used to uniquely identify the work from which this resource was derived, if applicable. For example, a PDF version of a novel might have a SOURCE element containing an ISBN number for the physical book from which the PDF version was derived.

| 12 | Language | LANGUAGE | General.Language |

Language(s) of the intellectual content of the resource. Where practical, the content of this field should coincide with RFC 1766. See http://ds.internic.net/rfc/rfc1766.txt

| 13 | Relation | RELATION | Relation.Kind, Relation.Resource |

The relationship of this resource to other resources. The intent of this element is to provide a means to express relationships among resources that have formal relationships to others, but exist as discrete resources themselves. For examples, images in a document, chapters in a book, or items in a collection. Formal specification of RELATION is currently under development. Users and developers should understand that use of this element is currently considered to be experimental.

| 14 | Coverage | COVERAGE | General.Coverage |

The spatial and/or temporal characteristics of the resource. Formal specification of COVERAGE is currently under development. Users and developers should understand that use of this element is currently considered to be experimental

| 15 | Rights Management | RIGHTS | Rights.Description |

A link to a copyright notice, to a rights-management statement, or to a service that would provide information about terms of access to the resource. Formal specification of RIGHTS is currently under development. Users and developers should understand that use of this element is currently considered to be experimental.

Figure 19.1   IEEE LOM/Dublin Core crosswalk.

educational resources to educators and students alike, and its financial and industry support worldwide would indicate that its implementation and success are highly probable in the near future.

NOTES

1. The current homepage of the IMS project is http://www.imsproject.org.

2. Andrew Sithers, "An Introduction to the Instructional Management Systems (IMS) Project." *Active Learning* 8 (July 1998).

3. IEEE Learning Technology Standards Committee, *LOM: Base Scheme - v3.5 (1999-07-15),* http://ltsc.ieee.org/doc/wg12/scheme.html.

4. The IMS Learning Resources Meta-Data Best Practices and Implementation Guide is located at http://www.imsproject.org/metadata/mdbest01.html.

5. The current homepage of the NEEDS project is http://www.needs.org.

6. An article on my experiences as a remote cataloger of computer courseware materials on the NEEDS project will be published in a future issue of *The Journal of Internet Cataloging.*

7. *Inside IMS,* 5 (January 10, 2000) and 6 (February 28, 2000), http://www.imsproject.org/insideIMS/index1.html.

20

A Picture Is Worth a Thousand Words:
Metadata for Art Objects and Their Visual Surrogates

Murtha Baca

INTRODUCTION

In contrast to the library world, where the MARC (Machine-Readable Cataloging) format has held sway for some three decades,[1] the museum world does not have a long-standing tradition of data standards, much less a tradition of formal cataloging. As information networks began to proliferate during the late 1980s, the art information community recognized the growing need for some kind of metadata standard for describing art objects and their visual surrogates. The Art Information Task Force (AITF), an initiative jointly sponsored by the College Art Association of America and the Getty Trust, was formed to address this need. The AITF was modeled after the National Information Systems Task Force (NISTF), which had been convened by the Society of American Archivists in the early 1980s to reach consensus on the data elements for the management of archives, records, and manuscripts.[2]

The AITF—consisting of art historians, museum registrars, technical specialists, visual resources curators, and other art information professionals—met and debated for several years about the data categories necessary for describing (and, just as important, retrieving information about) works of art and material culture. The result, released in 1995, was *Categories for the Description of Works of Art* (CDWA).[3]

CATEGORIES FOR THE DESCRIPTION OF WORKS OF ART
AND OTHER METADATA SCHEMAS FOR ART AND MATERIAL

Unlike MARC, which can be seen as a kind of technical "container"-cum-metadata standard—that is, a specific set of fields and subfields designed to contain specific types of data values, with specific rules for its application—*Categories for the Description of Works of Art* is a document that provides broad guidelines for the formulation of art information systems. The 225-plus categories and subcategories do not necessarily correspond to database fields, although database fields and/or a data dictionary could be—and indeed have been—formulated based on them. Another key difference between MARC and CDWA is in their scope or breadth. MARC contains a limited number of fields and subfields; CDWA is made up of hundreds of categories and subcategories and can be expanded or "contracted" to meet the needs of whoever is using it. Because the aim of CDWA is to be as inclusive as possible, it could never be implemented in its entirety—nor should it be. Rather, the subset of the CDWA data elements that are most relevant to the materials in hand, most useful to the target users, and most realistically implementable should be carefully identified before beginning any implementation of these data categories. The CDWA document provides the intellectual guidelines for descriptions of works of art, regardless of the technical environment (or even old-fashioned paper medium, for that matter) in which that information might reside. It can be used to map diverse art information systems or to create new ones from scratch. For example, CDWA formed the basis of a system for all of the state museums of Chile, called SUR (TM), developed by the Centro de Documentación de Bienes Patrimoniales in Santiago. In this implementation, some of the CDWA categories were collapsed together, and others were further atomized, to meet the specific needs of the Chilean museum documentation specialists and the materials in their collections.[4]

At the highest level, CDWA has eight categories that are designated as "core."[5] Table 20.1 presents these core categories, with examples of the kinds of data values that could populate them. The examples are based on three paintings of the same subject that have all been attributed to the fifteenth-century Flemish artist Rogier van der Weyden.

Table 20.1   Categories for the description of works of art: core categories, corresponding subcategories, and sample data values.

Category	Sample Data Values
Object/Work—Term	➤panel painting ➤painting
Classification—Term	➤European paintings ➤Netherlandish paintings ➤paintings
Titles or Names—Text	➤St. Luke Painting the Virgin ➤St. Luke Drawing the Virgin and Child ➤St. Luke Drawing a Portrait of the Madonna and Child ➤Sv. Luka, risujutsij Madonna ➤Lukasmadonna
Creation	➤Creator: Weyden, Rogier van der (Flemish painter and draftsman, ca. 1399–1465) ➤Creation date: ca. 1435
Measurements	➤137.1 × 10.8 cm. ➤185 × 125 ➤138 × 111cm.
Materials	➤oil and tempera on panel ➤oil on canvas transferred from wood
Subject Matter	➤*Description*: man; drawing; woman; mother; infant; child; interior ➤*Identification*: St. Luke; portrait of the Virgin; Madonna and Child ➤*Interpretation*:portraiture; first portrait; self-portrait of the artist; power of the artist; creativity
Current Location	➤Museum of Fine Arts, Boston (MA, USA) ➤Hermitage Museum, St. Petersburg (Russia) ➤Alte Pinakothek, Munich (Germany)

Of the CDWA core categories, Measurements and Current Location would correspond to nonrepeatable fields for each individual art object being described, and indeed, these data categories make it possible to distinguish the three similar paintings one from the other. To the dismay of many programmers and analysts who encounter art information for the first time, a work of art may be attributed to more than one artist, may be attributed to different artists at different points in time, may be associated with multiple dates, or may have many different titles assigned to it. Art-historical data can be notoriously "fuzzy," when it's not outright contradictory, and CDWA was designed to accommodate this.

After the publication of CDWA in 1995, a burgeoning of metadata schemas occurred for art objects and cultural materials, each with its own scope and weltanschauung. I will mention some but not all of these metadata schemas here:

- *Object ID* codifies the minimum set of data elements (ten in all) needed to identify an object as "cultural property" and to help protect or recuperate it from theft and illicit traffic. This metadata schema consists of a simple checklist of ten categories (Object Type, Materials and Techniques, Measurements, Inscriptions and Markings, Distinguishing Features, Title, Subject, Date or Period, Maker, and Descriptive Note, which turn out to be a subset of CDWA), and a requirement for visual documentation. Its target users include law enforcement personnel, fine arts insurers and appraisers, and customs agents—mostly "nonexperts" in documentation. Whereas the context—historical/cultural, architectural, archaeological—in which a work of art or material culture was created is of great interest to the research audience for which the CDWA was designed (though not essential for their unique identification), it is of absolutely no interest to the target users of Object ID, whose goal is to document, protect, and eventually recover works of art or antiques as cultural property. Object ID has been adopted as a standard by UNESCO, the FBI, and Interpol, among many other organizations.[6]
- The *Consortium for the Interchange of Museum Information (CIMI) Profile*, derived from the *CIDOC Data Model*[7] and CDWA, defines data elements for "deep" museum information in a fairly sophisticated technical environment.[8]

- The Foundation for Documents of Architecture's *Guide to the Description of Architectural Drawings* focuses on architectural documents (drawings, blueprints, plans, etc.) but includes categories to describe the architectural works themselves. It maps closely to CDWA, with less specificity in some areas and more specificity in others.[9]
- The *VRA Core Categories,* which took the CDWA as their point of departure, provide data elements for both the work of art or architecture and its visual surrogate (CDWA also accommodates information about the visual surrogate, in the category Related Visual Documentation). This metadata schema, developed by the Data Standards Committee of the Visual Resources Association, is designed for use by those who must describe, manage, and provide quick access to information on the original art object or work of architecture and on its visual surrogate, be it a photograph, slide, or digital image. The VRA Core 2.0, which consists of two sets of data categories (one to describe the Work and one to describe and manage the Visual Document), was recently conflated into VRA Core 3.0, which is a single set of categories mapped to the Dublin Core metadata elements.[10]

Is this proliferation of metadata schemas for art information a problem? Not necessarily. Even a cursory analysis of the data categories that these schemas include will reveal that they are basically all different slices or views of the same categories of information, depending upon the materials being described, who the intended end-users are, and the goals or mission of the communities that developed them. An analysis of the fields in the leading collection management systems for art museums, or even the AMICO (Art Museum Image Consortium) data dictionary, which is based on CDWA, reveals that we are talking about the same data elements again and again.[11] As long as any given metadata schema is applied consistently, it is a relatively easy task to map it to another schema that may be broader in focus (e.g., CDWA versus Object ID), more specific in focus (e.g., the *Guide to the Description of Architectural Drawings* versus CDWA), or from a different "point of view" (e.g., the AMICO data dictionary versus the VRA Core Categories). Also, the metadata categories that are considered "core" or essential from one perspective might be irrelevant from another. For example, the category "Current Location" is considered core in CDWA, which aims to uniquely identify a known work of art and to distinguish it from other, possibly very similar works. Knowing the current location of works of art helps a user to distinguish the painting *St. Luke Drawing the Virgin and Child* in the Museum of Fine Arts, Boston, from the painting of the same subject by the same artist in the Hermitage in St. Petersburg or the one in the Alte Pinakothek in Munich. For a customs agent or Interpol officer using Object ID to identify a work of art that might have been stolen or illegally taken out of a country, the physical appearance of the object is much more important than the analytical, conceptual, and contextual elements that are included in CDWA. To a visual resources curator, the category "Visual Document Source" from the VRA Core is crucial, for academic as well as legal purposes; hence it is not an optional category, as it is in CDWA.

In any case, as long as metadata schemas are applied carefully and data values are entered into them consistently, it is a fairly straightforward task to map them to one another, particularly if they deal with similar types of information (in this case, descriptive information about works of art, architecture, or material culture). This type of data mapping becomes forced when one attempts to map data for heterogeneous types of materials. In this author's opinion, this is one of the crucial flaws of the Dublin Core, or rather of the many attempts that have been seen recently to fit the most diverse types of objects and resources into this still-evolving metadata schema: there is no such thing as "one-stop metadata" for all types of objects and resources. This is precisely why the library and archival communities spent long years developing metadata schemas for the specific types of materials with which they work. I believe that Dublin Core is best implemented as a metadata schema for Web resource discovery, rather than as a universal set of metadata categories to be applied to everything from books to sound recordings to museum objects to museums themselves.

Table 20.2 maps the CDWA core categories to the VRA Core Categories 3.0.[12]

As we can see from the mapping, the VRA Core Categories, which focus on the work of art or architecture and its visual surrogates, do not include the creator's life dates; this makes sense for the purpose for which this particular metadata schema was created. While CDWA, which analyzes the work of art in greater detail, breaks up Subject Matter into three distinct levels—Description, Identification, and Interpretation[13]—VRA limits itself to a single category for this information. Whereas Materials and Techniques are accommodated within a single large category in CDWA, they are broken out into two distinct categories in VRA, and so on.

More problematic is VRA's decision not to include the broad category that is called "Classification" in CDWA; many implementers have found this to be a sometimes "unscientific" yet extremely useful category for grouping materials according to big classifications that often reflect the collections themselves (as in a specific museum) or the particular user group that a collection of materials is intended to serve (e.g., in a university image repository, "textbook" designations such as *Greek, Roman, Byzantine,* or even something as vague as *Ancient,* may be quite useful for students or professors who wish to easily locate images of certain types of art and architecture).[14]

Table 20.2   Mapping of CDWA core categories and VRA Core 3.0.

CDWA Core Categories	VRA Core Categories
Object/Work— Type	Work Type
Classification—Term	
Titles or Names—Text	Title
Measurements	Measurements
Materials and Technique—Materials	Materials
Creation— Creator—Names	Creator
Creation—Creator—Dates	
Creation—Creator—Role	Creator Role
Creation—Date	Date
Subject Matter—Description	Subject
Subject Matter—Identification	Subject
Subject Matter—Interpretation	Subject
Current Location—Repository Name	Location Current Repository or Location Current Site
Current Location—Geographic Location	Location Current Repository or Location Current Site
Current Location—Repository Numbers	ID Number

THE QUEST FOR IMAGES ON THE WEB: A RENAISSANCE FOR SUBJECT-BASED INDEXING?

As we have seen, metadata schemas for art objects have existed since at least the early 1990s; controlled vocabularies that can provide the data values for populating those schemas have been in existence for even longer (the *Art & Architecture Thesaurus,* for example, began in the early 1980s, and the ICONCLASS system began being made available in book form as early as 1973). But only with the advent—and more recently, the explosion—of the World Wide Web has the art museum community become acutely aware of the pressing need for implementation of these schemas and vocabularies: to put it quite simply, nothing really works on the Web without them. Thus in the last few years, art museums large and small, under pressure from their administrators to make their "content" available to as broad a public as possible, in kiosk systems as well as on the Web, have scrambled to get appropriate collection management systems in place and—a much more difficult task—to get properly organized and indexed information input into those systems. Most of us are familiar with the abysmal searching functionalities currently available on the Web; as I am all too fond of saying, "The Web is *not* a library." Searching for images is perhaps even more problematic than searching for text-based resources, as users must rely on how well the images are indexed with words if they can hope to retrieve them. (To date, I have not seen any convincing demonstration of machine recognition of visual patterns as a tool for art-historical research; even if machine "image recognition" worked better than it currently does, its utility as an art-historical research tool would still be highly debatable.)

Anyone familiar with art information knows that often the subject matter or theme of a work of art is not reflected at all in its title. Hence if I want to quickly find images of "family life in the nineteenth century," which could have an infinite variety of titles, I can only find them if the descriptive terms *family life* and *nineteenth century* have been applied to them by a human being who has looked at an image; interpreted the title, the visual information, and other available data; and made the decision to apply these data values to it. If a user wants to retrieve images of domestic utensils from pre-Columbian Mexico, the data values "pre-Columbian," "household utensils," and "Mexico" must have been associated with that image in order for it to be retrieved by such a search. Obviously, we have little or nothing on the Web like this today. Although some art museum Web sites offer fielded searching, and some offer picklists to help searchers avoid retrieving zero results, museums and image repositories (including, glaringly, AMICO) are far from offering accurate end-user searching of art objects on the Web. In other words, the museum world is discovering what the library world has known for a century: *Cataloging counts!*

VOCABULARIES AND CLASSIFICATION SYSTEMS PLAY A KEY

We're all familiar with the expression "A picture is worth a thousand words." In the world of online searching for images of art works, it is precisely *words* that users enter to try to find images, and *words* that indexers use to create access points for finding images. But as Marcia Bates has shown, there is almost always an "expertise gap" between users and indexers. Hence, "ideally, the challenge for the indexer is to try to anticipate what terms people with information gaps of various descriptions might search for."[15] Bates convincingly argues that a combination of human indexing, vocabulary tools, and information system design could greatly improve the online searcher's results. We still have a long way to go in this area.

Let's say that a user actually had access to an online resource with the kind of searching by data categories described in the previous section. What if he or she entered "pre-Conquest," "domestic objects," and "Mexican" instead of the data values specified at the end of the last section? He or she would retrieve no results, if the image had been indexed with the values "pre-Columbian," "household utensils," and "Mexico"—that is, unless a controlled vocabulary had been applied at the time of indexing (adding the variant forms of terms and names) or was interposed as "middleware" between the user and the resource being searched. Say a high school student were writing a report on ancient Egypt and wanted to find images of the little statues that the wealthy Egyptians put in their tombs as servants to wait on them in the afterlife. If the student searches on "Egyptian" and/or "images" or "statues," he is likely to retrieve either no results or thousands of inappropriate ones, depending upon the resource or resources he is searching. But if he can first query a "knowledge base" like the AAT,[16] he can simply search on "sculpture" and navigate down the hierarchy to "funerary sculpture," under which he will find *ushabti,* with the descriptive note "Egyptian figures of stone, wood, or clay that were placed in tombs for the purpose of serving the deceased in the afterlife." Or, if the application allowed him to search not only the terms in the thesaurus but also the descriptive notes, he could search on "Egyptian AND tombs" or "figures AND afterlife" or some other Boolean combination, retrieve a list of matching concepts, read the descriptive notes, and find the appropriate term. The vocabulary also provides the user with alternate spellings and singular and plural forms of this transliterated Egyptian word: *shabti, shawabti, shawtaby, shawtabys, ushabtis, ushabtiu, ushabty, ushabtys.* Or say a user remembered seeing a fantastic painting in the Kunsthistorisches Museum in Vienna of the god Jupiter in the form of a cloud enveloping a naked woman and wanted to do further research on this specific iconographic theme, about which he remembers only one thing.[17] A simple keyword search on "Jupiter" in the ICONCLASS system retrieves a list of entries that includes "love affairs of Jupiter," under which is the entry "Jupiter, shrouded in a cloud, woos Io, daughter of Inachus."[18] The same search could have begun with the Greek form of the name, "Zeus," from which the ICONCLASS keyword index provides a cross-reference to "Jupiter." Or an Italian visitor to the Getty Museum Web site enters a search for the artist he or she knows as "Gherardo delle Notti." Because the *Union List of Artist Names*[19] record "knows" that this was the Italian nickname (meaning "Gerard of the Nights," because this artist had a predilection for dramatically lit nocturnal scenes) for a Dutch follower of Caravaggio active in Italy in the seventeenth century (and the name stuck to the degree that virtually all scholarly literature in Italian on this artist refers to him as Gherardo delle Notti), the user retrieves the two objects in the museum whose wall labels identify the artist as *Gerrit van Honthorst.* Or a Spanish-speaking user wants to retrieve records in an information system relating to works of art created in Florence, Italy: he can enter *Florencia,* which is more intuitive for him, because behind the scenes a tool like the *Thesaurus of Geographic Names* (TGN) has been used to include the forms *Firenze, Florence, Florencia, Florenz, Fiorenza,* and *Florentia* clustered together in a single subject record.[20] Vocabulary tools like the AAT, TGN, and ULAN, and classification schemes like ICONCLASS, can be exploited either behind the scenes or presented directly to users to help them find material that they might otherwise miss. Of course, the user interface issues involved in implementing vocabulary tools to enhance searching are numerous and extremely thorny; I suspect that it will take years to find a satisfactory way of presenting thesauri and other vocabulary tools to nonexpert users in a way that they can easily understand and utilize without the assistance of an "intermediary."

MUSEUM METADATA ON THE WEB

I will repeat my assertion that the Web is not a library—far from it. However, there are some "cataloging standards," albeit quite primitive ones, for Web resources. (It would seem that Dublin Core might ultimately become the cataloging metadata for Web resources, but it remains to be seen if, and how, it will be broadly implemented by Web-resource creators, and if and how it will be utilized by Web search engines.) The metadata elements that are currently recognized and utilized by many Web search engines are META tags—"Keywords" and "Description" to be specific.[21] These, in combination with the "Title" HTML tag, can help make Web searching more accurate and search results lists on search

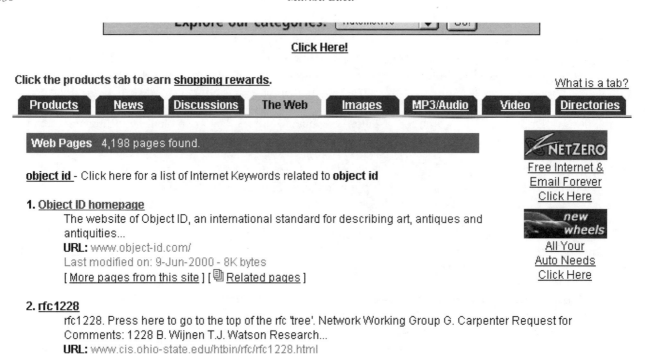

Figure 20.1   AltaVista search results for "art theft."

engines more comprehensible and useful. A well-tagged Web site can "lead" users to its home page by a careful use of the Keyword META tag. For example, if a searcher enters the keywords "art theft" in a Web search engine, he will retrieve the Object ID home page, even though those words do not appear on that particular page. Why? Because an intelligent tagger included this expression in the Keyword tag. In addition, because the page is properly tagged, figure 20.1 is how the Object ID site appears on a Web search results list (in this case, AltaVista), instead of the usual gibberish that one so frequently sees on Web search results lists.

In addition, since the person who created the Web page gave it a good Title HTML tag, when a user bookmarks this site, the bookmark will read "Object ID homepage," so that the bookmark will actually be useful in the future. (The many "Untitled documents" that we've all seen on search results simply mean that whoever created the particular Web page didn't bother to include an HTML Title tag.)

At the time of this writing (May 1, 2000), I examined the page source coding of the home pages of several major art museums; I will discuss only five here. The Metropolitan Museum of Art in New York, the Museum of Fine Arts, Boston, and the Los Angeles County Museum of Art (LACMA) all have no Description or Keyword META tags. Since there is no text on the LACMA home page itself, this results in a lacuna or ellipsis where the description or summary would normally appear on a Web search results list (see figure 20.2).

The home page of the National Gallery of Art in Washington, D.C., has Title and Description tags, but only one keyword expression in its Keyword tag: "art museum." Also, the Title tag is simply "National Gallery of Art," rather than "National Gallery of Art, Washington" to distinguish it from the National Gallery of Art in London. The London National Gallery has "Welcome to the National Gallery, London" as its Title tag, but since it has no Description META tag, search engines will display the only text that appears on the page, which produces the display shown in figure 20.3.

1. LACMA-Los Angeles County Museum of Art

...

URL: www.lacma.org/

Last Modified on: 1-Feb-2000-1K bytes-inEnglish

Figure 20.2   AltaVista search results for "LACMA."

1. Welcome to The National Gallery, London
Admission Free...
URL: www.nationalgallery.org.uk/
Last modifird on: 1-Apr-1999-7K bytes-in English
Figure 20.3 Display for The National Gallery, URL www.nationalgallery.org.uk.

Although the National Gallery in London home page doesn't have a Description META tag, it does have a Keyword tag, which appears to be machine-generated and includes keyword expressions like "unknown artist," "special events," and "North Galleries." It's difficult to imagine what users these keyword expressions might assist and what searches they might enhance. The Keyword tag also contains the titles of many or most of the major works in the museum and the names of many or most of the artists. While in principle this isn't a bad idea, we know that Keyword tags should contain no more than one thousand characters, including spaces, or they will be ignored by search engines, so this tag seems to be a wasted effort.

Thus we can see that far from offering accurate fielded end-user searching as is featured in online library catalogs, many art museum Web sites don't even have rudimentary metadata on their own home pages or have included metadata that is of little or no practical use to end-users.

THE ROAD AHEAD

The art museum and visual resources communities have finally begun to realize what the library and archival communities have known for many years: without metadata schemas and vocabulary and classification tools, creating accurate end-user access to information resources can be a difficult, if not insurmountable, task. They are also learning another lesson: that the implementation of such schemas and tools requires knowledge and especially training, to be truly effective. As more and more art museums seek to provide online access to their collections, and as image repositories like AMICO or the Academic Image Cooperative[22] continue to proliferate, metadata schemas and domain-specific vocabularies and classification systems will become increasingly important tools for managing, exchanging, and delivering images of art and architecture and related information.

NOTES

1. MARC was adopted as a national standard (ANSI Standard Z39.2) in 1971 and as an international standard (ISO Standard 2709) in 1973. See Lois Mai Chan, *Cataloging and Classification: An Introduction,* 2nd ed. (New York: McGraw-Hill, 1994), 404.

2. The resulting Data Elements Dictionary was used as the basis for development of the USMARC Format for Archives and Manuscript Control. See Richard H. Lytle, "An Analysis of the Work of the National Information Systems Task Force," *American Archivist* 7 (fall 1984): 357–365.

3. This document, which "lives" on the World Wide Web and was recently revised and updated, can be found at http://www.getty.edu/gri/standard/cdwa/. A special double issue of *Visual Resources: An International Journal of Documentation* 11, nos. 3–4 (1996), was devoted to the CDWA.

4. See Lina Nagel, "Using Standards in the Documentation of Museum Collections: Categories for the Description of Works of Art, Object ID, and Other Standardization Tools," *Spectra* 26, no. 1 (spring 1999): 36–39.

5. For reasons of clarity, I have simplified the presentation of the CDWA categories here. For the full structure, see the CDWA Web site indicated in the previous note 3.

6. Object ID is administered by the Council for the Prevention of Art Theft (CoPAT) in the UK. For more information, see http://www.object-id.com/.

7. CIDOC is the documentation committee of the International Council of Museums (ICOM). See http://www.cidoc.icom.org/guide/guideint.htm#int.

8. See http://www.cimi.org/downloads/ProfileFinalMar98/cimiprofile4.htm#6.4.3.2.

9. See http://www.getty.edu/gri/standard/fda/index.htm.

10. See http://www.oberlin.edu/~art/vra/wc1.html for VRA 2.0, and http://www.gsd.harvard.edu/~staffaw3/vra/vracore3.htm for VRA 3.0.

11. For obvious reasons, the AMICO data dictionary includes data categories for describing the work of art depicted in an image, as well as for the associated digital file. See http://www.amico.org/docs/AMICO.dd.9902.html.

12. For a full crosswalk of metadata schemas, including CDWA, VRA Core 2.0 and 3.0, MARC, and Dublin Core, see http://www.getty.edu/gri/standard/intrometadata/crosswalk.htm.

13. Based on Erwin Panofsky's classic *Studies in Iconology: Humanistic Themes in the Art of the Renaissance* (New York: Harper & Row, 1962).

14. See the article "Mapping Content and Structure of Metadata from the Spreadsheet to the Web-Based Searchable Database: The CIELO Project" by image curators Vickie Aubourg and Loy Zimmerman in the summer 2000 issue of the *VRA Bulletin*.

15. Marcia J. Bates, "Indexing and Access for Digital Libraries and the Internet: Human, Database, and Domain Factors," *Journal of the American Society for Information Science* 49 (November 1998): 1187.

16. Available on the Web at http://shiva.pub.getty.edu/aat_browser/.

17. This is typical of another phenomenon of online searching that Bates emphasizes in her study: "The user's task is to describe something that, by definition, he or she does not know." In this case, the user "describes the fringes of a gap in knowledge, and can only guess what the 'filler' for the gap would look like" (Bates, "Indexing and Access for Digital Libraries," 1186).

18. Available at http://iconclass.let.ruu.nl/home.html, as well as in CD-ROM and print form.

19. The ULAN data is available at http://shiva.pub.getty.edu/ulan_browser/.

20. Available at htttp://shiva.pub.getty.edu/tgn_browser. All three Getty vocabularies are updated on the Web on a monthly basis.

21. See Tony Gill, "Metadata and the World Wide Web," *Introduction to Metadata* (Los Angeles: J. Paul Getty Trust, 1998), 9–18. A revised version of this publication is available at http://www.getty.edu/gri/standard/intrometadata/.

22. See http://www.clir.org/diglib/artxdescription.htm.

21

Navigating LC's Cartographic Treasures

Elizabeth U. Mangan, transcribed by Mary Larsgaard

INTRODUCTION

As part of the Library of Congress's (LC) National Digital Library (NDL) initiative and the American Memory project, the Geography and Map Division (G&M) has scanned a substantial number of maps and created metadata for them.

In this chapter, I will take you on a journey of discovery, beginning on the LC homepage.[1] Then we'll go to American Memory, within that to Collection Finder, and then to Maps. (See figure 21.1.)

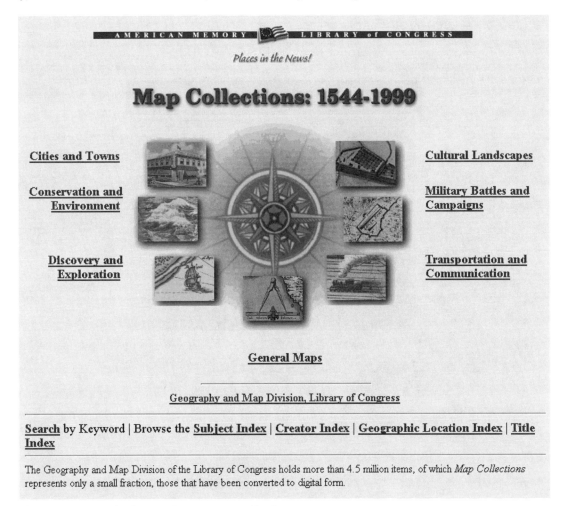

Figure 21.1 Maps in the American Memory collection.

Note that, in order for the maps to display quickly upon the users' computers, the digital images use LizardTech's MrSID (Multi-Resolution Seamless Image Database) compression technique.[2] Users can use standard Internet browsers to display American Memory maps. To download the .sid files to one's computer, it is first necessary to download the free viewing software from the LizardTech Web page.[2]

METADATA SOURCES

G&M has used several different sources in order to create records for its scanned maps. These sources are:

- Full-level cataloging
- Minimal-level cataloging
- Title-level cataloging
- Bibliography-based cataloging
- Databases

Full-Level Cataloging

Figures 21.2 and 21.3 show the scanned map for the Poole Brothers' "Bird's-Eye-View of the Business District of Chicago" of 1898. When full-level cataloging already exists for the original map, that catalog record is taken and the appropriate fields for the scanned map are added. The record for the 1898 Poole Brothers' map is LC record 75-693212. Figure 21.4 displays the enhanced record.

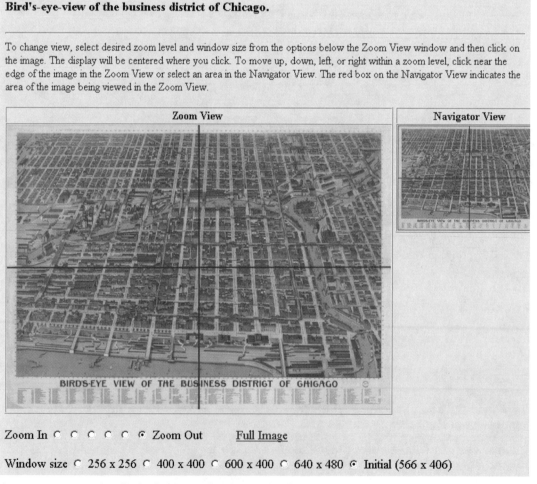

Figure 21.2   Image showing both zoom and navigator view boxes.

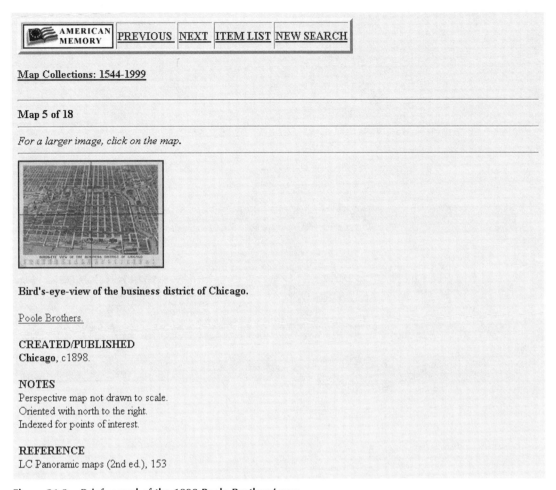

Figure 21.3   Brief record of the 1898 Poole Brothers' map.

The following fields were added in order to include American Memory bibliographic information:

- An availability note for the raster image in the MARC 21 field 530: "Available also through the Library of Congress Web site as a raster image"
- The URL/URN in the MARC 21 field 856
- A repository note in the MARC 21 field 852: "|a Library of Congress |b Geography and Map Division |e Washington, D.C. 20540-4650 USA |n dcu"

The following fields were added in order to include American Memory access information:

- The category name in the MARC 21 field 985: "|a GMD/CITYMAP |e ammem"
- The collection name(s) in field 985: "|GMD/PMMAP |e ammem"
- The geographic hierarchy in field 752: "|a United States |b Illinois |d Chicago"

Note that field 752 is in effect a hierarchical subject heading and, for this record, MARC 21 field 651 is "|a Chicago (Ill.) |x Aerial Views."

Minimal-Level Cataloging (MLC)

In some situations a catalog record exists for the paper map, but the record has been cataloged at the minimal level; see, for example, figure 21.5, LC record 93-686544, J. Ross Brown's 1908 view of "Stratford on Avon." Note that the end of the classification number (MARC field 050) has the mnemonic "MLC."

Tag	I1	I2	Subfield Data
035			‡9 (DLC) 75693212
906			‡a 7 ‡b cbc ‡c orignew ‡d u ‡e ncip ‡f 19 ‡g y-geogmaps
010			‡a 75693212
040			‡a DLC ‡c DLC ‡d DLC
050	0	0	‡a G4104.C6A3 1898 ‡b .P6
052			‡a 4104 ‡b C6
110	2		‡a Poole Brothers.
245	0	0	‡a Bird's-eye-view of the business district of Chicago.
260			‡a Chicago, ‡c c1898.
300			‡a col. map ‡c 94 x 145 cm. on 4 sheets 55 x 77 cm.
507			‡b Perspective map not drawn to scale.
500			‡a Oriented with north to the right.
510	4		‡a LC Panoramic maps (2nd ed.), ‡c 153
530			‡a Available also through the Library of Congress Web site as a raster image.
500			‡a Indexed for points of interest.
651		0	‡a Chicago (Ill.) ‡x Aerial views.
650		0	‡a Central business districts ‡z Illinois ‡z Chicago ‡x Maps.
752			‡a United States ‡b Illinois ‡d Chicago.
852	0		‡a Library of Congress ‡b Geography and Map Division ‡e Washington, D.C. 20540-4650 USA ‡n dcu
856	7		‡d g4104c ‡f pm001530 ‡g urn:hdl:loc.gmd/g4104c.pm001530 ‡u http://hdl.loc.gov/loc.gmd/g4104c.pm001530 ‡2 http
952			‡a AACR2
985			‡a GMD/PMMAP ‡e ammem
985			‡a GMD/CITYMAP ‡e ammem
991			‡b c-G&M ‡h G4104.C6A3 1898 ‡i .P6 ‡t Copy 1 ‡w MAPS

Figure 21.4   Catalog record LC-75-693212 showing the additional fields.

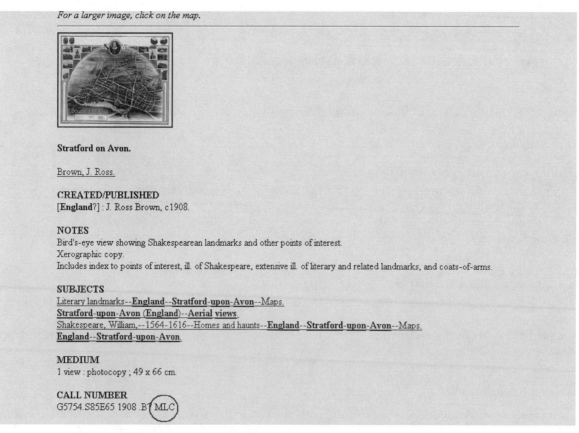

For a larger image, click on the map.

Stratford on Avon.

Brown, J. Ross.

CREATED/PUBLISHED
[**England**?] : J. Ross Brown, c1908.

NOTES
Bird's-eye view showing Shakespearean landmarks and other points of interest.
Xerographic copy.
Includes index to points of interest, ill. of Shakespeare, extensive ill. of literary and related landmarks, and coats-of-arms.

SUBJECTS
Literary landmarks--**England--Stratford-upon-Avon**--Maps.
Stratford-upon-Avon (England)--Aerial views.
Shakespeare, William,--1564-1616--Homes and haunts--**England--Stratford-upon-Avon**--Maps.
England--Stratford-upon-Avon.

MEDIUM
1 view : photocopy ; 49 x 66 cm.

CALL NUMBER
G5754.S85E65 1908 .B7 MLC

Figure 21.5   Brief record of Brown's 1908 map of "Stratford on Avon."

Tag	I1	I2	Subfield Data
035			‡9 (DLC) 93686544
906			‡a 7 ‡b cbc ‡c orignew ‡d u ‡e ncip ‡f 19 ‡g y-geogmaps
955			‡a ga05
010			‡a 93686544
034	0		‡a a
040			‡a DLC ‡c DLC ‡d DLC
050	0	0	‡a G5754.S85E65 1908 ‡b .B7 (MLC)
052			‡a 5754 ‡b S85
100	1		‡a Brown, J. Ross.
245	0	0	‡a Stratford on Avon.
255			‡a Not drawn to scale.
260			‡a [England?] : ‡b J. Ross Brown, ‡c c1908.
300			‡a 1 view : ‡b photocopy ; ‡c 49 x 66 cm.
500			‡a Bird's-eye view showing Shakespearean landmarks and other points of interest.
500			‡a Xerographic copy.
500			‡a Includes index to points of interest, ill. of Shakespeare, extensive ill. of literary and related landmarks, and coats-of-arms.
530			‡a Available also through the Library of Congress Web site as a raster image.
650		0	‡a Literary landmarks ‡z England ‡z Stratford-upon-Avon ‡x Maps.
651		0	‡a Stratford-upon-Avon (England) ‡x Aerial views.
600	1	0	‡a Shakespeare, William, ‡d 1564-1616 ‡x Homes and haunts ‡z England ‡z Stratford-upon-Avon ‡x Maps.
752			‡a England ‡d Stratford-upon-Avon.
852	0		‡a Library of Congress ‡b Geography and Map Division ‡e Washington, D.C. 20540-4650 USA ‡n dcu
856	7		‡d g5754s ‡f ct000162 ‡g urn:hdl:loc.gmd/g5754s.ct000162 ‡u http://hdl.loc.gov/loc.gmd/g5754s.ct000162 ‡2 http
952			‡a LMP
985			‡a GMD/CITYMAP ‡e ammem
991			‡b c-G&M ‡h G5754.S85E65 1908 ‡i .B7 MLC ‡t Copy 1 ‡w MAPS

Figure 21.6 "Stratford on Avon" catalog record, showing the additional fields.

Here again, the record for the paper map has the following American Memory bibliographic and access information fields added to it as appropriate. (See figure 21.6.)

- Raster image availability note in field 530
- URL/URN note in field 856
- Repository note in field 852
- Category name(s) (e.g., Citymap) in field 985
- Geographic hierarchy in field 752

Title-Level Cataloging

Of G&M's 4.5 million maps, about 180,000 are cataloged (at either full or minimal level). Access to the remaining maps is by geographic area. For these maps, basic bibliographic information is on each map folder; this always includes but is not always limited to geographic area and subject (when applicable). This portion of the Division's maps is called the "title collection." An example is a map of boundaries of Yellowstone National Park from 1895 (see figures 21.7, 21.8, and 21.9).

To create metadata for these maps, a bibliographic record must be created from scratch, using the bibliographic information on the map folder as a starting point. The title is transcribed from the item, the subjects and description are based on the information on the label on the outside of the folder, a call number is assigned based on geographic area, and (if necessary) a filing location is assigned. (See figure 21.10.) Note that the end of the classification number in the 050 field has a mnemonic "TIL." American Memory bibliographic and access information are also added to the record in a similar fashion as described previously.

[Yellowstone National Park boundaries].

CREATED/PUBLISHED
[S.l.], 1895.

NOTES
"From House Rept. 1763 53 C., 2 S."
National Park Exhibit, 1972. DLC
Accompanied by: United States House of Representatives Report no. 1763, 53rd Congress, 3rd Session.

SUBJECTS
Boundaries.
Parks.
United States--Wyoming--Yellowstone National Park.

MEDIUM
1 map : col. ; 34 x 38 cm.

CALL NUMBER
G4262.Y4 1895 .Y4 TIL

Figure 21.7   Brief record of "Yellowstone National Park Boundaries."

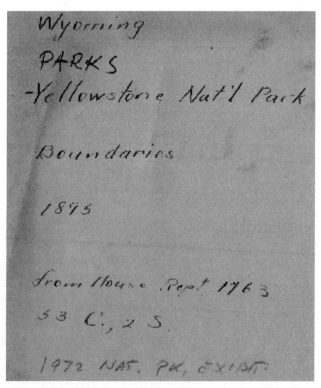

Figure 21.8   Yellowstone bibliographic information on map folder.

[Yellowstone National Park boundaries].

To change view, select desired zoom level and window size from the options below the Zoom View window and then click on the image. The display will be centered where you click. To move up, down, left, or right within a zoom level, click near the edge of the image in the Zoom View or select an area in the Navigator View. The red box on the Navigator View indicates the area of the image being viewed in the Zoom View.

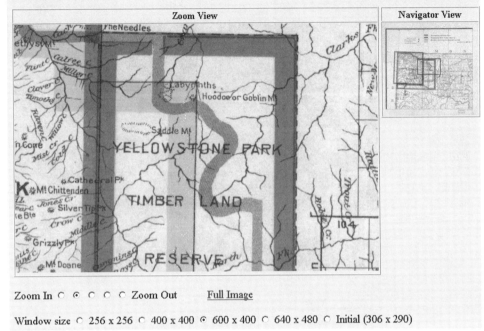

Zoom In ○ ◉ ○ ○ ○ Zoom Out   Full Image

Window size ○ 256 x 256 ○ 400 x 400 ◉ 600 x 400 ○ 640 x 480 ○ Initial (306 x 290)

Figure 21.9   Close-up view of "Yellowstone National Park Boundaries" map.

Tag	I1	I2	Subfield Data
035			‡9 (DLC) 97683574
906			‡a 7 ‡b cbu ‡c orignew ‡d u ‡e ncip ‡f 19 ‡g y-geogmaps
955			‡a ga32
010			‡a 97683574
034	1		‡a a ‡b 722500
040			‡a DLC ‡c DLC ‡d DLC
050	0	0	‡a G4262.Y4 1895 ‡b .Y4 TIL
052			‡a 4262 ‡b Y4
245	0	0	‡a [Yellowstone National Park boundaries].
255			‡a Scale [ca. 1:722,500].
260			‡a [S.l.], ‡c 1895.
300			‡a 1 map : ‡b col. ; ‡c 34 x 38 cm.
490	1		‡a House of Representatives. Report ; ‡v no. 1763, 53d Congress, 3d session
500			‡a "From House Rept. 1763 53 C., 2 S."
585			‡a National Park Exhibit, 1972. ‡5 DLC
500			‡a Accompanied by: United States House of Representatives Report no. 1763, 53rd Congress, 3rd Session.
530			‡a Available also through the Library of Congress Web site as a raster image.
650		4	‡a Boundaries.
650		4	‡a Parks.
752			‡a United States ‡b Wyoming ‡c Yellowstone National Park.
810	1		‡a United States. ‡b Congress. ‡b House. ‡t Report ; ‡v 53rd Congress, no. 1763.
852	0		‡a Library of Congress ‡b Geography and Map Division ‡e Washington, D.C. 20540-4650 ‡n dcu
856	7		‡d g4262y ‡f ye000018 ‡g urn:hdl:loc.gmd/g4262y.ye000018 ‡u http://hdl.loc.gov/loc.gmd/g4262y.ye000018 ‡2 http
985			‡a GMD/NPMAP ‡e ammem
985			‡a GMD/YEMAP ‡e ammem
985			‡a GMD/CNSVMAP ‡e ammem
991			‡b c-G&M ‡h G4262.Y4 1895 ‡i .Y4 TIL ‡t Copy 1 ‡w MAPS

Figure 21.10   Newly created catalog record for Yellowstone map.

Bibliography-Based Cataloging

Over the years, the Division has issued several heavily used cartobibliographies, such as Richard Stephenson's 1961 work *Civil War Maps*.[3] Bibliographies such as this are useful sources for creating metadata, which the Ditterline entry in figure 21.11 will illustrate.

The resulting cataloging record can be seen in figure 21.12, LC record 99-447499. It describes Ditterline's map of the "Field of Gettysburg, July 1st, 2nd, & 3rd." The bibliographic record for the hardcopy map is created and updated; also, the name authority file is checked, the descriptive information is verified by viewing the map, and a call number and filing location (if necessary) are assigned. In addition, a general note (MARC field 500), "Description derived from published bibliography," is added; this can be clearly seen on the brief record in figure 21.13. To complete the cataloging process, the American Memory bibliographic and access fields are added.

DATABASES

The last source for metadata that I will describe is data found in databases. This source has not been used yet but is planned for the G&M collection of fire-insurance maps. The Division has what is in effect a checklist of cities and years that records its holdings of fire-insurance maps.[4] The object will be to provide access to the scanned images by state, county, city, and date. First the database information will be verified, and then American Memory bibliographic and access information will be added.

Pennsylvania   336.7

331

Ditterline, Theodore.

Field of Gettysburg, July 1st, 2nd & 3rd, 1863. Prepared by T. Ditterline. P. S. Duval & Son lith., Philada. Colored. Scale ca. 1:25,500. 49 × 40 cm. *From his Sketch of the battles of Gettysburg* . . . New York, C. A. Alvord, 1863. 24 p.

Oval-shaped map depicting troop and artillery positions, relief by hachures, drainage, roads, railroads, and houses with names of residents.

332

Elliott, S. G.

Elliott's map of the battlefield of Gettysburg, Pennsylvania. Made from an accurate survey of the ground by transit and chain. F. Bourquin & Co., liths., Philada. [Philadelphia] S. G. Elliott & Co., ©1864. Uncolored. Scale 1:9051. 81 × 58 cm.

Shows breastworks and rifle pits, graves of Union and Confederate soldiers, "dead horses" reads and streets, relief by hachures, vegetation, drainage, houses and names of residents.

333

————Map of the battlefield of Gettysburg. Made from an accurate survey of the ground by transit and chain by S. G. Elliott, C.E. Published by H. H. Lloyd & Co., New York. ©1864. Colored. Scale 1:9051. 80 × 58 cm.

Inset: Plan of the National Cemetery.

Lower right corner: Sketch of the battle of Gettysburg.

[Text]

lines, fences, dwellings with names of inhabitants, points of interest on the battlefield, and in addition to the land owned by the association, that which is proposed to be purchased.

Union and Confederate positions are shown, with names of corps and divisions, sometimes including the name of the commanding officer, and the location of artillery.

See entry no. 329 for a similar map showing more extensive land holdings.

335

————Gettysburg and vicinity, showing the position of the troops July 1st and 3rd, 1863, and the land purchased and dedicated to the public by General S. Wylie Crawford and the Gettysburg Battlefield Memorial Association. Published by the Gettysburg Battlefield Memorial Association, 1885. Uncolored. Scale ca. 1:15,840. 41 × 31 cm.

Indicates Union troop positions and movements, points of interest on the battlefield, dwellings with names of inhabitants, drainage, fences, roads, and railroads.

336

————Gettysburg and vicinity, showing the position of the troops July 3, 1863 (third day's fight), and the land purchased and dedicated to the public by General S. Wylie Crawford and the Gettysburg Battlefield Memorial Association. Thos. Hunter, lith., Phila. Published by the Gettysburg Battlefield Memorial Association, March, 1883. Colored. Scale ca. 1:15,840. 41 × 31 cm.

"Land of battlefield Memorial Association tinted pink" and "land of General Crawford tinted blue."

Indicates troop positions and movements, roads, "Gettysburg and Hanover Railroad," houses, names of residents, fences, and drainage.

Figure 21.11   Ditterline entry from the 1961 annotated list.

Tag	I1	I2	Subfield Data
✦ 035			‡a (DLC) 99447499
906			‡a 7 ‡b cbc ‡c orignew ‡d u ‡e ncip ‡f 19 ‡g y-geogmaps
010			‡a 99447499
040			‡a DLC ‡c DLC ‡d DLC
050	0	0	‡a G3824.G3S5 1863 ‡b .D42 ‡u CW 331
052			‡a 3824 ‡b G3
072		7	‡a S5 ‡2 lcg
100	1		‡a Ditterline, T. ‡q (Theodore).
245	1	0	‡a Field of Gettysburg, July 1st, 2nd & 3rd, 1863 ‡c Prepared by T. Ditterline.
260			‡a [Philada. ‡b P. S. Duval & Son lith. ‡c 1863]
300			‡a 1 map ‡b col. ‡c 49 x 40 cm.
507			‡a Scale ca. 1:25,500,.
510	4		‡a LC Civil War Maps (2nd ed.), ‡c 331
500			‡a From his Sketch of the battles of Gettysburg . . . New York, C. A. Alvord, 1863. 24 p.
500			‡a Oval-shaped map depicting troop and artillery positions, relief by hachures, drainage, roads, railroads, and houses with names of residents.
500			‡a Description derived from published bibliography.
530			‡a Available also through the Library of Congress web site as raster image.
650		0	‡a Gettysburg (Pa.), Battle of, 1863 ‡v Maps.
651		0	‡a Gettysburg (Pa.) ‡v Maps.
653			‡a Gettysburg, Battle of.
752			‡a United States ‡b Pennsylvania ‡d Gettysburg.
852	0		‡a Library of Congress ‡b Geography and Map Division ‡e Washington, D.C. 20540-4650 ‡n dcu
856	7		‡d g3824g ‡f cw0331000 ‡g urn:hdl:loc.gmd/g3824g.cw0331000 ‡u http://hdl.loc.gov/loc/gmd/g3824g.cw0331000 ‡2 http
985			‡a GMD/CWMAP ‡e ammem
985			‡a GMD/MILMAP ‡e ammem
991			‡b c-G&M ‡o em

Figure 21.12   Newly created cataloging record of Ditterline's 1863 Gettysburg map.

For a larger image, click on the map.

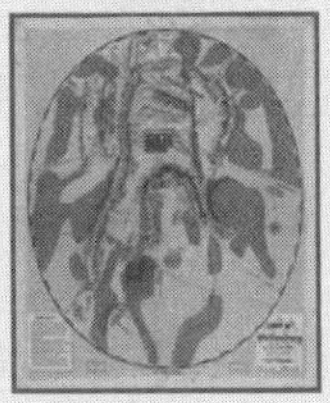

Field of Gettysburg, July 1st, 2nd & 3rd, 1863 Prepared by T. Ditterline.

Ditterline, T. (Theodore).

CREATED/PUBLISHED
[Philada. P. S. Duval & Son lith. 1863]

NOTES
Scale ca. 1:25,500,.
From his Sketch of the battles of **Gettysburg** . . . New York, C. A. Alvord, 1863. 24 p.
Oval-shaped map depicting troop and artillery positions, relief by hachures, drainage, roads, railroads, and houses with names of residents.
Description derived from published bibliography.

REFERENCE
LC Civil War Maps (2nd ed.), 331

SUBJECTS
Gettysburg (Pa.), Battle of, 1863--Maps.
Gettysburg (Pa.)--Maps.
United States--Pennsylvania--Gettysburg.

MEDIUM
1 map col. 49 x 40 cm.

Figure 21.13   Brief record of Ditterline's 1863 Gettysburg map.

CONCLUSION

As there is more than one way to skin a cat, there is also more than one way to generate metadata for scanned maps. I urge you to take a look at what the G&M Division has done and to compare and contrast access to the user, by taking your own voyage of discovery through the American Memory scanned maps.[5]

NOTES

1. "The Library of Congress," http://www.loc.gov/.
2. "LizardTech," http://www.lizardtech.com/.
3. Richard Stephenson, *Civil War Maps: An Annotated List of Maps and Atlases in Map Collections of the Library of Congress* (Washington, D.C.: Library of Congress, Map Division, 1961).
4. See *Fire Insurance Maps in the Library of Congress: Plans of North American Cities and Towns Produced by the Sanborn Map Company: A Checklist* (Washington, D.C.: Library of Congress; for sale by the Supt. of Docs, U.S. Government Printing Office, 1981).
5. "Library of Congress, American Memory: Map Collections, 1544–1999," http://Memory.loc.gov/ammem/gmdhtml/gmdhome.html.

22

VARIATIONS:
Creating a Digital Music Library at Indiana University

Constance Mayer

VARIATIONS TODAY

VARIATIONS, currently a joint project of the William and Gayle Cook Music Library and the Digital Library Program at Indiana University (IU), Bloomington, is known as one of the first digital library projects in music, particularly as regards streaming high-quality audio across a network to client workstations. Operational since April 1996, the project provides access to over 6,000 titles of near-CD-quality audio to users in the Cook Music Library and selected additional locations on the IU campus network. All course reserve listening assignments for students in the Indiana University School of Music, including over 1,500 titles per academic semester, are available online through VARIATIONS. Access statistics for spring semester 2000 revealed an average of 673 individual launches of the VARIATIONS player per day. During exam weeks, when everyone is in the library reviewing the same pieces at the same time, daily uses often exceed 4,000.[1] The project also serves as a test bed for research on multimedia digital libraries at Indiana University.

The current digital audio collection contains a wide range of musical materials, reflecting instructional emphases in the IU School of Music. While musical works from the canon of Western classical music still dominate the curriculum and the digital collection, recordings of jazz, rock, and world music are also making an appearance. Student digitizing technicians in the Cook Music Library add sound files to the collection daily, based upon requests from faculty for course reserves, requests from users for access to materials in archival sound recording collections, and other digitizing priorities set by the Collection Development Librarian. Source materials for digitization include compact discs, vinyl LPs, and tapes (reel-to-reel, cassette, and DAT) owned by the Cook Music Library.

This chapter will supplement previous discussions of the project[2,3,4] by focusing on the user interface and the ways in which decisions were made about integrating existing MARC records with locally designed systems for creating structural and administrative metadata. Our primary goal in the beginning was to create an intuitive, easy-to-use interface for access to the sound files that could also be economically maintained. Although we continue to review and improve aspects of the interface, we've found it to be amazingly robust from the points of view of both the users and the student assistants who create the metadata files.

DEVELOPING VARIATIONS: THE BEGINNINGS

VARIATIONS initially appeared as a named concept in a paper presented by Michael Burroughs and David Fenske at the International Computer Music Conference in Glasgow in 1990.[5] Combining their interests in music instruction, music libraries, and evolving multimedia technologies, Burroughs and Fenske envisioned a system in which library patrons would access a database of music information objects via a hypermedia graphical user interface. Each type of information source—text, graphics, scores, sound, and bibliographic information—would appear in its own window. Links from the catalog window to various content objects or links among content objects would connect related information sources. Links to outside information sources, as well as user-created linkages, would also be possible. VARIATIONS, from the musical term *theme and variations,* seemed an apt name for a system that would integrate the various formats needed to study a single musical work and provide networked access to users from a client workstation.

At about the same time, plans were underway for a new music library building for Indiana University, with an infrastructure supporting delivery of digital objects over a network. Designers visualized a library that would integrate physical and digital sources of musical information, with 130 computer workstations sharing space with a large collection of books, scores, sound and video recordings, microforms, and other media. Operational implementation of the VARIATIONS project began in conjunction with building the new library and initially focused on providing online access to audio recordings. Audio was a logical point of departure for several reasons:

- In the early 1990s, when the project began, the ability to provide CD-quality sound over a network without audio breakup presented a technical challenge that had not been solved by anyone else.
- Music study requires access to high-quality recorded performances of musical works.
- The size and scope of the Indiana University School of Music require multiple simultaneous access to the same study materials.
- The fragile formats of most audio recordings, particularly those on vinyl or magnetic tape, require preservation for continued use.

Although VARIATIONS was always viewed primarily as a digital music library project, not merely an electronic reserves system, project developers began building the collection with content from course reserves. Analysis of several years of archived course reserve lists reinforced librarian perceptions that instructors tended to choose instructional repertoires from a predictable canon of Western classical music and use the same materials again in subsequent semesters. Also, providing access to course reserve listening assignments for multiple simultaneous users was one of the existing service problems that VARIATIONS would be well equipped to solve. We theorized that this approach to digital collection building would rapidly lead to a core collection of online sound recordings that would meet the general course-related needs of the students in the School of Music. This assumption proved to be accurate and, after initial struggles to keep up with the digitizing backlog, we are currently able to meet most course reserves needs with only twenty hours per week of student digitizing time.

In 1995, prior to moving into the new building, we designed a prototype user interface based on a core course reserves list for an undergraduate music theory and literature class that was taught every semester to approximately two hundred students. We discussed options and made decisions about issues like sound-file parameters, the file-naming system, user access to supplementary textual information, navigation from the course reserves list and from the online catalog, and listings of internal tracks on the sound recording. Most of the decisions made at that time have proven viable and remain part of the operational user interface today.

DESCRIPTIVE METADATA: THE MARC RECORD

VARIATIONS developers chose to use the existing MARC bibliographic record in IUCAT, Indiana University's online catalog, as the primary source of descriptive metadata for helping users discover and identify digital sound files. The rationale stemmed partly from the fact that most of the music library's audio collection was already represented by catalog records created by expert catalogers using existing national standards, including authority control. Also, we could assume that users were already familiar with the IUCAT interface or would need to become so, from experiences searching for physical library materials. Using IUCAT as a primary interface would also integrate access to both physical and digital objects. A user searching the catalog for a sound recording of Beethoven's symphonies, for example, could identify library locations and call numbers for physical items and also access digital objects via a URL embedded in the 856 field.

After some discussion about the most effective means of defining sound files, we decided to equate one sound file with one compact disc, one side of an LP, or one side of a tape. This was done in part to simplify the decision-making process for the student digitizing technicians. We also wanted to create a system that would cause the least possible disruption for a listener who would come to the end of one sound file and have to retrieve another. Maintaining consistency with the divisions found on the original sources seemed to meet both requirements.

The centrality of the bibliographic record was also maintained in the file-naming schema, which is derived from the seven-character alphanumeric unique record identifier generated for each new bibliographic record by NOTIS, our current library automation system. An additional letter or number is added to accommodate multiple volumes: AFB1999A, AFB1999B, AFB1999C, and so forth. This system has been very effective in linking the sound files to their corresponding descriptive metadata but will require some adaptation when we migrate to new library automation systems in the future.

Library-created course reserves lists, based on descriptive metadata found in the IUCAT record, provide another point of access to the sound files. Library staff creates individual reserves lists for each course for which a faculty member requests reserve service. The original copy of the list, saved in ASCII text format in a "current semester reserves" directory, is created by following these steps:

1. Search IUCAT in staff mode and locate the bibliographic record corresponding to the instructor's reserve request.
2. Navigate to the associated holdings record. Select and copy the brief bibliographic information, including the call number.
3. Switch to the text-editing window and paste the information into the text file.
4. Edit out extraneous information, including field delimiters.
5. Add the seven-character NOTIS identifier to the line under the call number.

The entire directory of current reserves text files is FTP'd daily to the Web server, where a locally created program is run to add HTML markup to the files. The program also searches for sound files that match the NOTIS number entered on the last line and, if any are found, creates a link that displays as "Listen to online copy in VARIATIONS." (The NOTIS number disappears from view in any case.) Figure 22.1 illustrates a typical entry for online reserve sound recordings.

Using the MARC bibliographic record as a basis for helping users find digitized sound files, either through IUCAT or through the course reserves lists, has clear advantages. Some of the limitations appear in situations where more than one musical work is associated with one bibliographic record. These records can be confusing to users under the best of circumstances and, when they are condensed for incorporation into course reserves lists, may actually omit the very information a user needs.

The most intelligible transition from IUCAT record to course reserves listing is accomplished when the original sound recording contains one work by one composer. Figure 22.2 shows an example of a course reserves listing, copied and pasted from IUCAT, where students assigned to listen to *Beethoven's Symphony No. 9* can easily ascertain that they have found an appropriate example.

In a record containing two works by the same composer (see figure 22.3), it is less apparent to users that they have reached the correct entry for an assignment to listen to *Beethoven's Symphony No. 7*. The composer entry matches the inquiry and careful reading of the full title information reveals the presence of *Symphony No. 7,* but the uniform

Beethoven, Ludwig van, 1770–1827
    <Symphonies>
    9 symphonies <sound recording> / Beethoven.—Hamburg: Archiv Produktion;
    New York: Manufactured and marketed by PolyGram Classics & Jazz, p1994.
    CD .B414 G1-14
    Listen to online copy in VARIATIONS

Figure 22.1   Course reserves listing.

Beethoven, Ludwig van, 1770–1827.
  <Symphonies, no. 9, op. 125, D minor>
  Symphony no. 9 <sound recording>: "Choral"/Beethoven. -- New York: RCA
Victor Gold Seal: Manufactured and distributed by BMG Music, <1994>
(BMG classics)
<u>Listen to online copy in VARIATIONS</u>

Figure 22.2   Course reserves listing for one composer, one work.

Beethoven, Ludwig van, 1770–1827.
  <Symphonies, no. 5, op. 67, C minor>
  Symphony no. 5 in C minor, op. 67; Symphony no. 7 in A, op. 92 <sound
recording>/Beethoven. -- Albany, NY: Albany Records, <1993>
Listen to online copy in VARIATIONS

Figure 22.3   Course reserves listing for one composer, two works.

Schubert, Franz, 1797–1828
 <Songs. Selections>
 Goethe-Lieder <sound recording>/Schubert. -- New York, NY: London, p 1997
Listen to online copy in VARIATIONS

Figure 22.4   Course reserves listing for one composer, collective title.

title entry, correctly entered to match the first work on the disc, may lead the uninitiated to believe they've found a recording for the wrong symphony. Confusion of this sort often leads students to report that "you digitized the wrong recording."

The problem is exacerbated when a record contains multiple smaller works by the same composer. Figure 22.4 shows an example of a course reserves listing created in response to a faculty member's request for one of Schubert's lieder, "Der Erlkönig," from this collection. Fortunately for the students, the main entry is under the composer's name, so the record will file alphabetically in the expected location, but there's no indication from the brief record that "Der Erlkönig" is present on this particular recording. In a course where the instructor selects several Schubert songs from different recordings, each of which uses the uniform title "Songs. Selections," the brief record is clearly inadequate for locating and identifying the appropriate sound file in one click.

In figure 22.5, where the main entry is the name of the performer who is singing a collection of songs by various composers, the system breaks down almost entirely. Students looking for Schubert's "Der Erlkönig" could not be expected to find it filed alphabetically under "Lehmann, Lotte." In cases like this, if we know which selection is being used in the course or receive queries indicating confusion, we add bracketed title information and a cross reference to guide users.

STRUCTURAL METADATA: THE TRACK FILE

It was clear from the beginning that more detailed information about the contents of each sound file would be required for enhanced access and for internal navigability within the file. To address this need, VARIATIONS uses a locally defined structure to store both structural and administrative metadata. This information appears to the user as an interim screen that is accessible from the URL, embedded in either the catalog record or the reserves list, and provides:

- A link to the full catalog record
- Links to all sound files represented by the bibliographic record (each one is labeled "Side/Disc . . . ")
- Text of the contents, or "tracks," for each sound file
- Copyright information relevant to the original source material
- A link to a form for sending comments or reporting problems to the project staff

Figure 22.6 shows an example of a typical interim screen. When users click on a sound file, they launch a *VARIATIONS Player* application, developed by IU specifically to provide navigability within a sound file (see figure 22.7). The corresponding metadata file is retrieved along with the sound file so that information about composer, uniform title, track names, and track timings are available to users.

The player application allows stops, starts, and several means of moving from track to track or to specific points within tracks. An added feature displays the exact location of a musical example so that instructors can create their own course homepages or teaching tools by simply cutting and pasting URLs. The resulting links bypass the interim screen and open the player at the precise location defined by the instructor. This technique can be particularly helpful in cases where the descriptive metadata provided by the library points to the general rather than to the specific.

Lehmann, Lotte. prf
 Lotte Lehmann <sound recording>:26 Lieder (1928–1941). -- Newlands, South
Africa: Claremont Records, 1994.
Listen to online copy in VARIATIONS

Figure 22.5   Course reserves listing for Lieder by various performers, cataloged under the performer.

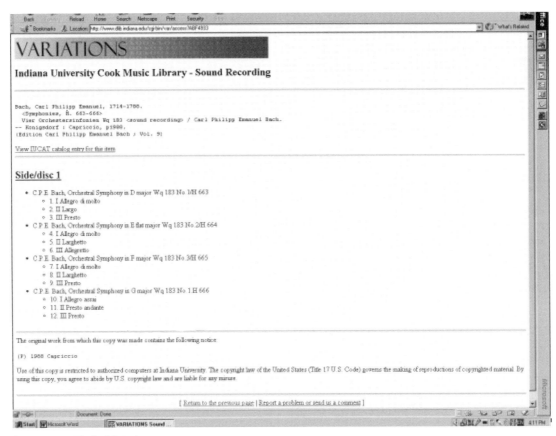

Figure 22.6   Typical interim screen.

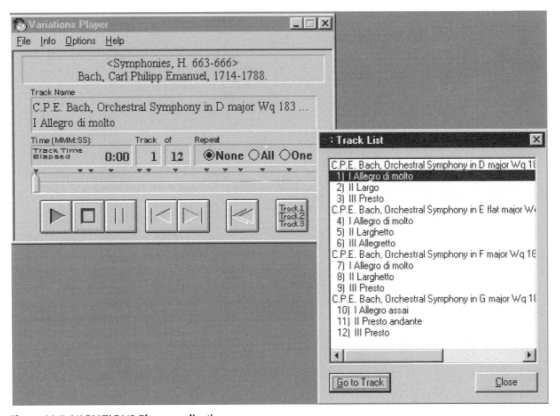

Figure 22.7 VARIATIONS Player application.

AUDIO CAPTURE AND METADATA FILE CREATION

Student technicians working under the supervision of the Reserves Coordinator in the User Services division of the Cook Music Library create the metadata files as part of the audio capture process. The administrative metadata entered into each file includes:

- Date of digitization
- Initials of the technician performing the work
- File format
- Equipment used
- Copyright notice from original item

Structural metadata, or track information, is added in a two-layer hierarchy—headings and tracks—that leaves some room for judgment on the part of the technician. At the very beginning of the project, we attempted to delineate guidelines that would allow the students to input data without having to make judgment calls but quickly found the rules inadequate in many cases and simply ridiculous in others. In general, students gather data from the original sources, including labels, covers, and liner notes, and strive for an aesthetically pleasing yet meaningful display of the contents of an individual sound recording. There is no attempt at authority control nor is there an attempt to standardize structural metadata across different representations of the same work, although we recognize the desirability of such functionality and see it as an important area for future work.

CONCLUSIONS AND FUTURE DIRECTIONS

VARIATIONS developers have achieved many of the original goals of the audio component of the project, including the development of a user interface that allows users to locate, play, and navigate from within sound files streamed from a multimedia server over a network. Students using the Cook Music Library depend upon VARIATIONS for their course reserve listening and have reacted very favorably to its reliability, comprehensiveness, and usability. The decisions about metadata have resulted in an application that allows patrons to find digitized sound files, discover their contents, and navigate to points within sound files.

As VARIATIONS and other digital music library projects move toward the future, some of the challenges will be:

- Defining standard file formats for sound, video, score images, score notation, and other musical information objects
- Developing standards for music metadata across data formats
- Working with music faculty to integrate digital library content with pedagogical applications
- Continuing to explore intellectual property issues as they relate to digital content and network distribution
- Integrating local and global information through one user interface
- Planning for preservation and migration of digital information to adapt to advances in technology

NOTES

1. Indiana University, "VARIATIONS Play and Retrieval Statistics," http://www.dlib.indiana.edu/variations/stats/.
2. David E. Fenske and Jon W. Dunn, "The VARIATIONS Project at Indiana University's Music Library," *D-Lib Magazine,* June 1996, http://www.dlib.org/dlib/june96/variations/06fenske.html.
3. Jon W. Dunn and Constance A. Mayer, "VARIATIONS: A Digital Music Library System at Indiana University," in *DL '99: Proceedings of the Fourth ACM Conference on Digital Libraries* (Berkeley, Calif.: Association for Computing Machinery, 1999), 12–19.
4. Indiana University, "VARIATIONS," http://www.dlib.indiana.edu/variations/.
5. Michael Burroughs and David E. Fenske, "VARIATIONS: A Hypermedia Project Providing Integrated Access to Music Information," in *International Computer Music Conference Glasgow 1990: Proceedings* (Glasgow, Scotland: International Computer Music Association, 1990), 221–24.

23

DDI, the Data Documentation Initiative: An Introduction to the Standard and Its Role in Social Science Data Access

Wendy Treadwell

Machine-readable social science data files date back to 1890, when Dr. Hollerith, an official of the U.S. Bureau of the Census, devised a means of encoding census data on punched cards and using a mechanical reader to process the information contained on those cards. His purpose was to speed up the analysis of the census data. In 1951, census data moved from being stored on a "machine-readable file" to being stored on a "machine-readable electronic file," as the bureau began to analyze census data by means of a UNIVAC I. It has been processed electronically since that time.

Social science data files are some of our oldest materials in electronic format. However, for the first twenty years of their existence, they tended to reside outside of libraries and outside of bibliographic control. Then, in January 1970, the Subcommittee on Rules for Machine-Readable Data Files was formed by the Descriptive Cataloging Committee of the American Library Association's Resources and Technical Services Division's Cataloging and Classification Section. This committee submitted its final report in 1976, resulting in a revision of a 1974 draft of a work entitled "Cataloging Machine-Readable Data Files—A Working Manual," originally compiled by Sue A. Dodd. In 1979, work on the compilation of a MARC format for machine-readable data files was begun by the Library of Congress.[1]

Today data files of many types are found within libraries and library catalogs. Major strides have been made to identify, describe, and provide access to social science data files through the bibliographic record. However, bibliographic control of these files is neither complete nor exhaustive in content and collection coverage. The reason for this is a combination of the nature of the materials being described and the specialized needs of the data user.

By nature, the data file is a social beast—it never resides alone. It is, as my son so precisely puts it, "a bunch of numbers." A social science data file without accompanying documentation has no meaning. A study, in fact, may consist of a number of related data files and one or more pieces of documentation relating to each of those files, separately or in combination. Names associated with files may have little to do with their content, and documentation can range from a well-formatted and complete publication to a folder of assorted pieces of paper containing such things as copies of questionnaires with handwritten notations of variable locations. When cataloging such materials, the question arises as to what one is actually describing. Is the cataloger describing the data file, the documentation pieces, or the study as a whole? More important, what is the implication of that decision for the user? All components are important to the user, and the selection of any one as the primary piece may result in insufficient bibliographic information.

Even when the cataloging description is complete, the data user has needs that extend beyond the standard information in a bibliographic record. In order to determine if a particular data set meets their needs, data users must be able to obtain information on the specific variables within a data file and the response categories within those variables. Ideally, the data user needs access to study, file, and variable information across data sets in a consistent and reliable manner. Most would then like to move from the documentation to the data itself in order to download, obtain subsets, or manipulate the data online.

In essence, the Data Documentation Initiative (DDI) committee was formed to address these issues. The DDI committee is a group of interested parties representing the European Community, Canada, and the United States. They represent producers, end-users, archives, and distributors of social science data. They are committed to the creation of a neutral nonproprietary standard and are considering future affiliation with a standards body. The first phase, DDI-I, was funded by National Science Foundation (NSF) grants, from membership dues to the Inter-University Consortium for Political and Social Research (ICPSR), and from the thousands of contributed hours by participants. The second phase,

DDI-II, will seek further funding from NSF to support continued work for the committee and ICPSR's efforts to produce metadata markup (XML-tagged codebooks).

In developing the eXtensible Markup Language (XML) Document Type Definition (DTD), the DDI sought to create a structured text that would improve human search capabilities and the ability to set up and use data. The committee wanted a structure that was machine understandable and allowed for automated processing of the information in the document, and that was nonproprietary and had archival integrity.

Version 1.0 of the DDI Codebook DTD (hereafter referred to as codebook.dtd) was published in March 2000. It addresses a convergence of user and producer needs to archive, analyze, discover, and manipulate/produce data.

ARCHIVE

- A nonproprietary, neutral standard
- Preserves both the content and the relational structure of the full documentation

ANALYSIS AND PRODUCTION

- Committed to both content and format standards based on standards currently in use and in development among data archives and data producers
- Robust and detailed, yet modular and flexible
- Functions as an interchange format, permitting transfer of particular contents to an unlimited array of systems and architectures

DISCOVERY

- Offers interoperability with resource-discovery and cataloging systems (Dublin Core, MARC, etc.)

The following changes are underway for the next version:

- Expansion to additional data formats such as aggregate and tabular data
- Better handling of logical data structures such as hierarchical, relational, and network
- Investigation of object meta-models such as those currently being developed by the U.S. Census Bureau (ISO 11179), NESSTAR, and others[2]

In focusing on the issues of description, identification, location, and access to resources (in this case, social science data), the codebook.dtd is essentially an extension of the traditional bibliographic record, which reflects the complexity of both the resource being described and the specialized needs of the user for identification and access.

The diagram of relationships in figure 23.1 shows the complexity of the situation facing data archivists and librarians. A data study is actually comprised of a number of disparate pieces, as shown on the lefthand side of the diagram. A bibliographic record, or (if all the individual pieces are being described) a set of bibliographic records (on the right), relays only a small amount of the total information available about a study and needed by the researcher. The XML document in the center, tagged in compliance with the DDI's codebook.dtd, provides a central source where the available information about a study can be recorded. It pulls together the descriptive elements found in a bibliographic record and integrates them with the breadth and depth of information found in the hard-copy codebook and supplemental materials. It acts as a central entry point to the study as a whole.

The concept of the XML-tagged codebook as an entry point or hub is important. Because it is an electronic file, it is no longer necessary to separate the bibliographic information from the finding aid or the finding aid from the object being described. Each of these sections contributes to aiding the researcher in locating and using data at different levels of the search process. It is possible, given this integrated structure, to develop search tools that would locate the

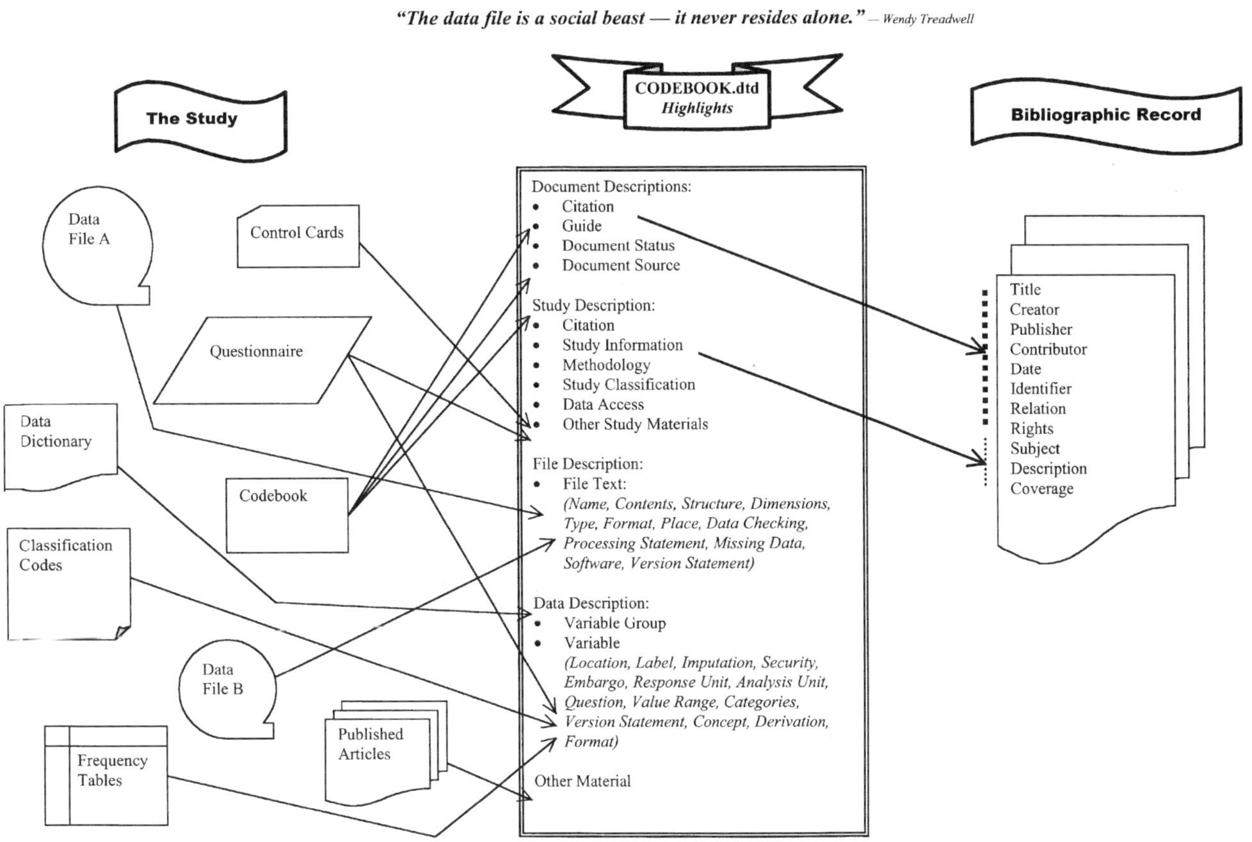

"The data file is a social beast — it never resides alone." — *Wendy Treadwell*

Figure 23.1   Diagram of relationships.

bibliographic elements of the codebook.dtd in the same manner as individual bibliographic records. Other search tools could be used to exploit the additional levels of information and complexity found in the codebook.dtd for either exploration purposes or for using the codebook to extract and manipulate data from the associated data file.

A complete schema of the codebook.dtd elements and their associated attributes can be found in figure 23.7 at the end of this chapter.[3] The level of detail represented by the schema is necessary to provide structural context for the information contained within the file and to ensure that the information can be processed accurately by a variety of search and extraction systems. The codebook.dtd is composed of five main modules, representing the major components of a traditional social science study codebook.[4]

DOCUMENT DESCRIPTION (MODULE 1)

This portion of the codebook.dtd will be most familiar to catalogers. It contains citation, guide, status, and source information. The citation section provides standard bibliographic information fields for describing the marked-up document. The majority of elements that map to the Dublin Core are found within this section. Specific terms and definitions used within the documentation are listed in the guide section. The status field provides a place to indicate that the document is being presented or distributed prior to being finalized (this is not an unusual situation in many data-processing strategies).

The Document Description also contains a section for full bibliographic information on the source document. Like other types of marked-up texts, the information in marked-up codebooks frequently comes from a previously existing print source. Unlike many other types of marked-up texts, the marked-up codebook does not simply replicate the print source with the addition of header, structural, and intellectual element tags. Existing codebooks, both print and electronic, rarely move smoothly into the marked-up structure. This is a result of the lack of structural consistency among print codebooks. Elements within existing codebooks are mapped into the structure from the primary source document. Others may be added using supplementary supporting materials, and some may be added from direct manipulation or analysis of the data. It is important to have accurate and full bibliographic information on each of these sources within the document. Figure 23.2 has an excerpt showing the citation information for a DDI-compliant codebook.[5]

STUDY DESCRIPTION (MODULE 2)

As noted earlier, a social science data collection is just that—a collection. The bibliographic information in the Document Description addresses only the marked-up document and the source materials used to create it. The study description addresses the data collection as a whole. A data collection may be as simple as a single data file with one accompanying codebook or as complex as a multiyear, multifocus study such as the National Longitudinal Survey, which

```
<docDscr>
 <citation>
  <titlStmt>
   <titl>An XML Codebook for a Nationally Representative Linked Sample of Population
         and Agriculture:  The United States in 1880</titl>
   <altTitl>1880 Agricultural Sample</altTit>
  </titlStmt>
  <rspStmt>
   <AuthEnty affiliation="Machine Readable Data Center">Block, William C.</AuthEnty>
  </rspStmt>
   <prodStmt>
    <producer affiliation="Machine Readable Data Center">Block, William C.</producer>
    <copyright>Copyright(c) William C. Block, 2000</copyright>
    <prodDate date="2000-03-15">March 15, 2000</prodDate>
    <prodPlac>2 Wilson Library, 309 19th Avenue South, Minneapolis, MN
          55455</prodPlac>
    <software version="Beta">MRDC Codebook Authoring Tool</software>
    <software version="2.0">XML-Pro for Unix/Linux</software>
   </prodStmt>
   <distStmt>
    <distrbtr abbr="MRDC" affil="University of Minnesota"
          URI="http://www.lib.umn.edu/mrdc">Machine Readable Data Center,
          2 Wilson Library, 309 19th Avenue South, Minneapolis, MN
          55455</distrbtr>
    <contact affil="Social Science Research Facility, University of Minnesota"
          email="block@socsci.umn.edu">William C. Block, 25 Blegen, 269 19th Avenue
          South, Minneapolis, MN 55455</contact>
    <contact affil="Machine Readable Data Center, University of Minnesota"
          URI="http://www.lib.umn.edu/mrdc" email="wendy@mrdc.lib.umn.edu">Wendy L.
          Treadwell</contact>
    <depositr affil="Social Science Research Facility, University of
          Minnesota">William C. Block</depositr>
    <depDate date="2000-05-01">May 1, 2000</depDate>
    <distDate date="2000-05-01">May 1, 2000</distDate>
   </distStmt>
    <biblCit>Block, William C., AN XML CODEBOOK FOR A NATIONALLY REPRESENTATIVE
          LINKED SAMPLE OF POPULATION AND AGRICULTURE:  THE UNITED STATES IN 1880
          [Computer file].  Minneapolis, MN:  University of Minnesota, Minnesota
          Population Center [producer], 2000.  Minneapolis, MN:  University of
          Minnesota, Machine Readable Data Center [distributor], 2000.</biblCit>
    <holdings location="Machine Readable Data Center, University of Minnesota">Both
          electronic and printed copies of the codebook are available at the
          Machine Readable Data Center, University of Minnesota, 2 Wilson Library,
          309 19th Avenue South, Minneapolis, MN  55455</holdings>
 </citation>
```

Figure 23.2   Document description example.

```
<stdyDscr>
 <stdyInfo>
  <subject>
   <keyword>Census</keyword>
   <keyword>Agriculture</keyword>
   <keyword>Agriculture Census</keyword>
   <keyword>Population Census</keyword>
   <keyword>Public Use Sample</keyword>
   <keyword>1880</keyword>
   <keyword>Census of Agriculture</keyword>
   <keyword>Linked Sample</keyword>
   <keyword>Population and Agriculture</keyword>
   <keyword>Microdata</keyword>
   <keyword>Economic</keyword>
   <keyword>Social</keyword>
   <keyword>Demographic</keyword>
  </subject>
   <abstract>Demographic, occupational, and economic information for a randomly selected national sample of rural households
in the United States in 1880 are presented in this dataset. The data were obtained from the manuscript population and agricultural
schedules of the 1880 United States Census. The dataset contains 23,806 individuals, 10,715 of whom are linked to an agricultural
schedule directly or are a family member of someone who was linked. Variables in the dataset include ...(continuation of ab-
stract)...(note: this list is not exhaustive; the agricultural schedule in 1880 was very detailed, asking a total of 100 questions in the
northern United States and 104 questions in the south. For a complete lists of questions, see the codebook.).</abstract>
    <sumDscr>
     <timePrd event="start" date="1879-01-01">January 1, 1879</timePrd>
     <timePrd event="end" date="1880-06-01">June 1, 1880</timePrd>
     <collDate ID="PCS" event="start" date="1989-11-01">November 1, 1989</collDate>
     <collDate ID="PCE" event="end" date="1993-07-21">July 21, 1993</collDate>
     <collDate ID="ACS" event="start" date="1990-08-01">August 1, 1990</collDate>
     <collDate ID="ACE" event="end" date="1998-07-21">July 21, 1998</collDate>
     <nation abbr="U.S.">United States</nation>
     <geogCover>This data contains counties sampled from the states of Alabama, California, Delaware, Florida, Georgia, Illinois,
Indiana, Iowa, Kansas, Kentucky, Louisiana, Maryland, Minnesota, Mississippi, Nebraska, New York, North Carolina, Ohio, Penn-
sylvania, Tennessee, Texas, South Carolina, West Virginia, and Wisconsin. Most of the counties sampled are complete; some of
the counties are only partial.</geogCover>
     <geogUnit>county</geogUnit>
     <anlyUnit>individuals</anlyUnit>
     <universe ID="PU" clusion="I">The resident rural population of the United States on June 1, 1880 living in sampled states and
counties.</universe>
     <universe ID="AU" clusion="I">agline > 0. Owners, Tenants, or Managers of farms greater than 3 acres in size or producing
and selling at least $500 in product during the year.</universe>
     <dataKind>census/enumeration data</dataKind>
    </sumDscr>
  </stdyInfo>
</stdyDscr>
```

Figure 23.3 Study description example.

consists of files for specific groups (such as youth, young women, mature women, young men, older men, and others)
and shelves of accompanying documentation. The Study Description, as shown in figure 23.3, includes sections for citation, scope, methodology, data access, and other study description information. It is within the study scope section
that you will find additional elements that map to the Dublin Core. Those items specifically pertain to subject classification, abstracts, and coverage. (A full description of Dublin Core mapping is provided later.)

FILE DESCRIPTION (MODULE 3)

While the first two modules provided information familiar to catalogers, the File Description module begins to address the structure and content of the data file itself. Data files have three levels of description. The overall structure

```
<fileDscr>
    <fileTxt>
        <fileName>1880ag.dat</fileName>
        <fileCont>Demographic, occupational, and economic information for a randomly selected national sample of rural house-
holds in the United States in 1880 are presented in...(continuation)...asking a total of 100 questions in the northern United States
and 104 questions in the south.  For a complete lists of questions, see the codebook.).</fileCont>
        <fileStrc type="rectangular">
        </fileStrc>
        <dimensns>
            <caseQnty>23806</caseQnty>
            <varQnty>142</varQnty>
            <logRecL>697</logRecL>
        </dimensns>
        <fileType charset="us-ascii">ASCII data file</fileType>
        <format>fixed-format</format>
        <filePlac>Social Science Research Facility, University of Minnesota</filePlac>
        <dataChck>The Data Producer produced a codebook for this dataset.  The Data Producer provided frequencies for this
dataset.</dataChck>
        <ProcStat>The Data Producer notes that the data at this stage has not undergone final cleaning and editing.  A new version,
soon to be released, will undergo
final cleaning and editing.</ProcStat>
        <dataMsng>Missing data are represented by blanks.</dataMsng>
        <software version="6.1">SPSS for Solaris</software>
    </fileTxt>
</fileDscr>
```

Figure 23.4   File description example.

of the file is the macro view. It provides the name of the file and information on the general content, such as the number of cases and records in the file. The next level is the record. Each record is made up of a number of variables. A case may have multiple records that relate to each other in a specific way—for example, a household consisting of zero or more families and one or more persons. This level of information is provided within the File Description (see figure 23.4).

DATA DESCRIPTION (MODULE 4)

The variables themselves are described in the Data Description. For each individual variable item such as name, description, weight, location, response categories, and question, the information is given (see figure 23.5). In addition, information about structural, logical, and thematic groupings of variables is provided. This is the level of information needed by the researcher to assess the ability of a data set to meet his or her current needs and which is not possible to provide within a bibliographic record. It is the information that makes machine processing of the data set possible.

OTHER MATERIAL (MODULE 5)

This module provides a home for the inclusion of all other materials that are related to the study, such as bibliographies, reports, data definition statements for specific software, and PDF files or other facsimile materials.

In developing the codebook.dtd, great care was taken to ensure compatibility with bibliographic standards. All citation elements contain the attribute MARCURI, which allows for a link to an existing MARC record for the citation item (marked-up codebook, source, study, and all related publication and other document sections). In identifying specific

VARIABLE AS EXPRESSED IN XML CODEBOOK | VARIABLE AS EXPRESSED IN TRADITIONAL PRINT CODEBOOK

```
<var ID="A13" name="owner" format="numeric"
Dcml="0" sdatref="ACS ACE AU">
  <location StartPos="33" EndPos="33"
width="1"></location>
  <labl>Owner</labl>
  <security>public</security>
  <respUnit>Respondent</respUnit>
  <anlysUnit>Farm</anlysUnit>
  <qstn>
    <qstnLit>Tenure.  Owner.</qstnLit>
  </qstn>
  <valrng>
    <range min="0" max="1"></range>
      <key>
       0 Not Owner
       1 Owner
      </key>
  </valrng>
  <TotlResp>2006</TotlResp>
  <sumStat type="medn">1</sumStat>
  <sumStat type="mode">1</sumStat>
  <sumStat type="vald">2006</sumStat>
  <sumStat type="invd">0</sumStat>
  <sumStat type="min">0</sumStat>
  <sumStat type="max">1</sumStat>
  <catgry>
    <catValu>0</catValu>
    <labl>Not Owner</labl>
    <txt>Individuals coded Not Owner appear
either as cash tenants or production
        tenants.</txt>
    <catStat type="freq">551</catStat>
    <catStat type="percent">27.5</catStat>
  </catgry>
  <catgry>
    <catValu>1</catValu>
        <labl>Owner</labl>
    <catStat type="freq">1454</catStat>
    <catStat type="percent">72.5</catStat>
  </catgry>
</var>
```

```
Q. Tenure.  Owner.

Var.   Name            Start    End   Size
A13    Owner              33     33      1
       (Universe: Farms)
       (0:1)

Not Owner*
Owner
                      Freq     %Freq

        0             551      27.5
        1            1454      72.5


* Individuals coded Not Owner appear either
as cash tenants or production tenants.
```

Figure 23.5 Data description variables (a comparison).

mapping, the Dublin Core was selected as a common standard for exchange. Given that most of the content and XML coding is not being prepared by librarians, the looser requirements and broader acceptance of the Dublin Core seemed more appropriate. However, the codebook.dtd provides additional entry detail to be positioned to map to a number of the more specific fields in the MARC 21 format. Elements within the codebook.dtd allow for identification of specific formats when entries meet more stringent authority controls. In table 23.1, the elements map to the Dublin Core and through that to the MARC 21 format.

The DDI Committee is concerned with continued compatibility with bibliographic as well as other electronic formats. The selection of XML was based not only on the features that it offered but also on its growing use in Web tools and by other major collections of electronic formats, such as the Encoded Archival Description (EAD) and Text Encoding Initiative (TEI). The goal of providing access to social science data from a variety of perspectives in an integrated manner compels its developers to seek compatibility with other descriptive schema at various levels. As long as compatibility does not compromise the ability of the codebook.dtd to describe the social science data collection without loss of information, the developers will continue to support compatible formats. The complete DDI codebook schema is shown in figure 23.6.

Table 23.1 Mapping from DDI to Dublin Core to MARC 21.

DDI Elements	Dublin Core	MARC 21
*Within the **docSrc**—**citation**—*		
• **title** (Title of the Marked-up Document)	Title	245 00$a (Title Statement/Title Proper)
• **AuthEnty** (Authoring Entity)	Creator	720 ##$a with $e=author
• **producer** (Producer of the Marked-up Document)	Publisher	260 ##$b with $e=publisher
• **othId** (Other Identity and Acknowledgement)	Contributor	720 ##$a with $e=collaborator
• **prodDate** (Date of Production of the Marked-up Document)	Date	260 ##$c [additional dates may map to other DDI date fields]
• The URL for the DDI Codebook is suggested, if applicable. Alternatively, use the **IDNo**	Identifier	024 8#$a [more specific use of Scheme=URL: 856 40$u possible]
• Partially maps to **docSrc** (within **docDscr**). No mapping currently exists for the relation type component.	Relation	787 0#$n
• **copyright** (Copyright)	Rights	540 ##$s
*Within the **stdyDscr**—**stdyInfo**—*		
• **keyword** (Keywords)	Subject	653##$a
• **topcClas** (Topic Classification)		
• **abstract** (Study Abstract)	Description	520 ##$a (Summary, etc. notes)
• **timePrd** (Time Period Covered)	Coverage	500$a (General note)
• **collDate** (Date of Data Collection)		[Date.DataGathered: 567 ##$a
• **nation** (Country)		Coverage.Spatial: 522 ##$a
• **geogCover** (Geographic Coverage)		Coverage:Temporal 513 ##$b]

DDI Codebook Schema

```
* == ELEMENT IS OPTIONAL & REPEATABLE
+ == ELEMENT IS MANDATORY & REPEATABLE
? == ELEMENT IS OPTIONAL & NON-REPEATABLE
  == ELEMENT IS MANDATORY & NON-REPEATABLE

codeBook (ATT == ID, xml:lang, source)
|— docDscr* (ATT == ID, xml:lang, source)
|   |— citation? (ATT == ID, xml:lang, source, MARCURI)
|   |   |— titlStmt (ATT == ID, xml:lang, source)
|   |   |   |— titl       (ATT == ID, xml:lang, source)
|   |   |   |— subTitl*   (ATT == ID, xml:lang, source)
|   |   |   |— altTitl*   (ATT == ID, xml:lang, source)
|   |   |   |— parTitl*   (ATT == ID, xml:lang, source)
|   |   |   +— IDNo*      (ATT == ID, xml:lang, source, agency)
|   |   |— rspStmt? (ATT == ID, xml:lang, source)
|   |   |   |— AuthEnty*  (ATT == ID, xml:lang, source, affiliation)
|   |   |   +— othId*     (ATT == ID, xml:lang, source, type, role, affiliation)
|   |   |— prodStmt? (ATT == ID, xml:lang, source)
|   |   |   |— producer*  (ATT == ID, xml:lang, source, abbr, affiliation, role)
|   |   |   |— copyright? (ATT == ID, xml:lang, source)
|   |   |   |— prodDate*  (ATT == ID, xml:lang, source, date)
|   |   |   |— prodPlac*  (ATT == ID, xml:lang, source)
|   |   |   |— software*  (ATT == ID, xml:lang, source, date, version)
|   |   |   |— fundAg*    (ATT == ID, xml:lang, source, abbr, role)
|   |   |   +— grantNo*   (ATT == ID, xml:lang, source, agency, role)
|   |   |— distStmt? (ATT == ID, xml:lang, source)
|   |   |   |— distrbtr* (ATT == ID, xml:lang, source, abbr, affiliation, URI)
|   |   |   |— contact*  (ATT == ID, xml:lang, source, affiliation, URI, email)
|   |   |   |— depositr* (ATT == ID, xml:lang, source, abbr, affiliation)
|   |   |   |— depDate*  (ATT == ID, xml:lang, source, date)
```

Figure 23.6 The complete DDI codebook schema.

```
|   |   |   +— distDate?  (ATT == ID, xml:lang, source, date)
|   |   |— serStmt? (ATT == ID, xml:lang, source, URI)
|   |   |   |— serName*  (ATT == ID, xml:lang, source, abbr)
|   |   |   +— serInfo*  (ATT == ID, xml:lang, source)
|   |   |— verStmt* (ATT == ID, xml:lang, source)
|   |   |   |— version?  (ATT == ID, xml:lang, source, type, date)
|   |   |   |— verResp?  (ATT == ID, xml:lang, source, affiliation)
|   |   |   +— notes?     (ATT == ID, xml:lang, source, type, subject, level, resp)
|   |   |— biblCit?   (ATT == ID, xml:lang, source, format)
|   |   |— holdings* (ATT == ID, xml:lang, source, location, callno, URI)
|   |   +— notes?      (ATT == ID, xml:lang, source, type, subject, level, resp)
|   |— guide?      (ATT == ID, xml:lang, source)
|   |— docStatus? (ATT == ID, xml:lang, source)
|   |— docSrc*     (ATT == ID, xml:lang, source, MARCURI)
|   |   |—titlStmt (ATT == ID, xml:lang, source)
|   |   |   |— titl       (ATT == ID, xml:lang, source)
|   |   |   |— subTitl*  (ATT == ID, xml:lang, source)
|   |   |   |— altTitl*   (ATT == ID, xml:lang, source)
|   |   |   |— parTitl*   (ATT == ID, xml:lang, source)
|   |   |   +— IDNo*     (ATT == ID, xml:lang, source, agency)
|   |   |— rspStmt? (ATT == ID, xml:lang, source)
|   |   |   |— AuthEnty*      (ATT == ID, xml:lang, source, affiliation)
|   |   |   |— othId*             (ATT == ID, xml:lang, source, type, role, affiliation)
|   |   |— prodStmt? (ATT == ID, xml:lang, source)
|   |   |   |— producer*      (ATT == ID, xml:lang, source,  abbr, affiliation, role)
|   |   |   |— copyright?      (ATT == ID, xml:lang, source)
|   |   |   |— prodDate*      (ATT == ID, xml:lang, source, date)
|   |   |   |— prodPlac*      (ATT == ID, xml:lang, source)
|   |   |   |— software*      (ATT == ID, xml:lang, source, date, version)
|   |   |   |— fundAg*        (ATT == ID, xml:lang, source, abbr, role)
|   |   |   +— grantNo*       (ATT == ID, xml:lang, source, agency, role)
|   |   |— distStmt? (ATT == ID, xml:lang, source)
|   |   |   |— distrbtr*    (ATT == ID, xml:lang, source, abbr, affiliation, URI)
|   |   |   |— contact*    (ATT == ID, xml:lang, source, affiliation, URI, email)
|   |   |   |— depositr*   (ATT == ID, xml:lang, source, abbr, affiliation)
|   |   |   |— depDate*   (ATT == ID, xml:lang, source, date)
|   |   |   +— distDate?  (ATT == ID, xml:lang, source, date)
|   |   |— serStmt? (ATT == ID, xml:lang, source, URI)
|   |   |   |— serName*  (ATT == ID, xml:lang, source, abbr)
|   |   |   +— serInfo*  (ATT == ID, xml:lang, source)
|   |   |— verStmt* (ATT == ID, xml:lang, source)
|   |   |   |— version?  (ATT == ID, xml:lang, source, type, date)
|   |   |   |— verResp?  (ATT == ID, xml:lang, source, affiliation)
|   |   |   +— notes?     (ATT == ID, xml:lang, source, type, subject, level, resp)
|   |   |— biblCit?   (ATT == ID, xml:lang, source, format)
|   |   |— holdings* (ATT == ID, xml:lang, source, location, callno, URI)
|   |   +— notes?      (ATT == ID, xml:lang, source, type, subject, level, resp)
|   +— notes?     (ATT == ID, xml:lang, source, type, subject, level, resp)
|— stdyDscr+ (ATT == ID, xml:lang, source, access)
|   |— citation+ (ATT == ID, xml:lang, source, MARCURI)
|   |   |— titlStmt (ATT == ID, xml:lang, source)
|   |   |   |— titl       (ATT == ID, xml:lang, source)
|   |   |   |— subTitl*  (ATT == ID, xml:lang, source)
|   |   |   |— altTitl*   (ATT == ID, xml:lang, source)
|   |   |   |— parTitl*   (ATT == ID, xml:lang, source)
|   |   |   +— IDNo*     (ATT == ID, xml:lang, source, agency)
|   |   |— rspStmt? (ATT == ID, xml:lang, source)
|   |   |   |— AuthEnty*      (ATT == ID, xml:lang, source, affiliation)
|   |   |   +— othId*             (ATT == ID, xml:lang, source, type, role, affiliation)
```

Figure 23.6 The complete DDI codebook schema. *(continued)*

```
|   |   |— prodStmt? (ATT == ID, xml:lang, source)
|   |   |   |— producer*        (ATT == ID, xml:lang, source, abbr, affilation, role)
|   |   |   |— copyright?       (ATT == ID, xml:lang, source)
|   |   |   |— prodDate*        (ATT == ID, xml:lang, source, date)
|   |   |   |— prodPlac*        (ATT == ID, xml:lang, source)
|   |   |   |— software*        (ATT == ID, xml:lang, source, date, version)
|   |   |   |— fundAg*          (ATT == ID, xml:lang, source, abbr, role)
|   |   |   +— grantNo*         (ATT == ID, xml:lang, source, agency, role)
|   |   |— distStmt?  (ATT == ID, xml:lang, source)
|   |   |   |— distrbtr*        (ATT == ID, xml:lang, source, abbr, affiliation, URI)
|   |   |   |— contact*         (ATT == ID, xml:lang, source, affiliation, URI, email)
|   |   |   |— depositr*        (ATT == ID, xml:lang, source, abbr, affiliation)
|   |   |   |— depDate*         (ATT == ID, xml:lang, source, date)
|   |   |   +— distDate?        (ATT == ID, xml:lang, source, date)
|   |   |— serStmt?  (ATT == ID, xml:lang, source, URI)
|   |   |   |— serName*  (ATT == ID, xml:lang, source, abbr)
|   |   |   +— serInfo*    (ATT == ID, xml:lang, source)
|   |   |— verStmt* (ATT == ID, xml:lang, source)
|   |   |   |— version?   (ATT == ID, xml:lang, source, type, date)
|   |   |   |— verResp?   (ATT == ID, xml:lang, source, affiliation)
|   |   |   +— notes?     (ATT == ID, xml:lang, source, type, subject, level, resp)
|   |   |— biblCit?    (ATT == ID, xml:lang, source, format)
|   |   |— holdings* (ATT == ID, xml:lang, source, location, callno, URI)
|   |   +— notes?     (ATT == ID, xml:lang, source, type, subject, level, resp)
|   |— stdyInfo* (ATT == ID, xml:lang, source)
|   |   |— subject? (ATT == ID, xml:lang, source)
|   |   |   |— keyword*   (ATT == ID, xml:lang, source, vocab, vocabURI)
|   |   |   +— topcClas*  (ATT == ID, xml:lang, source, vocab, vocabURI)
|   |   |— abstract*  (ATT == ID, xml:lang, source, date)
|   |   |— sumDscr*(ATT == ID, xml:lang, source)
|   |   |   |— timePrd*       (ATT == ID, xml:lang, source, event, date)
|   |   |   |— collDate*      (ATT == ID, xml:lang, source, event, date)
|   |   |   |— nation*        (ATT == ID, xml:lang, source, abbr)
|   |   |   |— geogCover*     (ATT == ID, xml:lang, source)
|   |   |   |— geogUnit       ATT == ID, xml:lang, source)
|   |   |   |— anlyUnit*      (ATT == ID, xml:lang, source, unit)
|   |   |   |— universe*      (ATT == ID, xml:lang, source, level, clusion)
|   |   |   +— dataKind*      (ATT == ID, xml:lang, source)
|   |   +— notes? (ATT == ID, xml:lang, source, type, subject, level, resp)
|   |— method*(ATT == ID, xml:lang, source)
|   |   |— dataColl*  (ATT == ID, xml:lang, source)
|   |   |   |— timeMeth*          (ATT == ID, xml:lang, source, method)
|   |   |   |— dataCollector*     (ATT == ID, xml:lang, source, abbr, affiliation)
|   |   |   |— frequenc*          (ATT == ID, xml:lang, source, freq)
|   |   |   |— sampProc           (ATT == ID, xml:lang, source)
|   |   |   |— deviat*            (ATT == ID, xml:lang, source)
|   |   |   |— collMode*          (ATT == ID, xml:lang, source)
|   |   |   |— resInstru*         (ATT == ID, xml:lang, source, type)
|   |   |   |— sources?           (ATT == ID, xml:lang, source)<-+
|   |   |   |   |— dataSrc*       (ATT == ID, xml:lang, source)   |
|   |   |   |   |— srcOrig*       (ATT == ID, xml:lang, source)   |
|   |   |   |   |— srcChar*       (ATT == ID, xml:lang, source)   |
|   |   |   |   |— srcDocu*       (ATT == ID, xml:lang, source)   |
|   |   |   |   +— sources*       (ATT == ID, xml:lang, source) —-+
|   |   |   |   NOTE: ELEMENT sources has recursive definition, so any  within a codebook
|   |   |   |            can themselves list multiple, subsidiary sources
|   |   |   |— collSitu*          (ATT == ID, xml:lang, source)
|   |   |   |— actMin*            (ATT == ID, xml:lang, source)
|   |   |   |— ConOps*            (ATT == ID, xml:lang, source, agency)
```

Figure 23.6   The complete DDI codebook schema. *(continued)*

```
|   |   |   |— weight*          (ATT == ID, xml:lang, source)
|   |   |   +— cleanOps*        (ATT == ID, xml:lang, source)
|   |   |— notes?       (ATT == ID, xml:lang, source, type, subject, level, resp)
|   |   |— anlyInfo?  (ATT == ID, xml:lang, source)
|   |   |   |— respRate*     (ATT == ID, xml:lang, source)
|   |   |   |— EstSmpErr*    (ATT == ID, xml:lang, source)
|   |   |   +— dataAppr*     (ATT == ID, xml:lang, source)
|   |   +— stdyClas? (ATT == ID, xml:lang, source, type)
|   |— dataAccs* (ATT == ID, xml:lang, source)
|   |   |— setAvail* (ATT == ID, xml:lang, source, media)
|   |   |   |— accsPlac*     (ATT == ID, xml:lang, source, URI)
|   |   |   |— origArch?     (ATT == ID, xml:lang, source)
|   |   |   |— avlStatus*    (ATT == ID, xml:lang, source)
|   |   |   |— collSize?     (ATT == ID, xml:lang, source)
|   |   |   |— complete?     (ATT == ID, xml:lang, source)
|   |   |   |— fileQnty?     (ATT == ID, xml:lang, source)
|   |   |   +— notes*        (ATT == ID, xml:lang, source, type, subject, level, resp)
|   |   |—useStmt* (ATT == ID, xml:lang, source)
|   |   |   |— confDec?      (ATT == ID, xml:lang, source, required, formNo, URI)
|   |   |   |— specPerm?     (ATT == ID, xml:lang, source, required, formNo, URI)
|   |   |   |— restrctn?     (ATT == ID, xml:lang, source)
|   |   |   |— contact*      (ATT == ID, xml:lang, source, affiliation, URI, email)
|   |   |   |— citReq?       (ATT == ID, xml:lang, source)
|   |   |   |— deposReq?     (ATT == ID, xml:lang, source)
|   |   |   |— conditions?   (ATT == ID, xml:lang, source)
|   |   |   +— disclaimer?   (ATT == ID, xml:lang, source)
|   |   +— notes? (ATT == ID, xml:lang, source, type, subject, level, resp)
|   +— othrStdyMat* (ATT == ID, xml:lang, source)
|       |— relMat*       (ATT == ID, xml:lang, source)
|       |   +— citation*     (ATT == ID, xml:lang, source, MARCURI)
|       |— relStdy*      (ATT == ID, xml:lang, source)
|       |   +— citation*     (ATT == ID, xml:lang, source, MARCURI)
|       |— relPubl*      (ATT == ID, xml:lang, source)
|       |   +— citation*     (ATT == ID, xml:lang, source, MARCURI)
|       +— othRefs*      (ATT == ID, xml:lang, source)
|           +— citation*     (ATT == ID, xml:lang, source, MARCURI)
|     NOTE: complete tree under citation element omitted for reasons of space
|— fileDscr* (ATT == ID, xml:lang, source, URI, sdatrefs, methrefs, pubrefs, access)
|   |— fileTxt? (ATT == ID, xml:lang, source)
|   |   |— fileName? (ATT == ID, xml:lang, source)
|   |   |— fileCont?   (ATT == ID, xml:lang, source)
|   |   |— fileStrc?   (ATT == ID, xml:lang, source, type)
|   |   |   |— recGrp*   (ATT == ID, xml:lang, source, recGrp, rectype, keyvar, recidvar)
|   |   |   |   |— labl*         (ATT =- ID, xml:lang, source, level, vendor)
|   |   |   |   +— recDimnsn?   (ATT == ID, xml:lang, source, level)
|   |   |   |       |— varQnty?        (ATT == ID, xml:lang, source)
|   |   |   |       |— caseQnty?       (ATT == ID, xml:lang, source)
|   |   |   |       +— logRecL?        (ATT == ID, xml:lang, source)
|   |   |   +— notes?  (ATT == ID, xml:lang, source, type, subject, level, resp)
|   |   |— dimensns? (ATT == ID, xml:lang, source)
|   |   |   |— caseQnty*    (ATT == ID, xml:lang, source)
|   |   |   |— varQnty*     (ATT == ID, xml:lang, source)
|   |   |   |— logRecL*     (ATT == ID, xml:lang, source)
|   |   |   |— recPrCas*    (ATT == ID, xml:lang, source)
|   |   |   +— recNumTot*  (ATT == ID, xml:lang, source)
|   |   |— fileType?    (ATT == ID, xml:lang, source, charset)
|   |   |— format?      (ATT == ID, xml:lang, source)
|   |   |— filePlac?    (ATT == ID, xml:lang, source)
|   |   |— dataChck?    (ATT == ID, xml:lang, source)
```

Figure 23.6   The complete DDI codebook schema. *(continued)*

```
|   |   |— ProcStat?     (ATT == ID, xml:lang, source)
|   |   |— dataMsng? (ATT == ID, xml:lang, source)
|   |   |— software*  (ATT == ID, xml:lang, source, date, version)
|   |   +— verStmt?   (ATT == ID, xml:lang, source)
|   |        |— version?    (ATT == ID, xml:lang, source, type, date)
|   |        |— verResp?    (ATT == ID, xml:lang, source, affiliation)
|   |        +— notes?      (ATT == ID, xml:lang, source, type, subject, level, resp)
|   +— notes?  (ATT == ID, xml:lang, source, type, subject, level, resp)
|— dataDscr* (ATT == ID, xml:lang, source)
|   |— varGrp*  (ATT == ID, xml:lang, source, type, var, varGrp, name, sdatrefs,
|   |                      methrefs, pubrefs, access)
|   |   |— labl*      (ATT == ID, xml:lang, source, level, vendor)
|   |   |— txt*       (ATT == ID, xml:lang, source, level)
|   |   |— defntn?    (ATT == ID, xml:lang, source)
|   |   |— universe?  (ATT == ID, xml:lang, source, level, clusion)
|   |   +— notes?     (ATT == ID, xml:lang, source, type, subject, level, resp)
|   +— var* (ATT == ID, xml:lang, source, name, wgt, wgt-var, qstn, files,
|        |          vendor, dcml, intrvl, rectype, sdatrefs, methrefs, pubrefs, access)
|        |— location*        (ATT == ID, xml:lang, source, StartPos, EndPos, width,
|        |                        RecSegNo, fileid)
|        |— labl*            (ATT == ID, xml:lang, source, level, vendor)
|        |— imputation?      (ATT == ID, xml:lang, source)
|        |— security?        (ATT == ID, xml:lang, source, date)
|        |— embargo?         (ATT == ID, xml:lang, source, date, event, format)
|        |— respUnit?        (ATT == ID, xml:lang, source)
|        |— anlysUnit?       (ATT == ID, xml:lang, source)
|        |— qstn*            (ATT == ID, xml:lang, source, qstn, var, seqNo, sdatrefs)
|        |   |— preQTxt*     (ATT == ID, xml:lang, source)
|        |   |— qstnLit*     (ATT == ID, xml:lang, source)
|        |   |— postQTxt*    (ATT == ID, xml:lang, source)
|        |   |— forward*     (ATT == ID, xml:lang, source, qstn)
|        |   |— backward*    (ATT == ID, xml:lang, source, qstn)
|        |   +— ivuInstr*    (ATT == ID, xml:lang, source)
|        |        NOTE: qstn ELEMENT may include mixed #PCDATA content
|        |— valrng*          (ATT == ID, xml:lang, source)
|        |   |— range*   (ATT == ID, xml:lang, source, UNITS, min, minExclusive
|        |   |— item*    (ATT == ID, xml:lang, source, UNITS, VALUE)
|        |   |— key?     (ATT == ID, xml:lang, source)
|        |   +— notes?   (ATT == ID, xml:lang, source, type, subject, level, resp)
|        |— invalrng*         (ATT == ID, xml:lang, source)
|        |   |— range*   (ATT == ID, xml:lang, source, UNITS, min, minExclusive
|        |   |— item*    (ATT == ID, xml:lang, source, UNITS, VALUE)
|        |   +— key?     (ATT == ID, xml:lang, source)
|        |   +— notes?   (ATT == ID, xml:lang, source, type, subject, level, resp)
|        |— undocCod*   (ATT == ID, xml:lang, source)
|        |— universe*   (ATT == ID, xml:lang, source, level, clusion)
|        |— TotlResp?   (ATT == ID, xml:lang, source)
|        |— sumStat*    (ATT == ID, xml:lang, source, wgtd, weight, type)
|        |— txt*        (ATT == ID, xml:lang, source, level)
|        |— stdCatgry*  (ATT == ID, xml:lang, source, URI)
|        |— catgryGrp* (ATT == ID, xml:lang, source, missing, missType, catgry, catGrp)
|        |   |— labl*   (ATT == ID, xml:lang, source, level, vendor)
|        |   +— txt*    (ATT == ID, xml:lang, source, level)
|        |— catgry*    (ATT == ID, xml:lang, source, missing, missType, country)
```

Figure 23.6   The complete DDI codebook schema. *(continued)*

```
|        |    |— catValu?    (ATT == ID, xml:lang, source)
|        |    |— labl*       (ATT == ID, xml:lang, source, level, vendor)
|        |    |— txt*        (ATT == ID, xml:lang, source, level)
|        |    +— catStat*    (ATT == ID, xml:lang, source, type, URI)
|        |— codInstr*   (ATT == ID, xml:lang, source)
|        |— verStmt*    (ATT == ID, xml:lang, source)
|        |    |— version?    (ATT == ID, xml:lang, source, type, date)
|        |    |— verResp?    (ATT == ID, xml:lang, source, affiliation)
|        |    +— notes?      (ATT == ID, xml:lang, source, type, subject, level, resp)
|        |— concept*    (ATT == ID, xml:lang, source, vocab, vocabURI)
|        |— derivation?  (ATT == ID, xml:lang, source, var)
|        |    |— drvdesc?    (ATT == ID, xml:lang, source)
|        |    +— drvcmd?     (ATT == ID, xml:lang, source, syntax)
|        |— varFormat?  (ATT == ID, xml:lang, source, type, formatname, schema,
|        |                              category, URI)
|        +— notes*      (ATT == ID, xml:lang, source, type, subject, level, resp)
+— otherMat* (ATT == ID, xml:lang, source, type, level, URI)  <——————————+
      |                                    |
      |— labl*   (ATT == ID, xml:lang, source, level, vendor)          |
      |— txt?   (ATT == ID, xml:lang, source, level)                   |
      |— notes?  (ATT == ID, xml:lang, source, type, subject, level, resp)  |
      |— table*  (ATT == ID, xml:lang, source)                         |
      | - citation?    (ATT == ID, xml:lang, source, MARCURI)          |
      |    NOTE: full tree for citation element omitted for reasons of space |
      +— otherMat*   (ATT == ID, xml:lang, source, type, level, URI) —————————+
              NOTE: otherMat is recursively defined
```

Figure 23.6   The complete DDI code bookschema. *(continued)*

NOTES

1. Sue A. Dodd, *Cataloging Machine-Readable Data Files: An Interpretive Manual* (Chicago: American Library Association, 1982), xv–xvii.

2. Ann Green and Peter Joftis, "The Data Documentation Initiative: Current Status, Future Plans, and Structure" (paper presented at the FASTER Metadata Workshop, Voorburg, the Netherlands, April 2000).

3. Data Documentation Initiative, "DDI Codebook Schema," April 12, 2000, http://www.icpsr.umich.edu/DDI/ddischem.html.

4. For the complete DDI DTD Version 1.0 Tag Library of Element and Attribute descriptions and structural scheme, consult the Data Documentation Initiative homepage at http://www.icpsr.umich.edu/DDI/codebook.html.

5. All codebook samples in this paper are from: William C. Block, "An XML Codebook for a Nationally Representative Linked Sample of Population and Agriculture: The United States in 1880" (Minneapolis, Minn.: University of Minnesota, Minnesota Population Center [producer], 2000).

24

Dublin Core for Digital Video Clips

Beth Picknally Camden

In 1998, the University of Virginia Library embarked on a new phase of its digital library development, looking at integrated management of and access to electronic resources. This project builds on a history of electronic collections that include the founding of the Electronic Text Center in 1992, followed by other electronic centers that support collections in a variety of digital media, including statistical data, maps, images, and sound. The digital library project seeks to manage these growing electronic collections, provide an integrated search interface, and provide users with the tools they need to use and manage electronic materials.

Cataloging Services has been involved in cataloging electronic collections from the start, including bibliographic records in TEI (Text Encoding Initiative) Headers for electronic texts, as well as in the online catalog. Other types of electronic media have often been cataloged at the collection level using MARC records. Catalogers, in general, have had little practical exposure to types of metadata other than MARC. Discussions between the digital library project staff and the Cataloging department highlighted the importance of metadata to the digital library and the need for the skills of catalogers to work on this part of the project.

As the digital library project developed, the staff began to pull together a test bed with samples of the various types of electronic media collections available in the library. These included texts, finding aids, statistical data, images, sound, and maps. Sample collections were identified that had existing metadata from various sources. One area that was obviously lacking from the test bed was digital video. So, a collection of digital video clips was selected to round out the test bed.

The video clip collection had originally been created for a history class called "Viewing America." The professor, Brian Balogh, and his graduate students created video clips that are an integral part of his course about the history and culture of the late twentieth century, as part of the university's Teaching & Technology Initiative. The brief clips (generally less than two minutes) were extracted from videos in the library's collection and edited initially using analog tools, with the assistance of the library's Digital Media Center. The center later digitized the clips, first on CD-ROM and later for Web delivery. The only "metadata" available was an Access database developed by the creator for file tracking.

Working with the digital library project staff and the Digital Media Center, Cataloging mapped a local Dublin Core (DC) scheme for these digital video clips, using the sources available at the time (early 1999). These included: version 1.0 of the *Dublin Core Element Set*,[1] Rebecca Guenther's *Dublin Core Qualifiers/Substructure*,[2] and CIMI's *Guide to Best Practice: Dublin Core*[3] (then in draft form). We decided to use the information in the creator's database as the basis for the Dublin Core record. This was supplemented by information supplied programmatically to all records. This allowed the catalogers to focus on subject analysis and other areas needing their intellectual skills. A look at the Dublin Core field definitions, from the *Dublin Core Element Set*,[4] version 1.1, along with a discussion of the choices Virginia made for each field, will illustrate one approach to developing a local Dublin Core mapping.

TITLE

Definition: *A name given to the resource.*

Virginia used a descriptive title, which was supplied by the creator. Since these were brief extracts from much larger works, this information was especially helpful to the cataloger in identifying the creator's intent and often guided subject usage. Unlike electronic texts, title is not necessarily part of the digital resource. Occasionally, the cataloger supplied an additional title.

CREATOR

Definition: *An entity primarily responsible for making the content of the resource.*

Virginia used the name of the professor who created the clip. This was supplied by programming to all records. This decision was based on thinking of the video clip as a unique entity, compared to the original film/video. However, this sense of "authorship" does not ring true with many users. In retrospect, "Contributor" might have been a more useful choice.

SUBJECT

Definition: *The topic of the content of the resource.*

Virginia used a number of subject fields, including Library of Congress (LC) subject headings, LC name headings when appropriate, LC classification numbers, and additional keywords, when not already included in the title or summary. This was the main focus of the catalogers when editing the records.

DESCRIPTION

Definition: *An account of the content of the resource.*

Two Description fields were included in each record. The first was "Runtime." This was supplied by the creator and sometimes corrected by the cataloger. The second Description field included a brief summary (one or two sentences) created by the catalogers.

PUBLISHER

Definition: *An entity responsible for making the resource available.*

Virginia used a standard AACR publisher statement for the Library: "Charlottesville, Va.: University of Virginia Library." This was supplied by programming to all records.

CONTRIBUTOR

Definition: *An entity responsible for making contributions to the content of the resource.*

The Digital Media Center was given credit in all records as a Contributor, since it was the center that digitized the clips. This was supplied by programming to all records, using the standard LC name heading.

DATE

Definition: *A date associated with an event in the life cycle of the resource.*

This field was used for the date of the event, as supplied by the Creator. This field could be considered somewhat controversial. Many dates are associated with these digital objects, including date of the event, date the film was made, date of the video version, and date of the digital version. Which dates are meaningful to users? For documentaries, date of the event is probably the best choice. For feature films, the date of the film is most meaningful to users (this is not the AACR choice).

TYPE

Definition: *The nature or genre of the content of the resource.*

The type "image.moving" was supplied by programming to all records. Virginia is also considering a local extension of this Dublin Core field to enable sorting by broad content type—for example, feature film vs. documentary.

FORMAT

Definition: *The physical or digital manifestation of the resource.* (May be used to determine necessary software.)
The format "image/mpeg" from the Internet Media Types (IMT) scheme was supplied by programming to all records.

IDENTIFIER

Definition: *An unambiguous reference to the resource within a given context.*
The file name supplied by the creator was used, with the scheme URL. Since the catalogers were working with CD-ROM copies of the video clips, the complete URL was unavailable. This identifier is translated into a URN (uniform resource name) when loaded into the digital library.

SOURCE

Definition: *A reference to a resource from which the present resource is derived.*
The Source field includes the title and call number of original video, supplied by the Creator. The cataloger updated as needed and added the date of the source. This field overlaps with our usage of the "Relation" field.

LANGUAGE

Definition: *A language of the intellectual content of the resource.*
The IS0 639 code "en" was supplied by programming to all records. Virtually all clips were in English. The cataloger updated as needed, removing for silent clips.

RELATION

Definition: *A reference to a related resource.*
The Relation field included the title and call number of the original video, supplied by the Creator. The cataloger updated as needed and added the date of the original. The type "IsPartOf" was used. This usage of the field overlaps with the "Source" field.

COVERAGE

Definition: *The extent or scope of the content of the resource.*
The University of Virginia used the Type "PeriodName" and included the decade that the clip covered—for example, 1970–1979. This was supplied by programming to all records, based on the creator's file-naming scheme, which included decade.

RIGHTS

Definition: *Information about rights held in and over the resource.*
A note restricting usage to the University of Virginia faculty, students, and staff was supplied by programming to all records. Since these clips were extracted from material under copyright, classroom/educational access had to be restricted under the fair-use guidelines. The digital library will also include administrative metadata to regulate access rights.

Following these Dublin Core mapping decisions, a programmer adapted an existing Web-based form for data entry (see figure 24.1). The data supplied by the Creator were mapped to records, along with the information we had decided to include in all records. The form included empty fields to prompt the cataloger for the most frequently added information. It also allowed for any field to be repeated as needed. Where appropriate, Scheme and Type qualifiers were included in drop-down menus. The goal was to simplify input for the catalogers and focus their time on the intellectual activity of subject analysis.

When the record was complete, the cataloger would save and then, with a single click, would invoke a "dcfilter" program. This program would add the appropriate Dublin Core tags and add the record to a different directory for later addition to the digital library, along with the related clip (see figure 24.2).

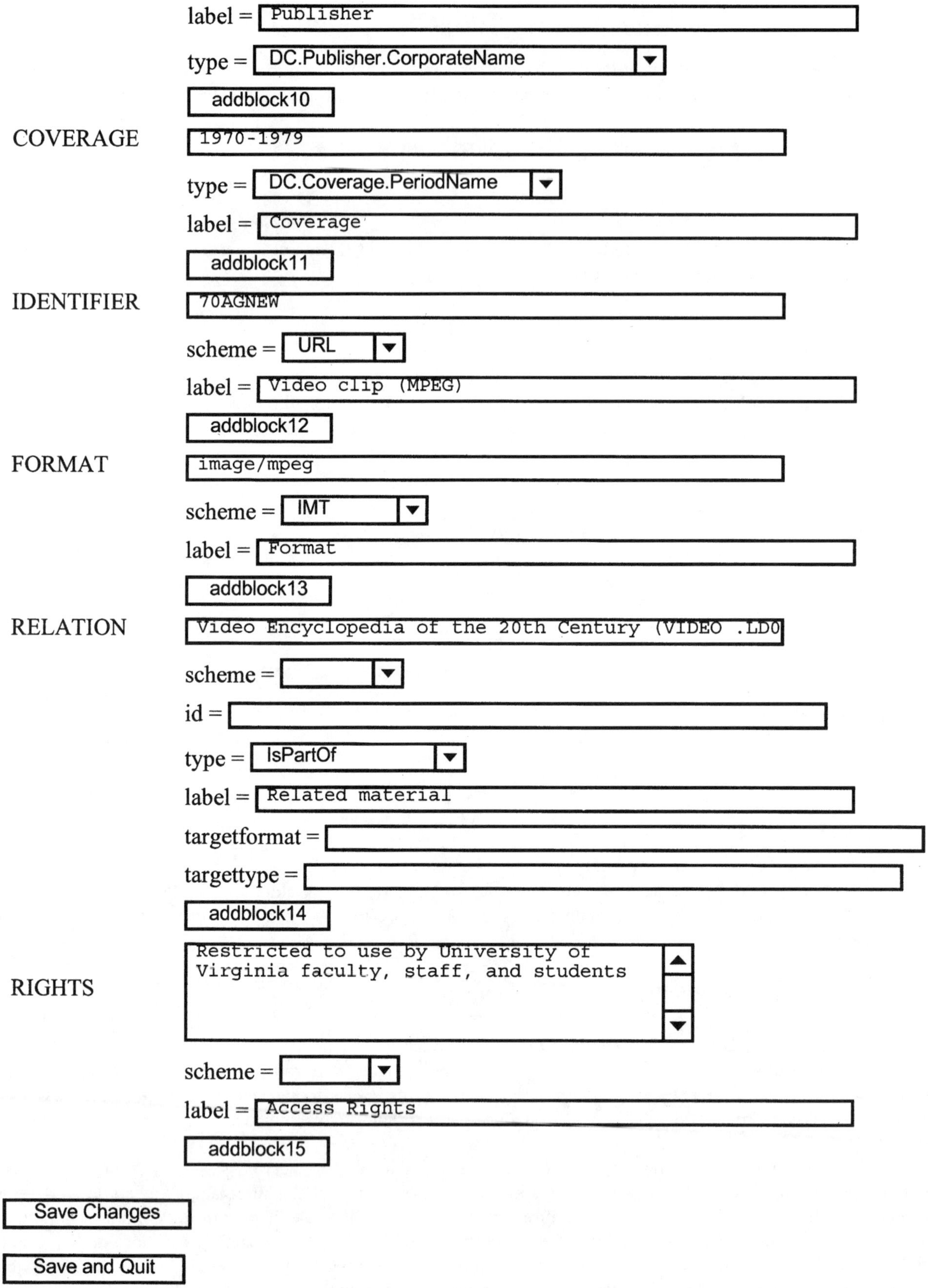

label = Publisher

type = DC.Publisher.CorporateName ▼

addblock10

COVERAGE

1970-1979

type = DC.Coverage.PeriodName ▼

label = Coverage

addblock11

IDENTIFIER

70AGNEW

scheme = URL ▼

label = Video clip (MPEG)

addblock12

FORMAT

image/mpeg

scheme = IMT ▼

label = Format

addblock13

RELATION

Video Encyclopedia of the 20th Century (VIDEO .LD0

scheme = ▼

id =

type = IsPartOf ▼

label = Related material

targetformat =

targettype =

addblock14

RIGHTS

Restricted to use by University of
Virginia faculty, staff, and students

scheme = ▼

label = Access Rights

addblock15

Save Changes

Save and Quit

Figure 24.1   Web-based data-entry form. (*continued*)

DESCRIPTION
```
Speech by Spiro Agnew attacking
intellectuals and the fourth estate, the
press.
```

scheme = [▼]

type = [DC.Description.Summary]

label = [Summary]

[addblock3]

DATE [1970]

scheme = [ISO8601 ▼]

type = [DC.Date.Created ▼]

label = [Date]

[addblock4]

TYPE [image.moving]

label = [Resource Type]

[addblock5]

SOURCE [Video Encyclopedia of the 20th Century (VIDEO .LD0]

scheme = [▼]

label = [Source]

[addblock6]

LANGUAGE [en]

scheme = [ISO639-1]

label = [Language]

[addblock7]

CREATOR [Balogh, Brian]

type = [DC.Creator.PersonalName ▼]

scheme = [LCNAF]

label = [Creator]

[addblock8]

CONTRIBUTOR [University of Virginia. Library. Digital Media Cen]

type = [DC.Creator.CorporateName ▼]

scheme = [LCNAF]

label = [Contributor]

[addblock9]

PUBLISHER [Charlottesville, Va.: University of Virginia Libra]

Figure 24.1 Web-based data-entry form. (*continued*)

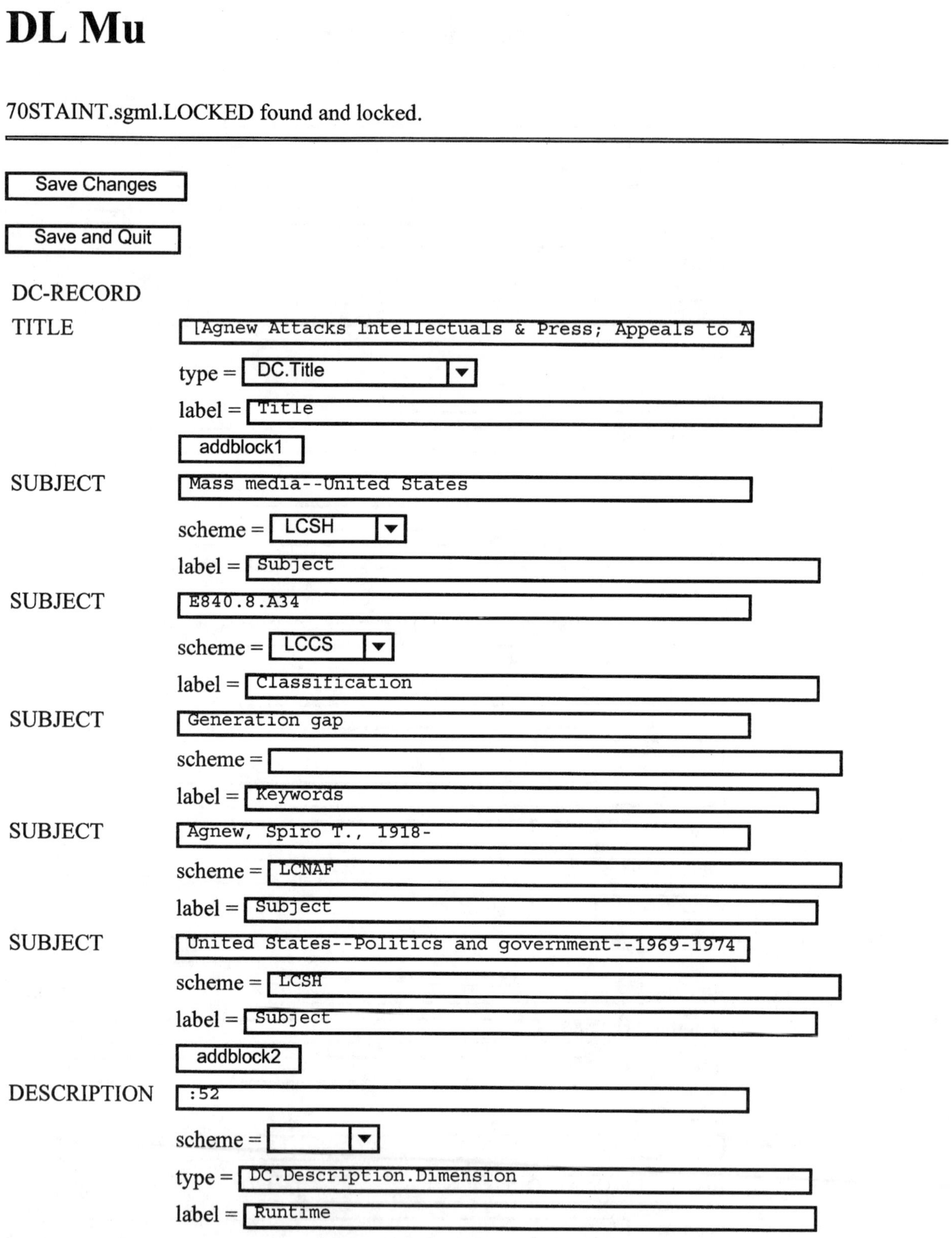

DL Mu

70STAINT.sgml.LOCKED found and locked.

| Save Changes |

| Save and Quit |

DC-RECORD

TITLE   `[Agnew Attacks Intellectuals & Press; Appeals to A`

       type = `DC.Title` ▼

       label = `Title`

       | addblock1 |

SUBJECT   `Mass media--United States`

       scheme = `LCSH` ▼

       label = `Subject`

SUBJECT   `E840.8.A34`

       scheme = `LCCS` ▼

       label = `Classification`

SUBJECT   `Generation gap`

       scheme =

       label = `Keywords`

SUBJECT   `Agnew, Spiro T., 1918-`

       scheme = `LCNAF`

       label = `Subject`

SUBJECT   `United States--Politics and government--1969-1974`

       scheme = `LCSH`

       label = `Subject`

       | addblock2 |

DESCRIPTION   `:52`

       scheme = ▼

       type = `DC.Description.Dimension`

       label = `Runtime`

Figure 24.1   Web-based data-entry form.

```
<DC-RECORD>
<TITLE type="DC.Title" label="Title">[Agnew Attacks Intellectuals & Press; Appeals to Average
American]
</TITLE>
<SUBJECT scheme="LCSH" label="Subject">Mass media—United States
</SUBJECT>
<SUBJECT scheme="LCCS" label="Classification">E840.8.A34
<SUBJECT scheme=""label="Keywords">Generation gap
<SUBJECT scheme="LCNAF" label="Subject">Agnew, Spiro T., 1918–
<SUBJECT scheme="LCSH" label="Subject">United States—Politics and government—1969–1974
<DESCRIPTION scheme="" type="DC.Description.Dimension" label="Runtime">:52
</DESCRIPTION>
<DESCRIPTION scheme="" type="DC.Description.Summary"label="Summary">Speech by Spiro
Agnew attacking intellectuals and the fourth
estate, the press.
</DESCRIPTION>
<DATE scheme="ISO8601" typc="DC.Date.Created" label="Date">1970
</DATE>
<TYPE label="Resource Type">image.moving
</TYPE>
<SOURCE scheme="" label="Source">Video Encyclopedia of the 20th Century (VIDEO .LD0669, pt.
25, B/13) published 1990
</SOURCE>
<LANGUAGE scheme="ISO639-1" label="Language">en
</LANGUAGE>
<CREATOR type="DC.Creator.PersonalName" scheme="LCNAF" label="Creator">Balogh, Brian
</CREATOR>
<CONTRIBUTOR type="DC.Creator.CorporateName" scheme="LCNAF"
label="Contributor">University of Virginia. Library. Digital Media
Center.
</CONTRIBUTOR>
<PUBLISHER label="Publisher" type="DC.Publisher.CorporateName">Charlottesville, Va.:
University of Virginia Library.
</PUBLISHER>
<COVERAGE type="DC.Coverage.PeriodName" label="Coverage">1970–1979
</COVERAGE>
<IDENTIFIER scheme="URL" label="Video clip (MPEG)">70AGNEW
</IDENTIFIER>
<FORMAT scheme="IMT" label="Format">image/mpeg
</FORMAT>
<RELATION scheme="" id=""type="IsPartOf" label="Related material" targetformat=""
targettype="">Video Encyclopedia of the 20th
Century (VIDEO .LD0669, pt. 25, B/13) published 1990
</RELATION>
<RIGHTS scheme=""label="Access Rights">Restricted to use by University of Virginia faculty, staff,
and students
</RIGHTS>
</DC-RECORD>
```

Figure 24.2   Data-entry form with Dublin Core tags.

During most of the project, the digital library test bed was still in development. Thus, all mapping decisions and most cataloging decisions were made in a vacuum. This was disconcerting for catalogers, who generally create records in a known context—OCLC or the local online catalog. Catalogers had to make choices without knowing how each video clip related to others or the rest of the digital library and without knowing how searching would work. However, catalogers found that working with Dublin Core and this project gave them the freedom to define their own rules. This was easy with the small number involved but would have been more difficult with a larger group. The project also brought to light concerns about merging multiple metadata schemes into the digital library. How will we reconcile various schemes, created with or without rules?

The digital video metadata project had a number of benefits for the University of Virginia Library. It provided a wider variety of digital objects in the digital library test bed, thus creating a model closer to reality. The project increased cooperation between digital library project staff and Cataloging and strengthened working relationships. It exposed more catalogers to Dublin Core and gave them practical working experience with it. Finally, it tested a model for future metadata projects, in which information from the digital object creator is supplemented by machine and enhanced by a cataloger. In the future, we look toward a greatly enhanced human/machine model for creation of the millions of metadata records that our digital library will need.

NOTES

1. Dublin Core Metadata Initiative, *Dublin Core Element Set, Version 1.0: Reference Description,* September 1998, http://purl.org/DC/documents/rec-dces-199809.htm.

2. Rebecca Guenther, *Dublin Core Qualifiers/Substructure,* October 15, 1997, http://www.loc.gov/marc/dcqualif.html.

3. Consortium for the Computer Interchange of Museum Information, *Guide to Best Practice: Dublin Core,* August 12, 1999, http://www.cimi.org/documents/meta_bestprac_final_0899.pdf.

4. Dublin Core Metadata Initiative, *Dublin Core Element Set, Version 1.1: Reference Description,* July 2, 1999, http://purl.org/DC/documents/rec-dces-19990702.htm.

VI

CONCLUSION:
WHERE ARE WE? WHERE ARE WE GOING?

25

Metadata: Hype and Glory

Michael Gorman

There is an old story about a fisherman fishing in a private river who, on being told, "You can't fish here!" replied, "But I *am* fishing here." This tale is illustrative not only of the difference between "may" and "can" that you should have learned at your mother's knee, but also of human beings' propensity to not realize that they are doing impossible things until they are told so. The impossible thing that librarians have been doing for a long time is classification—the reduction of the almost infinite dimensions of knowledge to a straight line from 000 to 999 or A to Z. Who but someone with the innate hubris of a cataloguer would dare to catch a flying complex subject and pin it to its exact place on that straight line to remain there forever? Now we have another impossible thing to do and we have to do it knowing that it is impossible—a thought that would never have occurred to, say, Melvil Dewey! This new impossible thing is to bring order to chaos, to trap lightning in a bottle, to take an electronic document with the lifespan of a mayfly (and, most likely, the cosmic significance of a mayfly) and make it part of an arranged and harmonious world—in short, to apply some kind of bibliographic control to the disorder of the Net and the Web. If, as politicians and futurists claim, untold intellectual riches are out there in cyberspace, what use are they if they cannot be found, and found, and found again with predictability and consistency? Until we have a Networld and a Webworld with the attributes of a well-organized major library, how will we ever know if those worlds have the potential to rival Libraryworld?

The attributes of a well-regulated library are well known to us all. They are organization, retrievability, authenticity, and fixity. There are those who claim that electronic documents and sites (assemblages of electronic documents) are different in kind and not just degree from all the other formats that human beings have used to communicate and preserve knowledge across the centuries. This is, essentially, an implausible notion—after all, at the end of the day we are still dealing with texts, images, sounds, and symbols—but its strongest support comes from the evanescence and mutability of electronic documents. Those characteristics, which any true librarian deplores, are really the logical outcome of the history of human communication—each format produces more documents than its predecessor, and each is less durable than its predecessor. It takes a long time to make many copies of stones bearing carved messages, but those messages can be read millennia later. You can send a message from Chicago to Addis Ababa in a twinkling of an eye, but that message may be expunged in a second twinkling. Many electronic documents are like those minute particles of matter that are only known because scientists can see where they have been during their micro-milliseconds of existence. Does an e-mail message exist if it is deleted unopened?

It seems to me that we should know, more precisely than we know now, exactly what we are dealing with when we talk of organizing documents and sites in cyberspace.

Ephemera. Libraries have always been far more selective than is generally acknowledged when it comes to their collections. I am not talking now of selection *within* formats (books, records, videos, etc.) but of ruling out, consciously or unconsciously, vast areas of recorded information. Much of the stuff that we used to ignore now shows up on the Net and the Web. To demonstrate this, just do a search on any subject and review the few thousand "hits" with a view to imagining their tangible analogues. Personal Web pages are the electronic versions of scrapbooks and diaries—of keen interest to their compilers but to few others. Restaurant reviews? Press releases in digital form? Association newsletters? Weather forecasts? Faculty lists of Australian universities? Syllabi? Advertisements? So, on and on it goes—acres of the cyberworld full of ephemera. What else is out there?

Print-derived resources. The one indisputably valuable sector of the Net is composed of many documents and sites that are derived from the print industry and are dependent on the success of that industry for their very existence. These do not, by and large, present much of a technical bibliographic control problem. We know, in principle, how to catalogue different format manifestations of texts and graphic publications—extending that knowledge into cyberspace is not a massive intellectual challenge. Further, print-derived electronic resources are far less transient than their purely electronic counterparts.

Commercial sites and pornography. People anxious to sell you something populate much of the electronic frontier. From e-tailers to business-to-business sites to pornographers, they are all pursuing the Great American Capitalist Dream, in the sure and certain knowledge that not only is there one born every minute but also that the one is likely to spend a lot of time online.

Here are the fundamental problems we encounter in trying to organize electronic documents and sites (other than those that are by-products of the print industries):

- There are too many of them.
- A lot of documents and sites have never been, and never will be, of interest to libraries and library users.
- The vast majority of such electronic documents are of temporary use, local use, or no use at all.
- We have little or no guarantee that any given electronic document is what it says it is.
- We have little or no assurance that any given document or site will be the same when next located or will even exist.
- There is nothing like the level of standardization of denotation and presentation that we find in books and other tangible library materials.

Far from being unique, these problems are uncannily like those of manuscripts and early printed texts. The manuscript swamp from which the early printed text emerged, taking fumbling steps at first, resembles nothing so much as the electronic swamp that we now confront. We are far from the exciting world of innovation and creativity that is presented by those who hope to make money from the "information age." What we are seeing is a cultural reversion, not cultural progress. The problem with the manuscript culture was that many texts were lost, many were altered in copying, many lacked such things as titles and discernible authors, and all lacked publishers and distributors. A library burning to the ground today is a local tragedy; in the past, a library of manuscripts burning to the ground was a cultural catastrophe from which there was no recovery. Anyone who has tried to catalogue electronic documents and sites will tell you that they are elusive and shape shifting, they often lack titles and discernible authors, they may or may not exist tomorrow, and they are subject to unpredictable change. Oh, and, once lost, they are lost forever. Sound familiar? There is, of course, one huge difference between the manuscript age and the looming electronic age. Pre-Gutenberg manuscripts were, by definition, created by an educated elite. Anyone doing a search using a search engine like AltaVista is soon made painfully aware that cyberspace is littered with the productions of stupid, semiliterate, and/or crazed individuals.

What shall we do about this reversion, this "back to the future" impending catastrophe? Those who throw up their hands in despair will surely be forgiven, but we librarians love action and will seek an answer no matter what. We need, first, to decide what we are seeking to organize. We can recognize pornography when we see it, as well as any Supreme Court justice. We can recognize commercial enterprises that need no help from us in bringing themselves to the attention of potential customers. We can probably recognize the ephemeral (though one librarian's ephemeron is another's invaluable cultural resource). That still leaves us with two large classes of material—print-derived resources and truly electronic resources of, at least, potential value to library users. As I have said, there is no doubt that we could relatively easily bring the print-derived resources into the world system of bibliographic control, using links from existing records, multilayered records, and full records using existing standards. Which, having eliminated the other slices of the electronic salami, still leaves us with a sizable chunk. That chunk consists of the potentially worthwhile scholarly and information resources that exist only in cyberspace and may or may not be retrievable at any given time, using search engines that use free-text keyword searching—well known to be the very worst information retrieval system conceived by human minds. Something is seductive about the "surfing" metaphor (especially when one remembers that surfing can be exhilarating, but you end up more or less where you started, only flat on your face in the sand), but, as a Californian, I think another Golden State metaphor—panning for gold—is more apt. Are we doomed to stand in the cold streams for the rest of our lives, engaged in the stoop labor of panning through the dross in ever-hopeful search of the glint of the one nugget among all the grit and stones? The answer is . . . maybe.

I have got this far in the chapter without mentioning the word *metadata* but will break that silence now. The idea behind metadata is that there is some Third Way, approximately halfway between cataloguing (expensive and effective) and keyword searching (cheap and ineffective). During the 2000 Annual ALA Conference, there was a program called (perhaps thinking wishfully) "Is MARC Dead?" I wish here to note the irony of one group of would-be revolutionaries meeting to proclaim the death of MARC, while others proclaim that the future belongs to metadata—the best-known example of which is the Dublin Core, an ill-formulated subset of the MARC record. Let us go back to the question of what we are going to do about the worthwhile purely electronic resources that we wish to separate from the rest of the Net and the Web. In my view, there are these possibilities. We can:

- Identify and catalogue them according to standards we use for other materials
- identify them and take a subset of MARC (a framework standard, not a content standard) and call it "metadata," if that makes us feel better, to be filled with content according to bibliographic standards (either fully applied or dumbed down) by cataloguers and paraprofessionals
- Identify them and take a subset of MARC and allow that framework to be filled with any content by anybody
- Leave them in the murky waters of the Net, to be discovered or not discovered as determined by the karma of the searcher on the day in question

These possibilities, obviously, range from the expensive and the effective to the inexpensive and the ineffective. There are also permutations and gradations, but those are essentially the choices before us. My belief is that "metadata," as presently conceived, will evolve toward standardization of elements and content and will be indistinguishable from real cataloguing in a relatively short time. That applies, of course, to those resources that are deemed "worthwhile." The rest will go their merry way to use, neglect, or oblivion with few tears shed.

Before we get to any kind of control, there is the question of identification of "worthwhile" materials. Again, we have choices. They are, first, a Grand Plan for cyber collection development and, second, a grassroots movement in which individual libraries, librarians, and groups of libraries choose and catalogue the documents, resources, and sites that they deem worthwhile. If you liked the drive for a national "information policy," you will love the years of striving for a national cyber collection policy. Not my cup of tea. The second approach will be a reprise of the history of libraries. Individuals and individual libraries built collections, one choice at a time, over many years. It was not until much later that union catalogues and library collectives brought those individual collections into a national system. The difference this time is that the benefits of the work of individual libraries and groups can be made available to all contemporaneously. Let a thousand INFOMINEs bloom, and record by record, collection by collection, "worthwhile" Net resources will be organized and made available in what will come to be a national system with nationally accepted standards.

Last, and most important, what is the point of all of this if the resources identified and catalogued are not preserved? Those more optimistic than I look to gigantic national electronic archives maintained by governments and private companies that will ensure the indefinite survival of the electronic records of humankind. The cost and practicalities of such schemes boggle the mind and defy credulity. We can, of course, ignore the problem and hope that it all turns out right in the end—after all, that is what we are doing now. Alternatively, we could turn to the only known way of preserving massive numbers of texts and images—print on acid-free paper. If you are inclined to laugh at that suggestion, I would recommend that you explore the financial costs and the cultural costs of the alternatives and keep an open mind.

Metadata is a buzzword that is losing its buzziness, but real problems and real issues lurk behind all the pomposity and techno-babble. What are we going to do about identifying and making accessible the valuable records of humanity that are only available in electronic form? How are we going to deal with the mutability and evanescence of those records? How are we going to preserve those resources and transmit them to posterity? We will only answer these questions if we employ wisdom and insight, are cognizant of the lessons of history, and work with the interests of all our users, present and future, in mind.

26

Future Developments in Metadata and
Their Role in Access to Networked Information

Clifford A. Lynch, transcribed by Sally C. Tseng[1]

The issues discussed in this chapter are important as context for understanding metadata, its roles, and its future. One hears too many discussions of metadata that seem to suggest that there is a divinely given, accurate, and comprehensive description of information objects that is represented in metadata, a sort of Platonic ideal of description. I don't believe this; in fact, I think that the proposition is misleading on two separate counts. First, while the preconference audience clearly and understandably has a particular interest in description and classification and the roles metadata can play there, metadata covers much more than description and classification—it covers information discovery and management very broadly and at many levels. We should recognize that metadata for classification and description is an important topic, but we must not limit our thinking about metadata to those applications. Second, and equally important, I think we need to recognize that metadata itself, as a concept and an area of inquiry, is not very helpful and doesn't get us very far. Metadata becomes interesting and useful when we *employ* it to construct information retrieval and management systems (with catalogs being only one rather specialized example), and when we *apply and exploit* it to make information more accessible or more manageable. The context of use is everything, and only when we talk about the contexts of use can we really talk about metadata in an informed and meaningful way.

It may be that the reason many discussions about metadata tend to focus on description and classification is that many of us share an implied context of use (such as catalogs and cataloging) because of common experiences, interests, and backgrounds. There is a specific intellectual framework and set of rules and practices, such as AACR2, that some view as providing the idealized, complete, and comprehensive set of metadata. This may be the source of the presumption that a "right" set of metadata exists—perhaps it does, within this particular use context. But even here I'm skeptical. I think we need to be skeptical and critical in our analysis: it is unclear to what extent AACR2 is a good match to the needs of users of modern information retrieval systems. While I'm certain it has parts that are highly relevant to this application, I'm equally confident that it has other parts that aren't very relevant and that it's not a comprehensive answer.

We need to be very aware of the changing contexts of metadata use. So much of our thinking about metadata is based on its use in highly controlled environments. An example of this is a shared cataloging service like that operated by OCLC, where there is a great deal of individual and organizational accountability about what goes on in the database, and where updating to that database is very carefully controlled and managed. Another example would be online catalogs at various libraries. Certainly, I think those of you who operate online catalogs generally would not be comfortable with the proposition of inviting the random public to add or modify records in your online catalog at will. In fact, though, that is what is happening on the Web to some extent—anyone can create metadata for a Web page.

Metadata moves from one place to another in very uncontrolled and sometimes poorly understood ways, which will lead to some new issues that are quite different from the ones we have worried about in the past. The commercial search engines that index the Web are one development in this area. New ones are coming all the time. For example, I would invite you to look at things like the Santa Fe Agreements from the Open Archives Initiative.[2] The Santa Fe Agreements are basically a fairly simple framework for harvesting bulk metadata at various times from sites so you can construct upper-level services, based on the metadata pulled out of those sites. I invite you also to look at some of the papers on a research system called Harvest, which was developed around 1992 or 1993 by Mike Schwartz, Mic Bowman, and some of their colleagues, mainly at the University of Colorado at Boulder. A Web site documented the project, which seems to have gone "off the air" recently. (See the notes at the end of the chapter for more on this. The disappearance of this site is a great tragedy and exemplifies the problems that will happen as we continue to fail to address digital preservation effectively—but this is another discussion, for another time.[3]) The term *harvesting* comes from this Harvest system, which was so well named that it now has become part of our language around metadata, even though the system never reached wide use outside of some organizational intranets. But, in fact, some very important architectural ideas are embodied in Harvest, and many of them have reoccurred elsewhere. Let me give you an example of the way metadata moves from place to place in the networked information environment and use this to illustrate some of the new considerations that are emerging.

We have heard quite a bit about the potential of attaching metadata to Web pages and how this can improve the quality of search systems. I certainly don't need to describe at length the various shortcomings of the public Web search engines, which are nonetheless very powerful and very useful tools (if you don't believe this, imagine a world without them!). But they are limited. For example, it would be helpful if they could distinguish pages *by* someone from pages *about* someone and if they could provide some kind of meaningful subject access. These are all things that are basic functions of descriptive metadata; if we could attach such metadata to Web pages, presumably the public search engines could collect and exploit the metadata to make Web searching more flexible and more capable.

You are also probably aware that there is an enormous amount of data on the Web that these Web-indexing systems cannot find. We sometimes call this the "dark matter" on the Web (as Vint Cerf terms it) or the "invisible" Web. The most prominent examples are databases that basically manifest themselves with a search form and then give you dynamically generated HTML pages in response to the search. Web search engines are unable to find and index these databases because no pages are there to index, other than maybe a few help or documentation screens. This is a major omission when we talk about indexing resources on the Web. Some of these databases are terabytes in size and are really comprehensive resources: think of EDGAR, PubMed, library online catalogs, and many other examples. Other parts of the "invisible Web" include sound, image, and video files that we mostly still describe and find through language, rather than content analysis. (Techniques for content-based retrieval of nontextual material, while a fascinating and important research area, are still at a relatively infant stage compared to what we can do with descriptions of these objects created by skilled human intellectual effort.) We should think about building surrogate metadata records that would allow these kinds of resources to be indexed in the Web search engines, based on this metadata.[4]

Those who run these search engines are not unaware of these problems; they are both smart and pragmatic. Moreover, they have significant resources to develop systems. Why haven't they picked up on metadata on public Web search engines? The reason is, and there is a terribly important message here, that the people who run the Web search engines are spending a great deal of their time dealing with those who run unpleasant Web sites full of pages that are designed to deceive Web search engines. These site operators do keyword stuffing and pagejacking and engage in other sorts of problematic activities. Basically, keyword stuffing tries to fool the Web search engines by building pages that are going to be machine processed differently from the way the human eye would evaluate the rendered HTML. By looking to see who is making a request—a human or a Web search engine's indexer program—a site intent on deception can provide different pages; the page the search engine indexes isn't the same page that the user will see if he or she clicks on the link to the page. That latter process is called pagejacking. There is, in fact, a good-sized technology "arms race" between the people who build search engines and those who build sites that try to game the Web search engines so that they can make their pages prominent in response to certain queries. If you talk to those who actually build search engines, you will find that they have put a lot of effort into developing computational techniques to try to filter out these bogus pages. They actually do statistical and linguistic analyses to try to see if the sites have plausible pages and plausible indexing terms. They work very hard at this and are now adding new techniques like link analysis to try to validate important pages as well, using the presence of many links from many sites to a page as supporting evidence for indexing and rating decisions. The search engine operators are having a lot of trouble dealing with content on the Web, however, even when all the evidence is before them in the form of the Web page itself for computational evaluation and indexing of Web pages.

What happens when we introduce metadata into the mix? When some metadata is attached to a Web page or is functioning as a surrogate for something that can't be directly indexed, like a nontextual file or a database, why should you believe it? In fact, Web search engines have compelling evidence that you should not always believe it, based on what they are finding. Of utmost importance, as we start thinking about creating and using metadata in this sort of uncontrolled public sphere, are indications of who authored the metadata and why we should believe it. This leads to a whole set of considerations about digitally signed metadata, where the digital signature allows linking a piece of metadata with a digital identity, and next to questions about the legitimacy of this digital identity, which then takes you into public key infrastructures (PKI). And beyond: just because you know *who* created the metadata, we still have the question of why you should believe that person. Knowing who to blame does not necessarily help to determine whether or not an individual should be believed. This is another kind of trust structure that we need to think about very hard; it reaches into questions about how reputations are established and managed. For an example of how some of these considerations might play out in actual systems, look at eBay, which tries to help broker trust among buyers and sellers who are not known to each other, or what Amazon.com is doing with book reviews and reviewers; note that systems of this type have major problems with people "gaming" the system. These are social and not just computational problems. Recognize that, ultimately, we need all of this—metadata provenance, identity, and trust and reputation management—as an underpinning for search processes that are themselves hard.

This will be very complicated. There have been some seemingly plausible propositions, like "Why not just believe metadata that has been created by librarians?" to simplify the situation. Let's explore this one for just a moment. First, obviously, librarians are not the only people who can create useful metadata, but let's leave that aside and just focus on trying to include librarian-created metadata. How do you know that a given piece of metadata was created by a librarian? In essence, you need to couple a public key infrastructure for identity with a controlled database from a trusted party that validates that certain identities belong to librarians. Who's going to do this (and think carefully about liability and jurisdictional issues here)? And then, of course, we have to deal with problems like "rogue" librarians who have turned to creating deceptive metadata. We are going to run into some very complex issues about trust and identity; it will be an integral part of making use of metadata for finding and managing information in the public Internet.[5]

Just to underscore this, I want to stress that today we are seeing metadata used in search engines that are being used to index controlled environments. Corporate or organizational intranets, for example, are starting to use various kinds of metadata on their content and are running various kinds of indexing engines that harvest not only pages but metadata. They can do this because they have institutional control and accountability over the Web sites on their intranet, as well as the metadata creation and quality-control practices that are used on these sites—they don't allow rogue sites or rogue metadata creators on their intranets. Because they are able to trust this metadata, they are using it to very good effect, providing much better searching than is possible on the public World Wide Web.

In fact, we are starting to see things that go beyond the organizational Internet. I'm thinking of developments like the subject gateways, the sort of work that the ROADS initiative does in the United Kingdom.[6] They are harvesting specifically identified sites that are known to be well behaved and managed in a rational way and building indexes with the metadata and content they extract from these sites. Here again, this is really a handcrafted trust relationship. Scaling up from there will require that we think about how to connect to the broader trust and identity infrastructure.

Let me make a final set of points about context for metadata, particularly as metadata moves from place to place and as different kinds of metadata created by different groups for different reasons may be marshaled together for a purpose such as searching. The problem is that the assumptions about exactly what objects are being described with a given set of metadata may not move along with the metadata. The object models are, after all, conceptual ideas that underpin the construction of systems and the construction of various kinds of metadata, but the metadata itself is tangible. It can be copied from place to place without our being sure that its contextual assumptions about object models move with it.

Different metadata schemes have been constructed by different communities for multiple purposes (virtually all of them descriptive, however). One of those schemes, Dublin Core, is a lowest-common-denominator metadata element set that is intended to span many communities and provide at least some basis for discovery. Some of you may also be familiar with conceptual models like the Warwick Framework.[7] It was originally developed as part of the Dublin Core work to provide a means of scoping the Dublin Core effort and making it clear how the Core could work with other richer and more detailed metadata sets developed by more specialized communities of practice. The Warwick Framework was also influential in the construction of the Resource Description Framework by the World Wide Web Consortium.[8]

Basically, what these models give us are pictures of multiple metadata sets, describing various properties and characteristics of an object for various communities of practice, and then these multiple metadata sets coming together, recombining, and being reused in various contexts. Every metadata set includes an implied perspective on the definition of digital objects. We are beginning to see a lot of issues about harmonizing object models in order to make multiple metadata sets work together. Hard, fundamental conceptual work will be needed here. Implicit here as well are questions about the role identifiers play, since often identifiers form the link between a set of metadata and the object that set describes. Object models are often implicit in identifier systems.[9]

There is tremendous activity in the identifier area. A lot of this activity is coming out of the desire to manage intellectual property and record intellectual rights. This often involves very complicated distinctions between objects, while at the same time ignoring other distinctions that may have traditionally been important for scholarship and hence for bibliographic description developed to support scholarship. Take a look at the work that is done on the <indecs> (Interoperability of Data in E-Commerce Systems) project, which is focused on recording intellectual property rights.[10] Or, look at some of the work being done by various groups working within the International Standards Organization (ISO), trying to come up with international standard work codes. You can see that there are those who are starting to establish identifiers with object models built in, primarily people with commercial motivations, and they are building up metadata sets around these identifiers. The Digital Object Identifier (DOI) is one identifier scheme that came out of the publishing community and is now being carried forward by the DOI Foundation.[11] Interestingly, it has until recently largely avoided grappling with questions around underlying object models. (It seems to basically identify anything that a publisher wants to identify, including a mechanism such as a Web page that might allow you to choose among and purchase various different formats that a piece of content might be available in.) It is particularly relevant here that, while the DOI Foundation was established to assign and manage identifiers, the developers quickly realized that they needed a whole metadata database hung around those identifiers for reverse lookup—a way to find the identifier corresponding to a digital object, or work, based on descriptive characterizations of that work. They are now building such a database. This will be particularly tricky to work with because of the ambiguities in the underlying object model—which they may try to address by adding object-typing information in the metadata, in effect introducing an object taxonomy rather than the more common practice of assigning identifiers to a certain specific class of objects within the framework of an object model.

IFLA has done some good work on object models for bibliographic description,[12] but this hasn't been well connected to discussions about identifiers yet—and we know that identifiers are very powerful in the networked environment because they are actionable.[13] More and more digital objects are coming with both identifiers and metadata designed to support electronic commerce and rights management and are being "packaged" within object models convenient for these interests. We need to think carefully about how these link up to our descriptive practices and descriptive metadata and to object models and identifiers more familiar to bibliographic and scholarly interests.

Perhaps a concise way of summarizing this set of points is to say that we need to ask questions about not only what kinds of metadata elements we need for what purposes, but also what the nature of the digital objects is to which this metadata applies, how we identify the objects, and when two objects are the same and when they are different.

I will conclude by following up on a set of points I made earlier about the need to think broadly about the information discovery and retrieval process and the kinds of metadata that can help to enhance this process. There is, I think, an unfortunate tendency to equate metadata with description. Not exactly with "formal" or "traditional" cataloging, but certainly, as elsewhere in this book, with the narrow view of cataloging, solely the descriptive view. In fact, if you look at information finding—and I think much of the reason for creating and studying metadata is as a basis for building information discovery systems—there is clearly a lot more to it than that. There is human intellectual analysis, classification, description, and things of this nature that we are familiar with from the tradition of cataloging and description. But two other major sources of information exist as well, which I think are, or should be, equally important and equally valid as part of the basis for discovering information. One of them is computational analysis. Computational analysis includes anything from now relatively traditional and well-understood full-text indexing to extracting the characteristics of images. So you can ask systems that house images questions like, "Show me some images with a lot of green on the bottom, and blue on the top, and some yellow bits in the green" (which is how you find pictures of meadows with flowers, among other things, in such a system; you can also, having found an interesting picture, ask it to find "more pictures like this one" and let the system figure out the characteristics—users need not learn the native languages of such content retrieval systems).

We need to think about how to represent and structure this kind of metadata, how to interchange it between systems, how to incorporate it into surrogate records that describe objects, and, of course, how to effectively relate it to and use it synergistically with intellectual description. We also need to explore underlying object models supporting computational or content analysis, which have not been well analyzed but tend to be, at least by tacit assumption, very literal (i.e., an object is a set of sequences of bits upon which the computation is done; two objects are the same if they are the identical set of sequences of bits; else they are different) and how they relate to the more nuanced object models typical in other frameworks.

The third great traditional source in information discovery is social behavior. This used to be handled person to person—asking a colleague for information—or through things like bestseller lists. In the digital world much more is possible, although it is starting to be explored, at least today, more in the commercial sector than in library-based information retrieval systems. Think about recommender systems (Amazon.com's recommendations: "other people with tastes similar to you bought this book, which you haven't bought yet"), popularity-tracking systems, and other approaches that track the behavior of populations as they use information. We can actually think of well-established approaches like citation analysis as one part of this kind of social context that can be exploited for retrieval.

As with computational analysis metadata, we need to think about when metadata related to social behavior can be isolated and abstracted from a particular system's context and usefully interchanged. This kind of information has been very poorly explored from the perspective of metadata and clearly has some strange properties; for example, it is often a function of a community that changes over time and that has to be defined in some fashion. On the other hand, it also illuminates broad characteristics of metadata that we don't typically focus much attention on. For example, in intellectual description, assignment of a subject term from a controlled vocabulary also has the property that it occurs at a point in time and isn't necessarily permanently valid, because the controlled vocabulary evolves over time, too. So, perhaps a deeper exploration of this kind of metadata, which space does not permit in this chapter, will help us to gain a better understanding of all types of descriptive metadata.

I hope this at least gives you a few things to think about as you contemplate the future evolution of work on metadata and the issues surrounding its creation, deployment, and use. My single strongest message is to always complement your thinking about the character and nature of metadata with an equal amount of thinking about how you move it from place to place; how metadata is going to be created, manipulated, and consumed; what exactly it applies to; and why you should trust it.

NOTES

1. This is a somewhat revised version of a talk originally titled "Vision for the Future: Accessing Web Pages," given at the ALCTS Preconference on Metadata. I'm deeply grateful to Sally Tseng of the University of California, Irvine, for preparing an initial transcript of that talk and for her subsequent help in refining the paper.

2. "The Open Archives Initiative," http://www.openarchives.org/.

3. The Harvest System's Web site was last seen at http://harvest.transarc.com; it probably vanished from there about the time that Mic Bowman left Transarc. I can no longer determine the earlier site addresses (if they existed), which may have included a site http://harvest.cs.colorado.edu or http://harvest.colorado.edu. Some of the Harvest software and manuals, as well as some subsequent work, are still available online. See "Harvest Web Indexing," http://www.tardis.ed.ac.uk/harvest/ (accessed August 21, 2000). See also C. M. Bowman, P. B. Danzig, D. R. Hardy, U. Manber, and M. F. Schwartz, "The Harvest Information Discovery and Access System," *Proceedings of the Second International World Wide Web Conference,* Chicago, Ill., October 1994 (n.p., 1994): 763–771; C. M. Bowman, P. B. Danzig, D. R. Hardy, U. Manber, M. F. Schwartz, and D. P. Wessels, *Harvest: A Scalable, Customizable Discovery and Access System,* Technical Report CU-CS-732-94 (Boulder, Colo.: Department of Computer Science, University of Colorado, 1994); C. M. Bowman, P. B. Danzig, D. R. Hardy, U. Manber, and M. F. Schwartz, "The Harvest Information Discovery and Access System," *Computer Networks and ISDN Systems* 28, nos. 1–2, (December 1995): 119–125.

4. For more on these issues and on search engines generally, see Clifford A. Lynch, "Searching the Internet," *Scientific American* 276, no. 3 (March 1997): 52–56, http://www.sciam.com/0397issue/0397lynch.html.

5. For a discussion of these issues, see Clifford A. Lynch, "When Documents Deceive: Trust and Provenance as New Factors for Information Retrieval in a Tangled Web," *Journal of the American Society for Information Science* (forthcoming).

6. Lorcan Dempsey, "ROADS to DESIRE: Some UK and Other European Metadata and Resource Discovery Projects," *D-Lib Magazine,* July/August 1996, http://www.dlib.org/dlib/july96/07dempsey.html. See also "ROADS Software/Documentation," http://www.roads.lut.ac.uk/.

7. See: Carl Lagoze, Clifford A. Lynch, and Ron Daniel, Jr., *The Warwick Framework: A Container Architecture for Aggregating Sets of Metadata,* TR96-1593, June 21, 1996, http://www.ifla.org/documents/libraries/cataloging/metadata/tr961593.pdf; Carl Lagoze, "The Warwick Framework: A Container Architecture for Diverse Sets of Metadata," *D-Lib Magazine,* July/August 1996, http://www.dlib.org/dlib/july96/lagoze/07lagoze.html.

8. W3C, "Resource Description Framework (RDF)," http://www.w3.org/RDF/.

9. Clifford A. Lynch, "Identifiers and Their Role in Networked Information Applications," *ARL Newsletter* 194 (October 1997):12–14. Also published with revisions in *Bulletin of the American Society for Information Science* 24, no. 2 (December/January 1998): 17–20, and in *CAUSE/EFFECT* 20, no. 4 (winter 1997–1998): 8–14. Reprinted in *Feliciter* 44, no. 2 (February 1998): 31–35. Also available online at: http://www.arl.org/newsltr/194/identifier.html. See also: Sandra Payette, Christophe Blanchi, Carl Lagoze, and Edward A. Overly, "Interoperability for Digital Objects and Repositories: The Cornell/CNRI Experiments," *D-Lib Magazine* 5, no. 5 (May 1999), http://www.dlib.org/dlib/may99/payette/05payette.html.

10. "Interoperability of Data in E-Commerce Systems <indecs>," http://www.indecs.org/.

11. "DOI: The Digital Object Identifier System," http://www.doi.org/.

12. IFLA Study Group on the Functional Requirements for Bibliographic Records, *Functional Requirements for Bibliographic Records* (Munich: Saur, 1998), http://www.ifla.org/VII/s13/frbr/frbr.pdf and http://www.ifla.org/VII/s13/frbr/frbr.htm.

13. See Lynch, "Identifiers and Their Role in Networked Information Applications."

Index

Note: Italic page numbers refer to illustrations.

About the Editors

Wayne Jones is head of serials cataloging at MIT. He is senior editor of *The Serials Librarian,* has edited two books (*Serials Canada* and *E-Serials*), and has published over twenty articles and book reviews.

Judith R. Ahronheim has at various times worked as cataloger, reference librarian, and document delivery specialist in public, special, and academic libraries. Formerly head of the Original Cataloging Unit at the University of Michigan Graduate Library, she currently serves the university as metadata specialist. She is the 1998 recipient of the Esther J. Piercy Award.

Josephine Crawford is head of information systems at the University of Minnesota Bio-Medical Library. She has twenty years of experience with online system development and managing information technology at three major universities, has been an active member of the American Library Association throughout this period, and is frequently called upon to give talks, present papers, and contribute to the professional literature. She also serves as an adjunct faculty member for the master's program in library and information science at Dominican University and the College of St. Catherine.

About the Contributors

Murtha Baca is head of the Standards Program at the Getty Research Institute. She holds Ph.D.s in art history and Italian literature from UCLA. During the last decade, her work has focused on data standards and structured vocabularies for indexing and accessing information on the visual arts and architecture. She edited *Introduction to Metadata* (Los Angeles: Getty Trust, 1998; Spanish translation, 1999) and the *Union List of Artist Names* (with James M. Bower; New York: G. K. Hall, 1994). She oversaw the publication of *Categories for the Description of Works of Art* and co-edited, with Patricia Harpring, a double issue of the journal *Visual Resources* (vol. 11, no. 34 [1996]) devoted to the *Categories*. She has written articles and taught workshops and seminars on indexing and accessing art information, thesaurus construction, and multilingual equivalency work at museums and other venues in North America, Latin America, and Europe.

Laura Bayard belongs to the library faculty at the University of Notre Dame, where she manages two units: Catalog & Database Maintenance and Government Documents Technical Services. In addition to participating on the Bibliographic Access Management Team, Laura is the library faculty affirmative action officer, is a member of the university's Academic Affirmative Action Committee, is the chair of the libraries' Training & Development Committee, and has served two terms as a faculty senator (1994/1995 and 1999/2000). She is active in LAMA and in the Indiana Library Federation as an at-large delegate on the Technical Services Executive Committee. She has co-authored articles in the areas of government documents and Web site cataloging.

Matthew Beacom is catalog librarian for Networked Information Resources at Yale University Library.

Stanley Blum is the research information manager at the California Academy of Sciences in San Francisco. By academic training, he is a systematic ichthyologist (classification of fishes; Ph.D., zoology, University of Hawaii, 1988). Since 1990, however, he has been working full-time in biodiversity and natural history collections informatics. The two most important themes in his work have been: (1) designing integrated information systems for natural history museums (i.e., systems that support a wide variety of collection disciplines, collection management practices, and uses of collection information); and (2) developing data standards and software architectures that will enable data to be integrated across distributed and heterogeneous collection databases.

Diane Boehr has been a cataloging unit head at the National Library of Medicine (NLM) since August 1998. She oversees both print monograph cataloging and serial cataloging in all formats. Prior to joining NLM, she served as a library services consultant for Costabile Associates, Inc., where she provided cataloging services in all formats for a wide variety of libraries, including working on metadata standards and creation for the Dept. of Veterans Affairs and the National Institute for Literacy. She is the current chair of the ALCTS Media Resources Committee and the former chair of the Cataloging Policy Committee of OLAC (Online Audiovisual Catalogers). Diane received her M.L.S. from the University of Maryland, where she now serves as an adjunct professor, teaching bibliographic control.

Beth Picknally Camden has been director of cataloging services at the University of Virginia since 1997. She held several positions previously at U.Va.: associate director of cataloging, library training coordinator, and head, copy cataloging. Before coming to Virginia in 1989, she worked at the University of Notre Dame as the head of Catalog and Database

Maintenance and as humanities cataloger. She is currently the chair of the ALCTS CCS Committee for Education, Training, and Recruitment for Cataloging. She received her M.S.L.S. at the Catholic University of America in 1984.

Brad Eden is currently head of cataloging for the University of Nevada at Las Vegas. Previous employment included coordinator of technical services for the North Harris Montgomery Community College District, remote cataloger for the NEEDS Project, and head cataloger at the NASA/Johnson Space Center. He holds master's and Ph.D. degrees in medieval musicology and often presents papers and research in this area. He has actively participated in ALA and ALCTS endeavors regarding metadata and is also an adjunct faculty member, conducting metadata seminars for the OCLC Institute. He is currently the editor of the *ALCTS Papers on Library Technical Services and Collections* and does book and multimedia reviews for a number of electronic library journals. His experiences on the NEEDS Project have recently been published in the *Journal of Internet Cataloging,* and a futuristic article has been included in the *Cybrarian Manual,* 2nd edition.

William Fietzer has been an assistant librarian at the University of Minnesota–Twin Cities since 1997. As digital resources and humanities cataloger, he works with a variety of TEI-related committees and initiatives in the campus community, including the Electronic Text Research Center and the Cooperative Online Resource Catalog Committee. On the national level he is a member of the ALCTS CC:DA Taskforce on Metadata and chair of ALCTS's Network Resources and Metadata Committee. He has presented talks on "Cataloging Electronic Resources in Music" for the Midwest Library Association and "Using the TEI Header" as part of "Creating, Encoding and Delivering Electronic Texts and Finding Aids for Scholarly Use" at the 1998 CIC Conference on Metadata. His publications include "Technical Services Librarians and Metadata: Reining in the New Frontier" and "Working Our Way through Wonderland: Technical Services and the Sociology of Metadata" in *Technicalities.*

William Garrison is head of cataloging at the University of Colorado at Boulder. He is active in the Program for Cooperative Cataloging, having served on the PCC Standing Committee on Standards and the BIBCO Operations Committee. He is currently vice-chair/chair-elect of the ALCTS/CCS and a member of the ALCTS Fundraising Committee. He has recently served on the ALCTS Membership Committee and the ALCTS Leadership Development Committee. He has also served on the ALCTS/CCS/Subject Analysis Committee, the ALCTS Policy & Research Committee, the LITA/ALCTS Authority Control Interest Group, and the ALCTS/CCS/Catalog Management Discussion Group and was elected secretary of ALCTS/CCS several years ago. He has been on the Metadata Task Force of the Colorado Digitization Project since its inception in the fall of 1998 and has attended two of the OCLC Institute's seminars on metadata. He has also chaired the Cataloging and Reference Group, which designed and implemented Prospector (the Colorado Unified Catalog).

Michael Gorman is dean of library services at the Henry Madden Library, California State University, Fresno. From 1977 to 1988 he worked at the University of Illinois, Urbana, Library as, successively, director of technical services, director of general services, and acting university librarian. From 1966 to 1977 he was, successively, head of cataloguing at the British national bibliography, a member of the British Library Planning Secretariat, and head of the Office of Bibliographic Standards in the British Library. He has taught at library schools in his native Britain and in the United States—most recently as visiting professor at the University of California, Berkeley, School of Library and Information Science (summer sessions) and as Bradshaw Lecturer at Texas Woman's University. He is the first editor of the *Anglo-American Cataloguing Rules,* second edition (1978), and of the revision of that work (1988). He is the author of all three editions of *The Concise AACR2* (1979, 1989, 1999); editor of, and contributor to, *Technical Services Today and Tomorrow,* 1st (1990) and 2nd (1998) editions; and editor of *Crossroads* (1984) and *Convergence* (1991) (proceedings of the 1st and 2nd National LITA Conferences), and *Californien,* published in 1991. *Future Libraries: Dreams, Madness, and Reality,* cowritten with Walt Crawford, was honored with the 1997 Blackwell's Scholarship Award. His most recent book, published by ALA in 1997, is entitled *Our Singular Strengths: Meditations for Librarians.* He is also the author of more than one hundred articles in professional and scholarly journals. He has contributed chapters to a number of books and is the author or editor of other books and monographs. He has given numerous presentations at international, national, and state conferences. He is a fellow of the [British] Library Association, the 1979 recipient of the Margaret Mann Citation, the 1992 recipient of the Melvil Dewey Medal, and the 1997 recipient of Blackwell's Scholarship Award. He was president of the Library and Information Technology Association (1999–2000).

Rebecca Guenther is senior MARC networking and standards specialist in the Network Development and MARC Standards Office of the Library of Congress. Her current responsibilities include work on national and international library automation standards, including MARC bibliographic, authority, classification, holdings, and community information formats, and MARC code lists for languages, countries, and geographic areas. She is also chair of the ISO 639 Joint Advisory Committee for language codes and a member of the NISO Standards Development Committee. Former positions include: section head of the National Union Catalog Control Section, Catalog Management and Publication Division; senior cataloger, German Language Section, Shared Cataloging Division (both at the Library of Congress); and cataloger, National Library of Medicine. She has been involved in discussions on metadata and accommodating online information resources into MARC 21 since the early 1990s. She participated in all of the seven Dublin Core metadata workshops and has been an active contributor to metadata discussions. In addition, she is a member of the Dublin Core Advisory Committee and the Dublin Core Usage Committee, and chair of the Dublin Core Type Working Group and Library Interest Group. She worked on the mapping between Dublin Core elements and MARC fields, between Dublin Core and GILS, and between GILS and MARC.

Diane Hillmann is head of the Technical Services Support Unit at Cornell University Library. She was a regular member of MARBI for two terms (1996/1997 to 1999/2000) and a liaison from 1989/1990 to 1992/1993, representing the American Association of Law Libraries. She has been involved with the Dublin Core Metadata Initiative since 1995 and currently serves as the chair of the DC-Guides Working Group and as a member of the Dublin Core Advisory Committee.

Jean Hirons is the coordinator of the CONSER Program at the Library of Congress. Her activities at LC have included editing the *CONSER Editing Guide* and the *CONSER Cataloging Manual.* She also founded and coordinates the Serials Cataloging Cooperative Training Program. She has been involved with the revision of AACR2 since she co-authored and presented the paper "Issues Related to Seriality" at the International Conference on the Principles and Future Development of AACR in 1997. In 1999 she issued a report with specific recommendations for revision of rules for serials and electronic resources for consideration by the Joint Steering Committee. Jean was awarded the 1996 Bowker/Ulrich's Serials Librarianship Award for her contributions to the education of serials catalogers.

Sheila S. Intner is a professor in the Graduate School of Library and Information Science at Simmons College, where she teaches cataloging and classification, collection development, bibliographic instruction, and preservation management. She has written or edited fifteen books and is working now on the third edition of her cataloging textbook *Standard Cataloging for School and Public Libraries.* She edits *Technicalities,* a monthly newsletter for technical services librarians and database managers, and *Frontiers of Access to Library Materials,* a monographic series published by ALA Editions, which included Dora Chen's book on serials management. She teaches workshops around the country and abroad on topics in cataloging and collection development—especially nonprint cataloging and the evaluation and strategic planning for collections—most recently at Bar-Ilan University in Ramat-Gan, Israel, but in the last few years, she also has taught cataloging at Hebrew University in Jerusalem, the University of Haifa, and in the Marshall Islands in Majuro and planning for collections in Wuhan, China, and Berlin, Germany, as well as at SEFLIN headquarters in Fort Lauderdale, Florida. She consults for public and academic libraries, both large and small, as well as the small special libraries of the Jewish Vocational Service of Boston and Temple Beth-El Library in East Longmeadow, Massachusetts. Some of her recent consulting included the City University of New York, Smith College, Union College, and Springfield (Mass.) Public Library. She currently is the immediate past president of ALCTS and served as an ALA councilor from 1995 to 1999. She has worked on numerous committees of CCS and CMDS and now is a member of ALA's Education Committee, the Spectrum Task Force, and several other ALA-wide task forces.

Kris Kiesling has been head of the Department of Manuscripts and Archives at the Harry Ransom Humanities Research Center, University of Texas at Austin, since 1990. Previously, she was employed in the Department of Rare Books and Special Collections at the University of Michigan, where she earned her MILS in 1988. She has presented numerous workshops on cataloging archival materials using MARC and *Archives, Personal Papers, and Manuscripts,* as well as on the implementation of Encoded Archival Description. She was a member of the EAD design team and is currently chair of the Society of American Archivists Standards Committee and the EAD Working Group. She is a fellow of the Society of American Archivists.

Clifford A. Lynch has been the director of the Coalition for Networked Information (CNI) since July 1997. CNI, jointly sponsored by the Association of Research Libraries and EDUCAUSE, includes about 200 member organizations concerned with the use of information technology and networked information to enhance scholarship and intellectual productivity. Prior to joining CNI, he spent eighteen years at the University of California Office of the President, the last ten as director of Library Automation. He holds a Ph.D. in computer science from the University of California, Berkeley, and is an adjunct professor at Berkeley's School of Information Management and Systems. He is a past president of the

American Society for Information Science and a fellow of the American Association for the Advancement of Science and the National Information Standards Organization. He currently serves on the Internet 2 Applications Council; he was a member of the National Research Council committee that recently published *The Digital Dilemma: Intellectual Property in the Information Infrastructure* and now serves on the NRC's committee on Broadband Last-Mile Technology.

Elizabeth U. Mangan started at the Library of Congress in September 1968 as a special recruit. Following her internship, she joined the Geography and Map Division as a map cataloger and became a supervisor in 1976. In March 1997 she became head of the Technical Services Section and served as acting chief from August 1998 to September 1999. She has been involved in the development and publication of numerous technical manuals, guides, and standards. She assisted in developing the MARC format for maps and co-authored the subsequent content designation manual. In addition, she was instrumental in the publication of the *Map Cataloging Manual, Geographic Cutters, MARC Conversion Manual: Maps,* and the G-schedule. She assisted the Federal Geographic Data Committee in developing the *Content Standards for Digital Geospatial Metadata.* She is directing the revision of *Cartographic Materials: A Manual of Interpretation for AACR2* for the Anglo-American Committee for Cataloging Cartographic Materials and is a deputy member for the Library on the U.S. Board on Geographic Names. She has been involved in the National Digital Library Program for Cartographic Materials since its inception in the early 1990s.

Lynn Marko is head of the Monograph Cataloging Division at the University of Michigan Library, a position that she has held for many years. From her perspective, one of the pleasures of working in an innovative library is the complexity of the problems and the creativity required to find their solutions. She views cataloging, with its present day expansion beyond AACR2/MARC, as a creative and important endeavor. She has published several articles and given many talks on the wider view of cataloging.

Constance Mayer is currently head of public services at the Eda Kuhn Loeb Music Library of the Harvard College Library at Harvard University. She has graduate degrees in music and library science from Indiana University, Bloomington, and worked in various capacities in the IU music library from 1986 to 2000, most recently as head of User Services and VARIATIONS project coordinator. During the years at IU, she participated in the development of the VARIATIONS project, particularly in the areas of user interface design, workflow management, structural metadata for music, and online score access. She has presented information on VARIATIONS in a variety of settings since its beginnings in the early 1990s.

Norm Medeiros is technical services librarian at New York University School of Medicine. A graduate of the University of Rhode Island School of Library and Information Studies, he has published in the areas of cataloging and Web site development and currently serves on two Dublin Core working groups. His research interests include the usability of Web-based OPACs and metadata as a means to resource discovery on the Web.

Eric Miller is a senior research scientist in the Office of Research at OCLC Online Computer Library Center, Inc. He is the co-chair of the W3C RDF Model and Syntax Working Group, chair of the W3C RDF Schema Working Group, and serves as the associate director of the Dublin Core Metadata Initiative.

Regina Reynolds has been head of the National Serials Data Program, the U.S. ISSN center, since 1992. She was a member of the CONSER AACR Review Task Force and is a corresponding member of ISBD(S) Review Group, as well as a member of the ISSN Manual Revision Working Group. She has done extensive writing and speaking on the topics of ISSN, cataloging of electronic serials, rule revisions, and standards to accommodate electronic serials. She was the 1999 winner of the Bowker/Ulrich's Award for Serials Librarianship. She was chair of the CONSER Task Force on Electronic Resources from 1994 to 1996. She has been a faculty member of several ALCTS Serials Cataloging Institutes, has presented workshops on cataloging online electronic serials, and is a former member of the ALCTS Networked Resources and Metadata Committee. She currently is a member of LC's BeOnline project team.

Juan Carlos Rodriguez is a science reference librarian and coordinator of information technology at the University of California, Riverside's Science Library. He is also co-Webmaster of the UCR Library Web site. He received his M.L.I.S. from UCLA in 1995 with a specialization in information systems. He is a member of ALA, LITA, ASIS, and REFORMA: The National Association to Promote Library and Information Services to Latinos and the Spanish-Speaking. He was co-chair of the REFORMA Information Technology Committee from 1997 to 2000 and has been a member of the INFOMINE Development Team since 1995. He has presented talks on "Searching the Web," "Demystifying Metadata," and "Providing Access to Internet Resources" at the local and national levels.

Carlen Ruschoff is director of technical services at the University of Maryland, College Park. She has been active in the development of the *Anglo-American Cataloguing Rules,* 2nd edition, through participation on the ALA Committee on Cataloging: Description and Access. She has been a planner and a trainer in many cataloging workshops and institutes sponsored by ALA, CAPCON, PALINET, and LC. Until 1999 she served on the editorial board for two journals: *The Journal of Academic Librarianship* and *Library Resources & Technical Services.* She has authored several papers on developments in cataloging, as well as retrospective conversion and outsourcing. Over the past year, she has employed her cataloging expertise in providing access to electronic information through metadata standards. In addition to cataloging activities, she represents the views of the American Library Association on standards developed under the auspices of the National Information Standards Organization. She assumed her role as president of ALCTS in 2000. She received her M.A. and B.A. degrees from the University of Minnesota.

Brian E. C. Schottlaender is university librarian at the University of California, San Diego. From 1993 to 1999, he worked at UCLA as associate university librarian for Collections and Technical Services and served, in 1998 and 1999, as senior associate to the university librarian of the California Digital Library with responsibilities for primary content development. From 1984 to 1993, he worked at UCLA as, successively, assistant head of the cataloging department and assistant university librarian for Technical Services. From 1974 to 1984, he held positions at Firma Otto Harrassowitz in Wiesbaden, Germany; Indiana University Libraries in Bloomington; and the University of Arizona Libraries in Tucson. A member of the American Library Association (ALA) since 1979, he has served on the ALA Committee on Cataloging: Description and Access since 1989 and chaired the committee in 1992 and 1993. Since 1995, he has served as the ALA representative to the Joint Steering Committee for Revision of the Anglo-American Cataloguing Rules. In 1997 and 1998, he chaired the Program for Cooperative Cataloging. Since 1999, he has served as chair of the Pacific Rim Digital Alliance. He has edited two books: *The Future of the Descriptive Cataloging Rules: Proceedings of the AACR 2000 Preconference* (1998) and *Retrospective Conversion: History, Approaches, Considerations* (1992). He has contributed articles to various professional journals, including *Rare Books and Manuscripts Librarianship* and *Journal of Internet Cataloging,* and has spoken widely on collections, bibliographic access, and digital library issues. He obtained his B.A. degree from the University of Texas, Austin, in 1974 (*ampla cum laude*). He received his M.L.S. degree from Indiana University in 1980, the same year he was admitted to Beta Phi Mu, the Library Science Honor Society. In 1995, he was one of fifteen individuals selected nationally to attend the Palmer School of Library Science at Long Island University as a senior fellow.

Wendy Treadwell has been the coordinator of the Machine Readable Data Center at the University of Minnesota since its creation in 1989. The MRDC provides research and instructional support for the use of social science data within the University of Minnesota Libraries, including access to ICPSR data sets. The MRDC also serves as a coordinating agency of the Minnesota State Data Center, providing archiving and custom services for Census and other federal data for the State of Minnesota. She has been an active member of the Association of Public Data Users (APDU) and the International Association of Social Sciences Information Service and Technology (IASSIST) since 1990, currently serving a two-year elected term as APDU president and an appointed term as IASSIST treasurer. She is also a member of the International Association of Office Statistics (IAOS) and serves on the Standing Committee on Regional and Urban Statistics (SCORUS).

Jennifer A. Younger has been the director of University Libraries at Notre Dame since October 1997, formally designated the Edward H. Arnold Director of Libraries since October 1999. Previously, she served in senior administrative positions at the Ohio State University and the University of Wisconsin–Madison, with experience as well at Northwestern University and the U.S. State Department Library in Washington, D.C. A Wisconsin native, she received all of her degrees (B.A., M.A., and Ph.D.) from the University of Wisconsin–Madison, completing the doctoral degree as a part-time student and full-time practicing librarian. She has held a number of positions in the Association for Library Collections and Technical Services, serving as the president in 1993–1994, and is currently the editor of the association's journal, *Library Resources & Technical Services* (LRTS). She is a frequent speaker at state and national conferences in areas that include library organization and management, access standards and technical services, with publications on these topics as well. She has also been a member of several external review panels appointed by the ALA Committee on Accreditation and chaired the panel visiting the University of Oklahoma in spring 2000.